# How the Qur'ān Works

# How the Qur’ān Works

*Reading Sacred Narrative*

Leyla Ozgur Alhassen

OXFORD
UNIVERSITY PRESS

OXFORD
UNIVERSITY PRESS

Oxford University Press is a department of the University of Oxford. It furthers the University's objective of excellence in research, scholarship, and education by publishing worldwide. Oxford is a registered trade mark of Oxford University Press in the UK and certain other countries.

Published in the United States of America by Oxford University Press
198 Madison Avenue, New York, NY 10016, United States of America.



Library of Congress Cataloging-in-Publication Data
Names: Ozgur Alhassen, Leyla, author.
Title: How the Qur'ān works : reading sacred narrative / Leyla Ozgur Alhassen.
Description: 1. | New York : Oxford University Press, 2023. |
Includes bibliographical references and index.
Identifiers: LCCN 2022060593 (print) | LCCN 2022060594 (ebook) |
ISBN 9780197654606 (hardback) | ISBN 9780197654620 (epub) |
ISBN 9780197654637
Subjects: LCSH: Qur'an as literature. | Qur'an—Language, style. |
Repetition in literature. | Repetition (Rhetoric)
Classification: LCC BP131.8 .O94 2023 (print) | LCC BP131.8 (ebook) |
DDC 297.1/224045—dc23/eng/20230119
LC record available at https://lccn.loc.gov/2022060593
LC ebook record available at https://lccn.loc.gov/2022060594

DOI: 10.1093/oso/9780197654606.001.0001

Printed by Integrated Books International, United States of America

# Contents

*List of Illustrations* vii
*Acknowledgments* ix

**1. Introduction: Why Repetition?** **1**

**2. Repetition in Structure: Parallels, Reversals, and Triangles** **9**
I. Introduction 9
II. Parallels, Reversals, and Swerves: Parents and Children 10
III. Parallels and Reversals: Family Members Doing Counterintuitive Things 15
IV. Parallels and Reversals: Mūsā Trusting Strangers 21
V. Parallels and Swerves: The Faith of Prophets 27
VI. Outliers 28
VII. Inverted Triangles 30
VIII. Conclusion 33

**3. Repetition in the Qur'ānic Story of Mūsā** **35**
I. Introduction 35
II. Types of Repetition 38
A. Root Word 39
B. Motif 40
C. Theme 42
D. Sequence of Actions 43
E. Type-Scene 44
III. What Is Done with Repetition 45
A. Deployed 45
B. Aborted 48
C. Suppressed 49
D. Suppressed: Focalization 51
E. Suppressed: Characterization 54
F. Suppressed: Reversal 55
G. Selective Giving and Withholding Information 55
IV. Repeated Elements 56
A. Length of Iterations 56
B. Introductions and Conclusions 59
V. Conclusion 60

**4. Repetition and the Portrayal of Time in the Story of Mūsā and Hārūn in the Qur'ān** **62**
I. Introduction 62

II. Mūsā and Hārūn with Minimal and No Leaps in Time and Space 64
III. *Sūrat Ṭaha* 66
IV. *Sūrat al-Shu'arā'* 72
V. Conclusion 75

**5. Echoing Phrases, Words, and Actions in Qur'ānic Stories: Exchange Encounters, Fasting, Feasting, and Faith 77**
I. Introduction 77
II. Zakariyyā's Fast (3:41 and 19:10) 79
III. Maryam's Fast (19:26–30) 80
IV. Fasting and Asking for Things from God (2:186) 81
V. Maryam's Provisions (3:35 and 3:37) 84
VI. Providing a Feast: Ibrāhīm and His Guests (11:69–76) 85
VII. Fasting from Water (2:249–251) 86
VIII. Consuming a Feast: The Table (5:112–115) 87
IX. How to Ask for Things from God 90
X. Conclusion 94

**6. Repetition in *Sūrat al-Shu'arā'*: Prophethood, Power, and Inspiration 96**
I. Introduction 96
II. Competing Sources of Power, Inspiration, and Revelation 97
III. God Gives People the Choice to Believe or Not 108
IV. What Messengers Expect from People 113
V. Responses to Revelation and Claims of Revelation 115
VI. Conclusion 120

**7. Repetition in *Sūrat al-Qamar* and a Comparison with *Sūrat al-Shu'arā'* 122**
I. Introduction 122
II. What Is Ordinary or Extraordinary? 124
III. God's Power Versus Human Weakness 129
IV. The Qur'ān as a Bridge 132
V. A Comparison of *Sūrat al-Qamar* with *Sūrat al-Shū'arā'* 136
VI. Conclusion 144

**8. Conclusion: Connections, Narrative, and Power 145**

*Appendices* 149
*Appendix A: Mūsā* 149
*Appendix B: Sūrat al-Shu'arā'* 159
*Appendix C: Sūrat al-Qamar and Comparisons of Sūrat al-Shu'arā' with Sūrat al-Qamar* 161
*Notes* 165
*Bibliography* 175
*Index* 183

# Illustrations

## Figures


2.1: Parallels, Reversals, and Swerves in Stories of Parents and Children 20
2.2: *Sūrat Maryam* as an Inverted Triangle 30
2.3: The Introduction of *Sūrat Yūsuf* as an Inverted Triangle 31
2.4: *Sūrat al-Baqara* as an Inverted Triangle 32
2.5: Descriptions of God in *Sūrat al-Fātiḥa* as an Inverted Triangle 32
5.1: The Intratextuality of Verses About Fasting in the Qur'ān 83
A.1: The Story of Mūsā in the Qur'ān 150
A.2: Number of Times Elements Are Repeated 154


## Tables


2.1: Parallels, Reversals, and Swerves in Stories of Parents and Children 22
3.1: Concentric Repetition in a Motif 42
3.2: Mūsā and Fir'awn: The Magicians 49
3.3: Mūsā and Fir'awn: God Talks to Mūsā 51
5.1: Exchange Encounters in Qur'ānic Stories 88
6.1: The Structure of *Sūrat al-Shu'arā'* 97
6.2: Struggles for Power and Privilege in Mūsā's Story in *Sūrat al-Shu'arā'* 99
7.1: The Structure of *Sūrat al-Qamar* 123
7.2: Repeated Themes in *Sūrat al-Qamar* 126
7.3: A Comparison of the Structure of *Sūrat al-Shu'arā'* and *Sūrat al-Qamar* 138
A.1: Stories of Mūsā and Fir'awn in the Qur'ān 151
A.2: Stories of Mūsā and the Book in the Qur'ān 155
A.3: Stories of Mūsā and His People in the Qur'ān 156
A.4: Story of Mūsā and the Wise Man in the Qur'ān 158
A.5: Verses Related to Mūsā, but Are Not Stories of Mūsā 158

B.1: Frequently Repeated Root Letters in *Sūrat al-Shu'arā'* 159
B.2: Infrequently Repeated Root Letters in *Sūrat al-Shu'arā'* 160
C.1: Frequently Repeated Root Letters in *Sūrat al-Qamar* 161
C.2: Infrequently Repeated Root Letters in *Sūrat al-Qamar* 162
C.3: Not Repeated Root Letters in *Sūrat al-Qamar* 163
C.4: Frequently Repeated Root Letters in *Sūrat al-Qamar* Versus *Sūrat al-Shu'arā'* 164
C.5: Infrequently Repeated Root Letters in *Sūrat al-Qamar* Versus *Sūrat al-Shu'arā'* 164

# Acknowledgments

I am grateful to Cynthia Read and Theo Calderara for their guidance on this project. Many thanks to Ris Harp and Suganya Elango for seeing me through the publication process. I am sincerely grateful for the generous feedback of the reviewers of the manuscript; they helped make this a better book.

Many thanks to Yasmin Amin, Rose Aslan, Michael Cooperson, Emad Hamdeh, Noor Hashem, and Charles Hirschkind for reading and giving feedback on earlier versions of some parts of this book. Thank you to Arielle Tonkin for friendship and great conversation. Many thanks to my family and friends for their support and love.

# 1

# Introduction

## Why Repetition?

One of the most frequent questions I am asked about Qur'ānic stories is about repetition. Why is there repetition in Qur'ānic stories? Oddly, we seem to ignore the incredibly widespread amount of repetition in our own cultures. For example, in popular American culture, there are Marvel movies; reboots of television shows, such as *The Wonder Years*; and the brilliant song "Satisfied" in *Hamilton*. Outside of American culture and a bit further in the past is the amazing Japanese film series by Ozu Yasujiro. And, of course, music has repetition in refrains. An educator might say that repetition is part of teaching: revisiting, recycling, and building upon information. One can certainly give psychological, historical, and anthropological answers to this question.

To understand how Qur'ānic stories work, this book focuses on Qur'ānic narrative, specifically, repetition in Qur'ānic stories. Analyzing repetition means that it looks broadly or holistically at the Qur'ān. When I mention reading the Qur'ān, that is shorthand for interacting with the Qur'ān, whether it is through reading, reciting, or listening to it. Reading and analyzing the Qur'ān means there is a relationship between the audience and the text, which Muslims believe is the word of God. So this is a process of meaning making. I approach the Qur'ān with the assumption that it deliberately uses language in particular ways to achieve particular goals. The Qur'ān is a foundational book for Islam and Muslims, and one of the results of the narratological way that I approach it is better understanding its theological beliefs.

Why does repetition matter? Results of repetition, as we will see, are scales, echoes, and the making of structure, all of which develop, complicate, and comment on the Qur'ān's messages. Repetition forges patterns, connections, and layers of meaning throughout the Qur'ān. It is part of the art of Qur'ānic literary technique. In addition, repetition develops subtleties and sophistication in the ideas the Qur'ān presents. For example, in Chapter 2, I discuss the displacement revealed through the use of the root *q-ṣ-y* in the Qur'ān and that it shows that the battle that had taken place, even though it was victorious, is

*How the Qur'ān Works*. Leyla Ozgur Alhassen, Oxford University Press. © Oxford University Press 2023.
DOI: 10.1093/oso/9780197654606.003.0001

still a sad affair (8:42). The rejection of a messenger and the breakdown of a community is a cause for displacement in the subtext—the messenger is physically and socially displaced. In addition, analysis of repetition lends insight into Qur'ānic structure, as we will see throughout the book.

In this book, I am looking at what kinds of repetition occur in Qur'ānic stories and what purposes they serve. This book is a rhetorical, semantic, and narratological analysis of the Qur'ān. Most of the chapters of the book examine multiple Qur'ānic chapters, which are comparative within the Qur'ān. While my work does not compare Qur'ānic stories to biblical stories or Arabic literature other than *tafsīr*, it takes inspiration from Robert Alter's *The Art of Biblical Narrative* and from Sandra Naddaff's *Arabesque: Narrative Structure and the Aesthetics of Repetition in the 1001 Nights*, in their methods of analysis. Both lend insight into repetition, how it is used, and what it does for a text.

This book is an exploration of repetition in Qur'ānic stories and how repetition forges connections. There are a number of ways to look at prophecy as repetition in regards to the Qur'ān: (1) What happened in history is repeated in text. (2) Repeated iterations of one prophet's story occur throughout the Qur'ān. Stories can be repeated in multiple iterations in different locations and lengths in the Qur'ān. The discourse—the narrative style—can be repeated. (3) Multiple messengers repeat parallel missions—the plot can be similar in stories of different prophets and people. (4) The Qur'ān encourages and rewards multiple readings, which is a repetition for the reader; this brings the reader into the world of the text. Taking inspiration from Sandra Naddaff, I argue that God in the Qur'ān is at the center of the story and the discourse, and with repeated iterations we move in time: the audience has a role in the repetition, through the multiple readings in which the reader may engage. This book thus explores Qur'ānic narrative and its intersections with repetition, time, theology, and the text and its readers.

Throughout this book, I use an intratextual approach, looking at relevant Qur'ānic verses on the topic at hand.[1] In the *tafsīr* tradition, there is a concept that the Qur'ān explains the Qur'ān (*al-Qur'ān yufassir ba'ḍuhu ba'ḍan*), and that some verses can best be understood in light of other verses.[2] A number of scholars, modern and classical, find an intratextual approach useful when looking at the Qur'ānic verses.[3] As I am interested in a literary approach, extra-Qur'anic and comparative sources are less important for this study.[4]

In the past two decades, there has been a major proliferation of books in Qur'ānic studies. However, analysis of Qur'ānic stories is often source critical, comparative, focused on *tafsīr*, or looks at the Qur'ān in its historical development. My book takes a different approach to Qur'ānic stories. It also varies from my previous book, *Qur'ānic Stories: God, Revelation and the Audience.*

*Qur'ānic Stories* focuses on one *sūra* per chapter and looks more comprehensively at narratological and rhetorical techniques as relevant to each *sūra*. This book compares different Qur'ānic stories across chapters and revolves around the specific technique of repetition, focusing on different types of repetition throughout the book.

I will argue that repetition is a narrative technique used in the Qur'ān to make theological points. What do I mean by theological points? These are the beliefs that the Qur'ān tries to instill in its audience. This answer reveals a rhetorical approach: the Qur'ān tries to make a change in the audience—in the way the audience thinks and acts. Thus, this book looks at the interactions between the audience, God, and the Qur'ān.

But how can one determine theological points from the Qur'ān? Shahab Ahmed's *What Is Islam? The Importance of Being Islamic* discusses the diverse array of opinions, cultures, behaviors, art, and literature that can be labeled as Islamic.[5] There are, of course, differences between Islam, Islamic, Muslims, the Qur'ān, and Qur'ānic. This question echoes debates in literary theory about whether the text presents meanings or if the reader brings meanings to the text. In the case of the Qur'ān and Muslims, of course people interpret it in different ways; they interpret it with their understanding, preferences and biases, and they choose to believe or follow or not. And then they can still consider themselves Muslims or not. I am not saying definitively what the Qur'ān says or what its intentions are. Rather, I am noticing patterns in the text and giving plausible explanations for what they are doing and what ideas they may be furthering. This is an interactive process of meaning making. Someone else can disagree and give a different set of reasoning, but their arguments should look comprehensively at the Qur'ān.

How can one discuss, in a sophisticated manner, what Qur'ānic theological statements or beliefs are? One way is via a comprehensive, narratological analysis, through which we see that the Qur'ān uses various techniques to scaffold these beliefs. For example, Ibrāhīm is repeatedly portrayed as a father or son, trying to convince others to believe in God, eventually leaving his father when he sees that his efforts are futile. In one of the *sūras* where his story is presented (*Sūrat Maryam*), the structure of the story sequence is an inverted triangle, in which family becomes less prominent and the relationship with God becomes foremost. So the narrative portrayal and the structure of the *sūra* promote a particular belief: if one has to choose between one's relationship with God or family, one should choose God.[6] How do we know that the Qur'ān is actually trying to make these theological points? (1) We can notice them through a variety of narrative techniques and a variety of levels of repetition; and (2) they are also stated in non-narrative verses.

Another way to think about repetition in the Qur'ān is through echo and resonance. This book explores the place of echo in the Qur'ān, comes to a theory of echo in the Qur'ān, and argues that echo has a place in Qur'ānic aesthetic values and in the way it makes and develops arguments. How do echoes advance the semantic, literary, and theological goals of the text? For example, when we think about refrains in the Qur'ān, we will see how refrains lend new meanings to a *sūra*. There can be the same refrain, but different characters and scenes, and the refrain brings whatever one learns from the previous story to the new story. In addition, sometimes the refrain itself may change, which also happens in the Qur'ān, then one can examine how and why the refrain changes. Here, we see that refrains and echoes make connections.

Echoes and resonance are more obvious with a voiced recitation. Thus, one can think about orality in relation to repetition, and there are at least three ways to think about orality and the Qur'ān. One is exploring the effects of sound on meaning, as Michael Sells does.[7] One can also see the Qur'ān as a form of literature that has an oral, performative aspect. Here, we can turn to Navid Kermani. Kermani writes about the recited Qur'ān and the "recitative character of the Qur'ān," which includes repetition and refrain,[8] both of which I analyze in this book. Orality may be a cause for repetition in the Qur'ān, and orality draws attention to repetition. To think about orality and the Qur'ān, one can also turn to Walter Ong's *Orality and Literacy: The Technologizing of the Word*. Ong points out that "many of the contrasts often made between 'western' and other views seem reducible to contrasts between deeply interiorized literacy and more or less residually oral states of consciousness."[9] He lists features common to oral literacy, which one can compare to the Qur'ān.[10] What is implied in the discussion of orality, the Qur'ān and its interpretation, is that scholarship that approaches the text as written alone and not oral is limited.

This book begins its analysis by looking at repetition on a large scale—structure—and moves to a small scale—root letters. It then looks at two *sūras* that have series of stories of prophets, and refrains, and analyzes them and compares them with each other.

## Chapter 2: Repetition in Structure: Parallels, Reversals, and Triangles

First, I approach repetition on a large, structural scale in the Qur'ān. I identify and discuss parallels, reversals, inverted triangles, and outliers found in Qur'ānic stories. In the Qur'ānic stories, there are many thematic reversals and parallels. I evaluate how these thematic parallels and reversals contribute to our understanding of the stories in question and their relationship to each other. For example, one way I examine reversals and parallels is through the semantic connections in the actions of throwing someone into something. We find this with the roots *q-dh-f* and *l-q-y* in the stories of Mūsā and his mother: Mūsā being thrown onto the riverbank (*l-q-y*), Mūsā delivering his message and people being so convinced of it that they are thrown in prostration (*l-q-y*), al-Sāmirī throwing out his idea to make the golden calf (*l-q-y*, 20:87), Yūsuf's brothers describing their action as throwing (*l-q-y*) Yūsuf into the depths of a well (12:10), and Yūsuf later telling someone to throw his shirt onto his father's face to recover his sight (*l-q-y*, 12:93). I analyze how these stories relate to and play off of each other, as well as other reversals, triangles, and parallels in Qur'ānic stories. I examine the different stories with a broad stroke to see how they interact with each other and to see the structural patterns within them.

## Chapter 3: Repetition in the Qur'ānic Story of Mūsā

Next, we have repetition on the level of the story, in the story of Mūsā in the Qur'ān. This chapter engages with Sandra Naddaff's discussions of narrative repetition in the *1001 Nights* and Robert Alter's *The Art of Biblical Narrative*. The story of the life of Mūsā is the most frequently mentioned story in the Qur'ān, with arguably forty-two iterations. In this chapter, the Qur'ānic stories about Mūsā in the Qur'ān are discussed and compared with each other. For example, through an analysis of focalization in the stories of Mūsā, we see that repetition in the Qur'ān is intimately connected to the ideas of power, storytelling, the right to tell a story or history, and truth. The chapter lends insight into Qur'ānic storytelling style: Qur'ānic stories can be told at length or in short pieces, chronologically all at once, or not. Focalization can be a tool for character development. History and dialogues can be told in different ways at different times.

## Chapter 4: Repetition and the Portrayal of Time in the Story of Mūsā and Hārūn in the Qur'ān

Next, I take up the idea of the portrayal of time in Qur'ānic stories, specifically looking at time leaps in various iterations of scenes, working with narratological discussions of the narrative portrayal of time. The portrayal of time in Qur'ānic stories is an area ripe for exploration. While there exists scholarship on the portrayal of time in the Qur'ān, little uses narratological theories of time to explore and explicate on the portrayal of time in the stories. The chapter compares the portrayal of time in the Qur'ānic story of Mūsā and Hārūn in particular, and it uses a narratological lens to analyze a few iterations of the stories, in which we see Hārūn gradually appearing in a scene, as well as Mūsā and Hārūn leaping in time and space to have a dialogue with Fir'awn. Through the exploration of the portrayal of time in this story, we see not just a movement in time but also a conversation about a time and place, and then a leap into that time and space. We see what purpose time leaps serve the reader, and that they are reflected in the storytelling, are not just didactic, but are performative. I argue that the narrator of the Qur'ān uses the narrative to shape the perceptions and norms of the reader about time and space and to thereby reinforce theological beliefs that the Qur'ān expresses in its metanarrative.

## Chapter 5: Echoing Phrases, Words, and Actions in Qur'ānic Stories: Exchange Encounters, Fasting, Feasting, and Faith

The fifth chapter moves to repetition on a small scale, in echoing words and phrases in the Qur'ān, focusing on fasting and feasting throughout the Qur'ān. I propose that the Qur'ānic narrative portrayal of fasting and feasting can be seen as exchange encounters in which something is given and something is received. This analysis develops to demonstrate that these stories are united both thematically and stylistically, that the exchange encounters connect with the idea of asking for things from God, and that the manner of asking reflects one's belief. Through these stories, we see that not only do Qur'ānic narratives exist, but also they are woven together, with metanarrative, to reinforce theological beliefs.

## Chapter 6: Repetition in *Sūrat al-Shu'arā'*: Prophethood, Power, and Inspiration

Chapter 6 is paired with the next, this one focusing on *Sūrat al-Shu'arā'* and the next on *Sūrat al-Qamar* and then a comparison of the two *sūras*. *Sūrat al-Shu'arā'* is made up of an introduction, conclusion, and seven stories of prophets. The chapter analyzes repetition in the *sūra*, in the series of stories, which lends insight into its structure, in the root letters, and in the *sūra*'s themes. I also analyze root letters within the series of stories and refrains. This analysis lends insight into underlying themes in the stories. For example, in this *sūra*, we see a theme of power, privilege, and inspiration. Throughout the series of stories, there is the idea of lying and calling others liars, and there is the breakdown of communication. Connected to this theme, there is a contrast between Fir'awn as a father figure or enslaver and Ibrāhīm's father, which then pivots from Ibrāhīm's father to God. We see through the analysis in this chapter how repetition occurs at various levels of scale throughout *Sūrat al-Shu'arā'* and how it is used to contrast and complicate various ideas.

## Chapter 7: Repetition in *Sūrat al-Qamar* and a Comparison with *Sūrat al-Shu'arā'*

In this chapter, I analyze repetition in *Sūrat al-Qamar* then compare it with *Sūrat al-Shu'arā'*. I first examine the structure, refrains, echoing roots, and themes in *Sūrat al-Qamar*. Both *Sūrat al-Qamar* and *Sūrat al-Shu'arā'* include a number of Qur'ānic stories, one after another, with refrains. This allows us to compare stories and repetition within a *sūra* and stories and repetition between *sūras*. It also provides the opportunity to compare the refrains, echoing roots, focalization, and prominent themes within and between the *sūras*. Through the echoing roots, themes, stories, and *sūras*, we examine repetition on various scales. As a result of this analysis, we will see that sometimes the same prophets feature in a sequence of stories in different *sūras*, but their stories are told in different narratological ways and with different topics of focus. In both *sūras*, we see how repeated themes, root letters, and refrains draw connection and contrast. Through this analysis, we see that *Sūrat al-Qamar*, with the interplay of its stories and refrain, emphasizes the relationship between the audience and the Qur'ān.

## Conclusion: Connections, Narrative, and Power

The conclusion reviews the various narratological features that the book analyzed and connects them to the issues of repetition and Qur'ānic theology. It also looks at underlying themes discussed throughout the book, and then it discusses venues for further research inspired by the book's analysis.

## Appendices

The appendices include comprehensive tables of all the stories about Mūsā in the Qur'ān: the four stories with forty-two iterations that are the basis of my analysis in Chapter 3, as well as tables useful in the analysis of *Sūrat al-Shu'arā'* and *Sūrat al-Qamar*.

This book takes a journey through the Qur'ān, often expansive, moving from one verse to another, one story to another, focusing on narratological elements while conducting a fine reading of Qur'ānic material to understand how these techniques enhance a theological agenda. It helps us better understand particular Qur'ānic stories, Qur'ānic literary style, and Qur'ānic theology.

# 2

# Repetition in Structure

## Parallels, Reversals, and Triangles

## I. Introduction

One manifestation of repetition in Qur'ānic stories is on a large, structural scale. Raymond Farrin, Nevin Reda, and Michel Cuypers have explored the structural patterns of concentric circles in the Qur'ān.[1] Karen Bauer looks at some parallel stories through their shared emotional resonances or "emotional plots."[2] Celene Ibrahim analyzes some parallel stories and some contrasting stories, reversals, in the Qur'ān.[3] Al-Qushayrī mentions a parallel in the story of Yūsuf.[4] In fact, if we look at some of the Qur'ānic stories, such as that of Yūsuf, we find a concentric pattern, within which we can find parallels and reversals. In this chapter, I seek to identify some structural and thematic reversals, parallels, swerves, and triangles in Qur'ānic stories and see patterns in them. I evaluate how these structures contribute to our understanding of the stories in question and the Qur'ān more broadly.

In the examples in this chapter, we will see parallels, reversals, outliers, inverted triangles, and what I call swerves. We will find that some stories have multiple reversals. I use the term "swerve" when something first looks like a parallel, then it varies from the original, but it does not vary enough to be a reversal. For example, we start with the stories of Maryam and Zakariyyā being told they will have children. Here we see parallels with some slight variations—within parallels, there are, of course, small variations. Then comes Ibrāhīm, first with a reversal of the stories of Maryam and Zakariyyā. Then, we see a pattern and an example of a lack of repetition in Ibrāhīm's story. There are reversals in the stories of Mūsā's encounters with strangers. In the stories of family members doing counterintuitive things, there are parallels and contrasts. Then, in the faith of prophets, we see swerves. Finally, we look at parallels and reversals in the ways that outliers function in Qur'ānic stories. Through this analysis, we will come to an understanding of repetition in large structural frameworks and themes in the Qur'ān. This will add insight to our understanding of repetition in the Qur'ān and structural patterns and logic of

*How the Qur'ān Works*. Leyla Ozgur Alhassen, Oxford University Press. © Oxford University Press 2023.
DOI: 10.1093/oso/9780197654606.003.0002

the Qur'ān. Through the exclusion of a parallel story in *Sūrat Maryam*, we will see that repetition is a deliberate literary technique that serves to make theological points.

As far as each story is concerned, the use of repetition on a large scale encourages the audience to compare characters that one may not have thought to compare. For example, we will see a comparison between Ibrāhīm, Mūsā's mother, and Yūsuf's brothers below. Repetition or its opposite, reversals, bring out themes in the stories. Through a focus on repetition, we see the themes of theft and agency in *Sūrat Yūsuf*. Parallels, swerves, and reversals also show how Qur'ānic *sūras* interact with each other. We will see, through parallels, swerves, and reversals, connections made between seven *sūras*. The patterns of parallels, swerves, reversals, and triangles serve to organize information and stories in the Qur'ān, directing the audience to make comparisons between characters and stories while bringing out certain themes and theological points.

## II. Parallels, Reversals, and Swerves: Parents and Children

We can start with the theme of parents and children in the structural pattern of parallels and swerves. I discuss the structure of the story of Maryam and Zakariyyā in *Sūrat Maryam* in detail elsewhere.[5] Essentially, there is a series of stories, and in the first one, Zakariyyā prays to have a child and is told that he will have one (19:3–6). With many parallel words, in the second section, Maryam is told she will have a child, even though she did not ask to have one. So here is a parallel, a parent being told they will have a child, and a variation in that one parent asks to have a child and the other does not. Maryam is told not to speak, and her baby speaks instead (19:30-3). Here, the child takes on a more prominent role than in Zakariyyā's story, and this is a turning point in the series of stories. One detail that will come up later is that Zakariyyā describes the child as a "successor," *walī* (19:5), and he says he wants the child to inherit from him and the family of Ya'qūb, *yarithunī* (19:6).[6]

As we continue reading *Sūrat Maryam*, there is a reversal in the story of Ibrāhīm (19:41–50):

> 19:42 He said to his father, "Father, why do you worship something that can neither hear nor see nor benefit you in any way?
>
> 43 Father, knowledge that has not reached you has come to me, so follow me: I will guide you to an even path.

44 Father, do not worship Satan—Satan has rebelled against the Lord of Mercy.
45 Father, I fear that a punishment from the Lord of Mercy may afflict you and that you may become Satan's companion [in Hell]."

Here is a reversal, in which Ibrāhīm, the child, wants to give something (knowledge instead of inheritance) to his father. Al-Zamakhsharī emphasizes that Ibrāhīm does not use the knowledge that he has been given to insult his father or to prop himself up. Rather, this knowledge is the reason his father should follow him and is a basis for faith.[7] 'Īsā began a shift in the parent-child relationship (19:30–33), but here it is a reversal. Ibrāhīm speaks with kindness and an endearing term to his father (19:44 and 19:45); his father responds by threatening him and telling him to go away (19:46). The harsh words of Ibrāhīm's father contrast with Maryam's mother's prayers for her baby in utero: "Imran's wife said, 'Lord, I have dedicated what is growing in my womb entirely to You; so accept this from me. You are the One who hears and knows all'" (3:35). Ibrāhīm leaves his father and people (19:48) and is blessed with a child and grandchild (19:49–50), symbolizing movement into the future, rather than being stuck in and following the past (21:51–73, 26:69–89, and 43:23–29).

While analyzing the story of Ibrāhīm in the Qur'ān, in terms of the larger question of repetition, parallels, and reversals, one will also notice that Ibrāhīm's story in other places in the Qur'ān includes the birth of a miraculous child. This story is a parallel to those of Zakariyyā and Maryam. For an example, we can focus on this story in *Sūrat al-Dhāriyāt*, where it clearly echoes *Sūrat Maryam* (51:28–30; 19:9, and 19:21). In the story, some guests visit Ibrāhīm and his family; he offers them a calf to eat, and when they do not eat, he becomes fearful (51:24–27). Ibrāhīm was

51:28 beginning to be afraid of them, but they said, "Do not be afraid." They gave him good news of a son who would be gifted with knowledge [*fa-awjasa minhum khīfatan qālū lā takhaf wa-bashsharūhu bi-ghulāmin 'alīm*].

29 His wife then entered with a loud cry, struck her face, and said, "A barren old woman [*fa-aqbalati imra'atuhu fī ṣarratin faṣakkat wajhahā wa-qālat 'ajūzun 'aqīm*]?"

30 but they said, "It will be so. This is what your Lord said, and He is the One who has the knowledge to decide [*qālū kadhāliki qāla rabbuki innahu huwa al-ḥakīmu al-'alīm*]."

First, we can notice that there are three or more angels and that they are described as guests. Ibrāhīm offers them food; Zakariyyā and Maryam do not offer food to their mysterious guests (I discuss this further in Chapter 5). Ibrāhīm and his wife do not ask God for a child, but the angels tell them they will have one. The child is described with the root *b-sh-r*, as are the children of Zakariyyā (3:39 and 19:7) and Maryam (3:45). The *b-sh-r* root is used repeatedly in the Qur'ān for Ibrāhīm's children (11:71, 15:53, 15:54 twice, 15:55, 37:101, 37:112, and 51:28 above). The word *ghulām* is used for the children of Ibrāhīm (15:53, 37:101, and 51:28 above), Zakariyyā (3:40, 19:7, and 19:8), and Maryam (19:19 and 19:20). And the biggest parallel is in the verse 51:30: "but they said, 'It will be so. This is what your Lord said, and He is the One who has the knowledge to decide,'" *qālū kadhāliki qāla rabbuki innahu huwa al-ḥakīmu al-'alīm*. This echoes what the messenger tells Maryam, "and he said, 'This is what your Lord said: "It is easy for Me—We shall make him a sign to all people, a blessing from Us,"'" *qāla kadhāliki qāla rabbuki huwa 'alayya hayyinun wa-li-naj'alahu āyatan li-l-nāsi wa-raḥmatan minnā wa-kāna amran maqḍiyya* (19:21). The phrase in the beginning is almost the exact same, with a difference in the plural versus the singular speaker: '*qālū kadhāliki qāla rabbuki*' (51:30) and '*qāla kadhāliki qāla rabbuki*' (19:21). The response to Zakariyyā is also very similar (19:9). Thematically, Zakariyyā and his wife and Ibrāhīm and his wife are parallels in that they are to have children in their old age and are surprised about it. Zakariyyā and Ibrāhīm's wife explicitly express this surprise (19:8 and 51:29).

Despite the parallels in the main plot (someone surprisingly having a child), and the semantic echoes, the story of Ibrāhīm having a child is missing from *Sūrat Maryam*. I am arguing that since repetition serves a purpose in Qur'ānic stories, the story of Ibrāhīm having an unexpected child is not in *Sūrat Maryam*, despite the parallels, because it would serve little purpose there. In other words, *Sūrat Maryam* includes stories of miraculous births of children, but it does not include Ibrāhīm's, probably because it would be simply repetitive and too similar to Zakariyyā's and Maryam's stories. Instead, *Sūrat Maryam* has the reversal in which Ibrāhīm takes on the role of father in his relationship with his father. This reversal allows the *sūra* to move from a focus on family to a focus on God, as I discuss elsewhere.[8] We see, then, that repetition is not simply for the sake of repetition or the collection of knowledge. It has other purposes. And repetition here pivots to a reversal to make a theological point.

We can further develop our understanding of the portrayal of Ibrāhīm in another verse in the Qur'ān. First, God somehow tests Ibrāhīm, Ibrāhīm passes the test, and earns a special epithet and perhaps ranking from God. Ibrāhīm then asks God about his children:

> 2:124 When Abraham's Lord tested him with certain commandments, which he fulfilled, He said, "I will make you a leader of people." Abraham asked, "And will You make leaders from my descendants too?" God answered, "My pledge does not hold for those who do evil."

It is striking that Ibrāhīm asks about his children after receiving such special words from God, that God will make him a leader for people, "*lil-nāsi imāman.*" There is no other story in the Qur'ān in which God designates one person as an *imām*. Elsewhere, this word is used to describe God's revelation (11:17 and 46:12), in the plural (9:12, 21:73, 28:5, 28:41, and 32:24), as a record (17:71 and 36:12), as something that people pray to be (25:74), and as a highway (15:79), but not to refer to a particular individual appointed by God. In the context of Ibrāhīm representing the pulls between a person and God versus a person and family, this makes sense.[9] Here he is given a special place and title with God, but he is still concerned about his progeny. And this time his concern is his children—the generation forward rather than his father. Here is, again, the pattern of Ibrāhīm embodying the clashes between faith and family. In terms of Qur'ānic parallels and reversals, this is parallel to the story of Zakariyyā and his wanting to pass something on to his child.

A resolution to the pulls between faith and family in the story of Ibrāhīm occurs in *Sūrat al-Baqara*. Here, Ibrāhīm builds the Ka'ba with his son and then is remembered by his descendants.

> 2:127 As Abraham and Ishmael built up the foundations of the House [they prayed], "Our Lord, accept [this] from us. You are the All Hearing, the All Knowing.
>
> 128 Our Lord, make us devoted to You; make our descendants into a community devoted to You. Show us how to worship and accept our repentance, for You are the Ever Relenting, the Most Merciful.
>
> 129 Our Lord, make a messenger of their own rise up from among them, to recite Your revelations to them, teach them the Scripture and wisdom, and purify them: You have the power to decide."
>
> 130 Who but a fool would forsake the religion of Abraham? We have chosen him in this world and he will rank among the righteous in the Hereafter.
>
> 131 His Lord said to him, "Devote yourself to Me." Abraham replied, "I devote myself to the Lord of all worlds,"
>
> 132 and commanded his sons to do the same, as did Jacob: "My sons, God has chosen [your] religion for you, so make sure you devote yourselves to Him, to your dying moment."

> 133 Were you [Jews] there to see when death came upon Jacob? When he said to his sons, "What will you worship after I am gone?" they replied, "We shall worship your God and the God of your fathers, Abraham, Ishmael, and Isaac, one single God: we devote ourselves to Him."

First, Ibrāhīm is devoted to God in a long-lasting, foundational way, with his son, building the Ka'ba, which becomes the direction of prayer and location of hajj for Muslims. Then, Ibrāhīm is portrayed as being remembered by his descendants, who say they will worship the God of their father and their forefather, Ibrāhīm (2:133). Here we see the unifying power of belief in God, where a family all worships God together and remembers each other through their shared belief in God. In terms of parallels and reversals, this is a reversal of the scene of Ibrāhīm with his father. In the larger story of Ibrāhīm, we move from Ibrāhīm trying to teach his father and people, to his leaving them, his moving into the future through his children and grandchildren, him being told he will have a child, him being told to sacrifice his child and then not having to, him being tested by God and being told he is an *imām* and asking God if that includes his children, and finally this, where his child is worshipping God with him and together building a center of worship for God.

In the theme of parents having children, there are parallels and reversals. First there are two parallel stories in *Sūrat Maryam*: those of Zakariyyā and then Maryam being told they will have children. Then there is a reversal in Ibrāhīm trying to encourage his father to inherit from his knowledge. Meanwhile, elsewhere is a parallel story, with echoing phrases, of Ibrāhīm having an unexpected child. This then leads to an examination of Ibrāhīm and his representation of the conflicts that people might feel between their loyalty to their faith and their family. Ibrāhīm's story finds resolution to this conflict in the building of the Ka'ba with his son. We see here how parallels and reversals draw connections between characters and stories, while they can also complicate and develop theological beliefs across verses and *sūras*. Here, those beliefs are that God is central to human lives: God is the source of children, there may be conflict between faith and family, but faith in God always takes priority over family. One must move forward in one's faith in God, moving generations into the future, rather than being held back by a parent stuck in the past and the past ways of believing. Ideally, as a family, one can worship God together with God at the family's center. This would have been a compelling and relevant message for people coming to a new faith, sometimes leaving their families to do so.

## III. Parallels and Reversals: Family Members Doing Counterintuitive Things

Related to the theme of parents and children, we can turn to parallels and reversals in stories of family members doing something counterintuitive to each other. When Mūsā is a baby, his mother fears that Fir'awn and his people will have him killed because they were killing the sons of Banī Isrā'īl. God inspires Mūsā's mother with a surprising way to save him: "We inspired [*awḥaynā*] Moses' mother, saying, 'Suckle him, and then, when you fear for his safety, put him in the river: do not be afraid, and do not grieve, for We shall return him to you and make him a messenger'" (28:7). This is also in *Sūrat Ṭaha*, when God tells Mūsā:

> 20:38 We inspired [*awḥaynā*] your mother, saying,
> 39 "Put your child [*iqdhifihi*] into the chest, then place him [*fa-qdhifihi*] in the river. Let the river wash him on to its bank, and he will be taken in by an enemy of Mine and his." I showered you with My love and planned that you should be reared under My watchful eye.

Twice, the Qur'ān uses the same word to say that God inspired Mūsā's mother, *awḥaynā*, and there is some discussion in commentary on how God inspires her.[10] Also noteworthy is that the verb *qadhafa* describes how the mother should put the baby in the box and then in the river. M. A. S. Abdel Haleem translates *qadhafa* gently, as "put" and "place," but the word can be used for casting or throwing stones, arrows, or speech. So, a nursing mother is inspired by God, when she fears for her child's life, to throw him in a box and then throw him into a river, and an enemy of his and of God's will take the baby (20:39), and she follows these commands. This is counterintuitive.

A parallel, counterintuitive story is when Ibrāhīm sees in a dream that he should sacrifice his son (37:83–113). This story is a reversal of the story of Ibrāhīm and his father (19:41–49), which in turn is a reversal of the stories of Zakariyyā and Maryam (19:2–40), as discussed above. This time, Ibrāhīm, in the role of father, tells his son that he has knowledge from God, and the son believes him and tells him to do what he was commanded to do. In both stories, a father threatens a son with violence, but here, the son complies because of a shared respect and faith. Through the Qur'ānic narrative style, namely repetition in reversals and parallels, the stories interact across chapters and generations.[11]

The stories of Mūsā's mother and Ibrāhīm are parallels to each other: both are asked by God to do something counterintuitive—to put their child's life in danger—and they do so. The similarity in the parallels in the plots draws the audience to compare two stories with different characters and in different *sūras* with each other. The stories address the conflicts between faith and family discussed above and assert that faith in God should take priority over family. In the end, however, probably because of God's mercy, the parents do not have to give up their children permanently and are reunited with them. So, if one must make a decision, one should choose faith in God over family, but God is so merciful that God reunites families.

While making this theological point, these parallels also draw comparison, interestingly, between Mūsā's mother and Ibrāhīm. To further the comparison, this time with contrast, we can note that Mūsā's mother receives *waḥy* about the actions she should take, whereas Ibrāhīm sees it in a dream (37:102). Because Mūsā's mother is described as receiving *waḥy*, some consider her a prophet.[12] However, it is worth noting that the root *w-ḥ-y* is used in the Qur'ān for beings not traditionally considered prophets, such as the disciples of ʿĪsā (5:111), angels (8:12), the earth (99:5), the skies (41:12), and bees (16:68). The fact that Mūsā's mother is a parallel to Ibrāhīm would certainly strengthen the argument that she is a prophet. Her being a prophet would also make a parallel in terms of the parent and child in each story being a prophet. Of course, one could argue that she is not a prophet, and this element is instead a source of contrast between the stories. Indeed, we can contrast the age of the children in the stories. Ibrāhīm's son is old enough to understand and respond to his father's words, agreeing that his father should sacrifice him (37:102), while Mūsā is a nursing baby that can be placed in a box in water (20:38–39).

We have now seen that Ibrāhīm has a role as a child and a parent in Qur'ānic stories, and so does Maryam. Ibrāhīm clashes with his father on faith, whereas Maryam is a fulfillment or perhaps even a pinnacle of her mother's faith (3:35–36). Probably as a result of her mother's faith and prayer to God (3:35–36), Maryam is blessed by God (3:37 and 3:42) and blessed above the women of the world (3:42). In contrast, Ibrāhīm is threatened by his father (19:46).

Moving back to Ibrāhīm's sacrifice, it is striking that he sees a dream, and the story of Yūsuf also begins with a dream. However, the language used to describe them is different. In *Sūrat Yūsuf*, it says:

> 12:4 Joseph said to his father, "Father, I dreamed of eleven stars and the sun and the moon: I saw them all bow down before me,"
>
> 5 and he replied, "My son, tell your brothers nothing of this dream, or they may plot to harm you--Satan is man's sworn enemy."

Despite the translation, Yūsuf says *ra'aytu*, "I saw." And his father refers to it as "*ru'yāka*," your vision or, most literally, the thing you saw. There are, of course, other dreams in *Sūrat Yūsuf*: those of the prisoners (12:36) and the king (12:43), all described with the same root, *r-'-y*. The exception is the king's advisers refer to them as *aḥlām*, "dreams" (12:44). Ibrāhīm tells his son *innī arā fī al-manām*, "I saw in a dream" (37:102). Yūsuf's brothers do indeed plot against him (12:5)—the Qur'ān does not say if they somehow heard or overheard the dream—and then throw him in a well (12:8–15). There is a contrast in that Ibrāhīm saw the dream and is to commit the sacrifice, whereas Yūsuf saw the dream and is to be sacrificed.

This brings us to a surprising reversal on these stories in the Qur'ān, in the story of Yūsuf's brothers throwing him into a well. Here, also, family members do something surprising and counterintuitive to another family member. An additional link is that God says that he inspired Yūsuf when he is in the well, *awḥaynā* (12:15). In contrast, the brothers were inspired by their souls, *sawwalat lakum anfusukum amran* (12:18 and 12:83) or by Shayṭān, *nazagha al-shayṭān* (12:100). Here, we see a contrast in sources of inspiration. In fact, we see this theme throughout *Sūrat Yūsuf*: What makes people act the way they do? Where does inspiration come from?

There are some important semantic connections in the actions of throwing someone into something. Mūsā's mother's action is described with the root *q-dh-f* (20:39) and *l-q-y* (28:7). The root *l-q-y* is present throughout *Sūrat Ṭaha*.[13] After Mūsā's mother casts him into a box (*q-dh-f*) and casts the box into the river (*q-dh-f*), "the river will throw [*l-q-y*] it onto the bank" (20:39).[14] Later, the magicians are thrown in prostration (*l-q-y*) after being convinced of the truth of Mūsā's mission and the existence of God (20:70). There is a movement and culmination from Mūsā being thrown onto the riverbank (*l-q-y*) to being found and raised in Fir'awn's house, to Mūsā delivering his message and people being so convinced of it that they are thrown in prostration (*l-q-y*). This is contrasted with al-Sāmirī throwing out his idea to make the golden calf (*l-q-y*, 20:87).[15] Meanwhile, one of Yūsuf's brothers describes their action as throwing (*l-q-y*) Yūsuf into the depths of a well (12:10), then God describes it with *j-'-l* (12:15). Later in the story, Yūsuf tells someone to throw (*l-q-y*) his shirt onto his father's face to recover his sight (12:93), the person throws the shirt (*l-q-y*) and Ya'qūb is able to see again (12:96). So here, then, is another reversal, highlighted with a semantic echo: the brothers throwing Yūsuf into the well (12:10), and the pain it causes their father finds its healing in the throwing of Yūsuf's shirt over Ya'qūb's face (12:93 and 12:96).

The brothers taking Yūsuf looks like theft, and in Yūsuf's story, the idea of theft has at least three reversals. First, there is the theft in which Yūsuf's brothers steal him from their parents (12:8–18). They do have permission to take him, but they do not return him to their father, and they lie about what befell him. Then there is the accusation that the brothers are thieves (12:70), then specifically that the youngest brother stole the king's cup (12:70–76), and the brothers say that the youngest brother had a brother who also stole (12:77),[16] in verses that explicitly use language of theft. In fact, Yūsuf frames his brother in order to keep his brother with him. When the other brothers ask him to keep one of them instead of the youngest, Yūsuf says he does not want to steal a brother who did not steal in the first place (12:79). But none of his brothers stole the cup. However, ironically, they did steal Yūsuf, and so, they are, indeed, *sāriqūn* (12:70). The parallels and contrasts here make one wonder why Yūsuf framing his brother and "stealing" him are morally justified, but his brothers stealing him is not. First, though, one can mention that Yūsuf tells his younger brother who he is beforehand, so perhaps, in this way, he prepares him for what is to come (12:69). Yūsuf's actions with the cup are followed by God describing them as God's plotting (12:76). It would seem, then, that the key is the source of inspiration, the intention, or the inherent goodness in it. We can also add that everything belongs to God (e.g., 2:107 and 3:189), so if God takes something, it is not theft. Yūsuf's actions with the cup lead to the brothers' repentance (12:91) and reunite the family with understanding and an explicit mention of no blame (12:92). If we broaden theft to the idea of taking something that one does not have a right to, we can add the people who take Yūsuf from the well and sell him (12:19–20), the purchase of Yūsuf (12:21), the wife's attempt to seduce Yūsuf (12:23–29), and Yūsuf asking for his brother to be brought to him (12:59–66).

Noticing this pattern of repetition through parallels and swerves helps resolve some issues of interpretation in *Sūrat Yūsuf*. When Yūsuf is in prison, he correctly interprets the king's dream, and the king calls for Yūsuf to be brought to him (12:50). Yūsuf sends the messenger back and tells him to ask the king to investigate the matter of the women of the city (12:50). So, Yūsuf will not leave prison unless it is on his terms. The king investigates, finds Yūsuf innocent, and sends for him again. The phrase is the exact same both times: "*wa-qāla al-maliku i'tūnī bih*," "The king said, 'Bring him to me'" (12:50 and 12:54). The second time, Yūsuf agrees and says what position he wants to be placed in: "Joseph said, 'Put me in charge of the nation's storehouses: I shall manage them prudently and carefully'" (12:55). So, Yūsuf exerts his agency in both of these interactions. This completely counters the previous cases of Yūsuf being stolen from his family, from the well, and, even, from himself.

Some commentators, readers, and listeners might express surprise that Yūsuf does not seem eager to leave prison and instead asks for his innocence to be proven first (12:50). For example, al-Ṭabarī gives two *ḥadīth* to explain this verse: the first is that Prophet Muḥammad said that Yūsuf had a lot of patience; if someone was going to let me out of the prison, I would have gotten out of there quickly. The second *ḥadīth* adds that Prophet Muḥammad said he would not have asked to be absolved of guilt.[17] So here, Prophet Muḥammad, himself, is expressing surprise at Yūsuf's behavior. The analysis of patterns resolves this issue of interpretation. Yūsuf asking for his case to be investigated is a show of his agency over himself—he will leave prison when and under the conditions that he stipulates. Additionally, some commentators probably find it unpalatable that Yūsuf asks for a position from a person (12:55), so they explain that this is not out of a desire for his own self,[18] rather it is to spread God's rules, truth and justice, and because he knows that other people cannot do what he can do.[19] Yūsuf's story has a pattern of people taking things that they have no right to, and this theme is resolved in Yūsuf insisting upon his own agency. Not only is Yūsuf unwilling to leave prison unless his innocence is first acknowledged, but he is also going to choose the position of privilege that he will be granted. So, the commentator's confusion or surprise are explained through the analysis of parallels and reversals, which brings to light the themes of theft and agency. It is also helpful to rewind the story to revisit how Yūsuf ends up in prison in the first place. He prays to God to put him in prison (12:33), and the people put him in prison after seeing signs (12:35).[20] So he is again choosing his path. Perhaps this is what allows him to forgive his brothers later in the story—he chooses where to be and when to be there, so he asserts his agency, after having lost it as a child. Through the analysis of the patterns of repetition, we have found that theft and agency are themes in *Sūrat Yūsuf*.

Going back to the three stories in question (Mūsā's mother, Ibrāhīm, and Yūsuf and his brothers), the similarities in all of them is in family members doing counterintuitive things to each other; all the family members being reunited; and in two of the stories, God revealing something to one of the family members. In addition to Mūsā and Yūsuf both being thrown into things by family members, there are other parallels in their stories in the Qur'ān.[21] However, the variations are that God reveals to the person acted upon, Yūsuf, in one case, and to the actor in another case, Mūsā's mother; both use the same root, *w-ḥ-y*. The similarities and contrasts draw one to reflect upon the themes of family, inspiration from God, on what basis people choose to act, reunion, being spared from a difficult fate, and the sometimes opposing pulls between faith and family. One is also led to reflect on similarities and differences between the main actors in the stories: Mūsā's mother, Ibrāhīm, and Yūsuf's brothers on one hand, and Mūsā, Ismāʿīl, and Yūsuf on the other hand. In the first category, we also see the striking categorization of Yūsuf's brothers with their sin and crime, with Mūsā's mother and Ibrāhīm. One is then led to think about what makes their actions morally different.

We can broaden our scope and think about how the theme of parents and children, and family members doing counterintuitive things are related. Figure 2.1 shows these connections. We can start with the story of Zakariyyā asking to have a child and move to its parallel story, in the same *sūra*, of Maryam being told she will have a child. Then, in different *sūras*, comes a parallel of Ibrāhīm and his wife being told they will have a child. A reversal is Ibrāhīm being asked to sacrifice his son. Parallel to this is Mūsā's mother being inspired to throw her baby in a river. A reversal to this is Yūsuf's brothers throwing him into a well. A reversal of this is when Yūsuf's shirt is thrown on his father to heal him (12:93 and 12:96). Another reversal to Yūsuf's being thrown in the well is the accusation that the king's cup is stolen. A reversal to this is Yūsuf keeping his brother. Going back to *Sūrat Maryam*, a reversal to the stories of people having children is Ibrāhīm's interaction with his father.

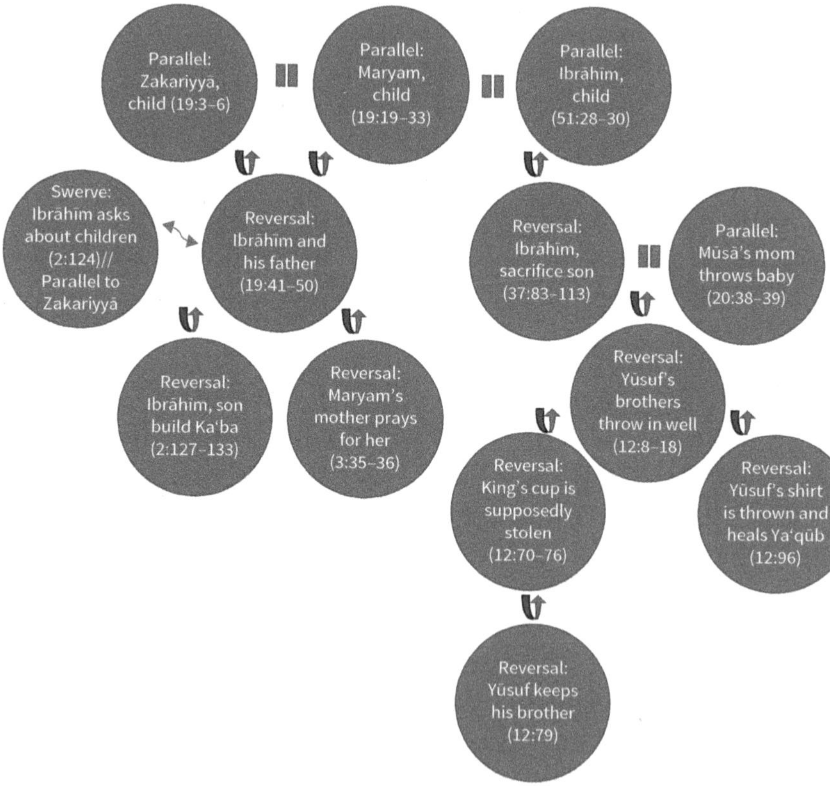


**Figure 2.1** Parallels, Reversals, and Swerves in Stories of Parents and Children

A swerve is when Ibrāhīm asks God about his children. Two final reversals, and really resolutions, are when Ibrāhīm and his son build the Ka'ba, and when Maryam's mother dedicates her to God.

This can also be envisioned as a table, Table 2.1, showing the connections between stories, with "P" for parallel, "R" for reversal, and "S" for swerve.

Here, there are thematic and semantic connections between seven *sūras* (*sūras* 2, 3, 12, 19, 20, 37, and 51, and some of the stories have repeated iterations, which are not included here). In this way, the stories of Maryam's mother, Maryam, Zakariyyā, Ibrāhīm, Mūsā's mother, and Yūsuf are all connected. Through an exploration of parallels, reversals, and swerves, we come to find that the theme of parents and children is are very much connected with the theme of family members doing counterintuitive things.

## IV. Parallels and Reversals: Mūsā Trusting Strangers

Within Mūsā's story in the Qur'ān, there are more parallels and reversals, specifically in the theme of meeting people and their influences on each other. First, Mūsā hears a person yelling for help, he goes to help and not only does he accidentally kill a man (28:15), but he also later finds out that the man crying out for help is himself an instigator (28:18–19):

> 28:15 He entered the city, unnoticed by its people, and found two men fighting: one from his own people, the other an enemy. The one from his own people cried out to him for help against the enemy. Moses struck him with his fist and killed him. He said, "This must be Satan's work: clearly he is a misleading enemy."
>
> 16 He said, "Lord, I have wronged myself. Forgive me," so He forgave him; He is truly the Most Forgiving, the Most Merciful.
>
> 17 He said, "My Lord, because of the blessings You have bestowed upon me, I shall never support those who do evil."
>
> 18 Next morning, he was walking in the city, fearful and vigilant, when suddenly the man he had helped the day before cried out to him for help. Moses said, "You are clearly a troublemaker."
>
> 19 As he was about to attack the man who was an enemy to both of them, the man said, "Moses, are you going to kill me as you killed that person yesterday? You clearly want to be a tyrant in the land; you do not intend to put things right."
>
> 20 Then a man came running from the furthest part of the city and said, "Moses, the authorities are talking about killing you, so leave—this is my sincere advice."
>
> 21 So Moses left the city, fearful and wary, and prayed, "My Lord, save me from people who do wrong."

**Table 2.1** Parallels, Reversals, and Swerves in Stories of Parents and Children

| Person, event | Zakariyyā, child | Maryam, child | Ibrāhīm, child | Ibrāhīm and his father | Ibrāhīm, sacrifice son | Mūsā's mother throws baby | Ibrāhīm asks about his children | Maryam's mother prays for her | Ibrāhīm, son, build Kaʿba | Yūsuf's brothers throw in well | King's cup is supposedly stolen | Yūsuf keeps his brother | Yūsuf's shirt is thrown on Yaʿqūb |
|---|---|---|---|---|---|---|---|---|---|---|---|---|---|
| Zakariyyā, child | P | P | P | R | R | | P | | | | | | |
| Maryam, child | P | P | P | R | R | | | | | | | | |
| Ibrāhīm, child | P | P | P | R | R | | | | | | | | |
| Ibrāhīm and his father | R | R | R | | | | | R | R | | | | |
| Ibrāhīm, sacrifice son | R | R | R | | | P | | | | R | | | |
| Mūsā's mother throws baby | R | R | R | | P | | | | | R | | | |
| Ibrāhīm asks about his children | P | | | S | | | | | | | | | |

| Person, event | Zakariyyā, child | Maryam, child | Ibrāhīm, child | Ibrāhīm and his father | Ibrāhīm, sacrifice son | Mūsā's mother throws baby | Ibrāhīm asks about his children | Maryam's mother prays for her | Ibrāhīm, son, build Kaʿba | Yūsuf's brothers throw in well | King's cup is supposedly stolen | Yūsuf keeps his brother | Yūsuf's shirt is thrown on Yaʿqūb |
|---|---|---|---|---|---|---|---|---|---|---|---|---|---|
| Maryam's mother prays for her | | | | R | | | | | | | | | |
| Ibrāhīm, son, build Kaʿba | | | | R | | | | | | | | | |
| Yūsuf's brothers throw in well | | | | | R | R | | | | | R | | R |
| King's cup is supposedly stolen | | | | | | | | | | R | | R | |
| Yūsuf keeps his brother | | | | | | | | | | | R | | |
| Yūsuf's shirt is thrown on Yaʿqūb | | | | | | | | | | R | | | |

*Note:* "P" for parallel, "R" for reversal, and "S" for swerve.

22 As he made his way towards Midian, he was saying, "May my Lord guide me to the right way."

In the beginning of this story, Mūsā helps a person he should not have helped and in a way that was also bad, resulting in accidentally killing someone. Mūsā asks God for forgiveness and swears that he will never again help a criminal (28:16–17). Not only does Mūsā realize that this man presumably frequently picks fights with people (28:18), but also one of the men accuses Mūsā of being a tyrant who has no interest in doing good (28:19).

There is a complication in this story. Mūsā prays to God and says he will not "support those who do evil" (28:17), but then he sees men fighting again, is on the verge of helping again, and finally does not (28:18–19). Why does Mūsā seem to come so close to making the same error again? Perhaps the narrator is showing the audience that it takes time to change oneself. In the story of Mūsā's people, we see similar lessons: despite the people seeing Mūsā's God-given miracles (20:23, 27:13, 43:47–54, and 79:20) and being freed from slavery at least partly as a result of them (20:77), when they see people worshipping an idol, they also want one (7:138–140), and when al-Sāmirī proposes making a golden calf for them, they agree and are adamant in worshipping it (20:85–91) to the extent that Hārūn fears for his own life (7:150). Mūsā almost makes the same mistake twice, and his people do indeed make the same mistake more than once. So in Mūsā and his people, we see that it takes time for people to change their actions, inclinations, and beliefs. At the same time, we see a leader who has gone through similar challenges as his people: the leader reflects the people. Another way to look at this scene is that through repetition Mūsā gets a second chance; he gets a chance to avoid making the same mistake twice.

Returning to the story, in a twist, or a reversal, a man comes and warns Mūsā that the counselors—*al-mala'* again—are deliberating about having Mūsā killed (28:20). Mūsā believes him and runs away, praying to God to protect him from wrongdoers (28:21). The contrast is clear: first, Mūsā trusts the wrong person and does the wrong thing, then he almost trusts the wrong person again, then he trusts the right person and does the right thing. Some questions this brings forward are how can someone judge the people they just met, and how can one judge one's own reason or another's morality?

Perhaps not surprisingly, Mūsā flees to Madyan, where he again sees people who need help and he again helps (28:23–24):

28:23 When he arrived at Midian's waters, he found a group of men watering [their flocks], and beside them two women keeping their flocks back, so he said, "What is the matter with you two?" They said, "We cannot water [our flocks] until the shepherds take their sheep away: our father is a very old man."

24 He watered their flocks for them, withdrew into the shade, and prayed, "My Lord, I am in dire need of whatever good thing You may send me,"

Mūsā meets and trusts the two women whom he helps and their father (28:23–25). He tells the father his life story and then makes an agreement with the man to work for him and marry one of his daughters (28:25–28). There are a number of reversals in this story: Mūsā again helps people, and in this case they are good people. Instead of something bad happening as a result (him accidentally killing someone), good things happen (he gains employment and gets married). Mūsā also trusts the women's father, and the women and their father trust him.

There are clear reversals in the stories where Mūsā helps the man and accidentally kills someone, where he almost again helps a person in a fight, where another man tries to help him by telling him to flee, and when Mūsā is in Madyan. Each of the scenes, which is a parallel or reversal, has the word *madīna* or Madyan, all with the letters *m-d-y-n*. In fact, in Arabic script, the main parts of the words are the same and are differentiated with an *alif* and *lam* in the beginning and a *tā' marbuta* in the end of the word *al-madīna*. First, Mūsā enters the city, *al-madīna* (we do not know where he was before or why this is an important detail), and accidentally kills someone (28:15). Then comes the scene the next day, when Mūsā almost gets involved in a fight again, with the word *al-madīna* (28:18). The third time we have the word *al-madīna* is when the man comes from the outskirts of the city to warn Mūsā (28:20). And then, Mūsā finds himself at Madyan (28:22). Clearly, the Qur'ān is drawing attention to the parallels and reversals in these stories, with the echoing words and letters. Here, the Qur'ān uses semantic echoes to draw attention to parallels and reversals in its stories. The shared root is a semantic parallel in stories with thematic parallels. The semantic choices reflect the thematic choices, all of which draw comparison between the various stories.

The parallels and reversals in these stories bring to light the issue of trust. In fact, the woman uses the word trustworthy to describe Mūsā, *al-amīn*: "One of the women said, 'Father, hire him: a strong, trustworthy man is the best to hire'" (28:26). Why did the women, their father, and Mūsā trust each other, and why were they correct to do so? Why was Mūsā wrong to trust before but right to trust now? One reason it was right for Mūsā to trust these strangers in Madyan is because he had prayed to God to bless him with good (28:24). In fact, after Mūsā accidentally kills the man, he asks God for forgiveness and swears that he will never again help a criminal (28:16–17), then he narrowly avoids getting involved in another fight and then the man comes and correctly tells him to flee. So a difference is in Mūsā's praying to God, who is the correct being to trust. Another difference is that in the conflicts with the men, Mūsā trusts someone from his tribe and sees the other as the enemy; perhaps he is to learn not to judge based only on tribe or appearance.

Another story in which Mūsā deals with trust is in *Sūrat al-Kahf*, when he meets a person who has knowledge from God (18:65). The man is often called al-Khiḍr or al-Khaḍir in extra-Qur'ānic sources. Mūsā seems to be looking for this person, so he is possibly not entirely a stranger. Mūsā asks if he can follow him around so he can learn from what the man has been taught (18:66), and the man says Mūsā will not be able to be patient, for how can he be patient with things he does not understand (18:67–68)? Mūsā says he will try to be patient, and the man tells him not to ask him any questions until he explains things to him (18:69–70). The man does three surprising things, and Mūsā asks him about his actions each time, until the man finally tells him not to continue with him (18:71–78). He is generous enough to explain his actions before they part (18:79–82). In regards to the issue of strangers and trust, it appears that perhaps Mūsā had heard about this man and he knew he had some knowledge from God (18:60–64 and 18:66); yet, Mūsā does not trust him enough to keep his promise of not questioning his actions. So this is a swerve on the other stories of Mūsā trusting strangers. In this case, the stranger is one that Mūsā should trust, despite his surprising and normally objectionable actions. And yet, Mūsā has a hard time trusting him. The Qur'ān does not tell us if this occurs after the other stories, and Mūsā has learned his lesson to not trust too readily, or if the man's actions are just so strange that Mūsā cannot help but question him.

Mūsā, in the Qur'ān, is dealing with the issue of whom to trust. Ironically, Yūsuf was betrayed by his brothers, and later his adoptive mother tries to seduce him and then blames him; in his case, his betrayals are by family members, not strangers. So Yūsuf could easily be a character through which to explore trust, but he is not. Yūsuf, one could speculate, might have difficulty trusting people as a result of being betrayed by his family members. In contrast, Mūsā, if anything, is too trusting. The issue of trust is a fundamental part of believing in a message, having faith, and believing in God. This is especially clear in Mūsā's story, when, for example, a messenger comes and warns him (28:20–21). This is clearly a parallel to prophets: they come with a message and warn people, fulfilling the role of a *nadhīr*, a warner. It is as if Mūsā gets a foreshadowing of himself in this messenger. Through the theme of Mūsā trusting strangers, as well as his learning whom to trust, the Qur'ānic audience reflects on messages, messengers, and trust.

## V. Parallels and Swerves: The Faith of Prophets

We have seen parallels and contrasts in Mūsā and Yūsuf and their lives. We can examine parallels from a different perspective, in the theme of how prophets come to believe. There are two stories that serve as parallels and swerves to each other. First, there is the story of Ibrāhīm looking at the moon and stars to think about faith (6:74–83):

> 6:74 Remember when Abraham said to his father, Azar, "How can you take idols as gods? I see that you and your people have clearly gone astray."
>
> 75 In this way We showed Abraham [God's] mighty dominion over the heavens and the earth, so that he might be a firm believer.
>
> 76 When the night grew dark over him he saw a star and said, "This is my Lord," but when it set, he said, "I do not like things that set."
>
> 77 And when he saw the moon rising he said, "*This* is my Lord," but when it too set, he said, "If my Lord does not guide me, I shall be one of those who go astray."
>
> 78 Then he saw the sun rising and cried, "*This* is my Lord! This is greater." But when the sun set, he said, "My people, I disown all that you worship beside God.
>
> 79 I have turned my face as a true believer towards Him who created the heavens and the earth. I am not one of the polytheists."
>
> 80 His people argued with him, and he said, "How can you argue with me about God when He has guided me? I do not fear anything you associate with Him: unless my Lord wills [nothing can happen]. My Lord encompasses everything in His knowledge. How can you not take heed?
>
> 81 Why should I fear what you associate with Him? Why do you not fear to associate with Him things for which He has sent you no authority? Tell me, if you know the answer, which side has more right to feel secure?
>
> 82 It is those who have faith, and do not mix their faith with idolatry, who will be secure, and it is they who are rightly guided."
>
> 83 Such was the argument We gave to Abraham against his people—We raise in rank whoever We will—your Lord is an all-knowing judge.

In this story, Ibrāhīm looks at the outside world, at large celestial bodies, to think about faith and to explore it with others. I discuss this scene elsewhere, in the context of other stories of Ibrāhīm.[22] We see here his thought process as he thinks about faith. It is noteworthy that Ibrāhīm is not in a dialogue with God, but, it says that God gave him this proof (6:83).

A parallel story is found in Mūsā's dialogue with God about his staff and hand. These are signs for him to show Firʿawn, but they also are metaphors for him to understand his role. God summons Mūsā, tells him He is God, and tells him to worship God (20:12–16).[23] Then God asks Mūsā what is in his hand (20:17). Since God is omniscient, this is an interesting question. And Mūsā's answer is also interesting, mentioning its particular and abstract uses (20:18). God commands Mūsā to throw the staff, he does, and it becomes a snake (20:19–20). Mūsā is scared, God tells him not to fear, and then God returns the staff to its original form (27:10 and 20:21). Similarly, God changes the nature of Mūsā's hand: God tells Mūsā to put his hand under his arm and then it becomes white (20:22). A staff that one presumably uses frequently—Mūsā has it with him on the very occasion of this dialogue—and one's hand, which one then places under one's arm, are very intimate and local objects. They show Mūsā how something can change into something else, just as Mūsā can change from a flawed person to a messenger who leads his people out of slavery, and Mūsā can change from a son/subject fleeing from his father figure/ruler to a messenger demanding a tyrannous ruler to free the people he enslaves. Interestingly, both Ibrāhīm and Mūsā have problematic relationships with their father and father figure, respectively.

In the stories of Mūsā, his hand and staff, and Ibrāhīm and the celestial bodies, the parallels are in the exploration of the faith of prophets, how they believe in God and themselves. Contrasts are found in the large and small, celestial and human, distanced and local and intimate. These parallels and swerves enable the audience to think about faith, how one comes to faith, and to ponder similarities and differences between Mūsā and Ibrāhīm. In addition, this form of repetition enables characterization. Why does Ibrāhīm think about celestial bodies in his exploration of faith? Perhaps he is more interested in or awed by celestial bodies and thinks about faith on a grand, majestic scale. Perhaps Mūsā's gaze is more localized and personal because he needs to reexamine himself and see himself as being empowered by God. Maybe he sees faith on a personal and intimate level. Thus, the repeated parallel themes and differences draw us to think about how Ibrāhīm and Mūsā think about faith, and this in turn lends insight into their personalities and the nature of belief. Some may come to faith by looking at large signs and others may come to faith by looking at small signs. Here, Qur'ānic stories perfectly embody verses, such as "On earth there are signs for those with sure faith– and in yourselves too, do you not see?' (51:20–21).

## VI. Outliers

In a discussion of structural patterns and repetition in the Qur'ān, it is useful to also discuss thematic outliers. In the Qur'ān, we find repetition, but sometimes there are outliers. For an example, we can focus on the root *q-ṣ-y* and all of its five appearances in the Qur'ān.[24] In two of the occurrences, with echoing phrases and words, a man comes from the outskirts of a city to warn someone or people—one of these is the verse examined above, when a man warns Mūsā that the chiefs are talking about killing him (28:20 and 36:20). In the third example, Maryam is pregnant, goes to "a distant place" (*qaṣiyyā*, 19:22), delivers her baby, 'Īsā, and then goes back to her people with him. Maryam is a messenger of the messenger—and she brings the word of God to the people (4:171). In the fourth verse with *q-ṣ-y*, God moves the Prophet to "the furthest [*al-aqṣā*] place of worship" (17:1). In these four times that the root *q-ṣ-y* appears in the Qur'ān, there is a message and/or messenger that is associated with the outskirts of a place.

The remaining time we see the *q-ṣ-y* root in the Qur'ān is in the following:

> 8:42 Remember when you were on the near side of the valley, and they were on the far [*al-quṣwa*] side and the caravan was below you. If you had made an appointment to fight, you would have failed to keep it [but the battle took place] so that God might bring about something already ordained.

The context given for this verse is that it is telling the Prophet and his people about the Battle of Badr. This verse clearly contrasts with the previously discussed ones. It addresses the second-person plural, so the Prophet Muḥammad is implied as part of the group (8:42) but is not mentioned specifically. Also noticeable is that *q-ṣ-y* refers to the enemy. So the messenger is in a different location than we have seen until now—the messenger is displaced. Here is a contrast and a reversal: there is the diminished presence of a messenger, and he is rejected by some. The contrast brings a sadness to the verses: the messenger is physically displaced and spiritually rejected by some. The battle took place two years after the hijra, so the Prophet and other Muslims were indeed physically displaced in their migration to Madīnah. The Muslims were victorious in this battle, so it is significant that the undertones of the verse are negative. This is not a boastful celebration of prowess. Perhaps this reflects the people's initial hesitation to fight or an inherent sadness in fighting with others, which is a breakdown of communication and amity. The verse clearly alludes to God's hand in all of this—God's will—that also connects to the previous verse (8:41), specifying that one-fifth of the spoils goes to God and those that God mentions in the verse.

The existence of an outlier is not a surprise; it is similar to a reversal. Elsewhere in the Qur'ān, we see patterns being made and then broken, as we did with parallels, swerves, and reversals. What I label as outliers can be swerves or reversals, but they are clearly different from the other usages of the root. The existence of outliers makes us realize the sophistication of Qur'ānic style and that it trusts the careful audience will be able to identify patterns and outliers and will contemplate reasons for the contrasts. We also find the breaking of patterns in Qur'ānic rhyme, which some explain as preventing monotony. Outliers are reflective of Qur'ānic style and how the Qur'ān comments on itself, complicating and adding layers of meaning to itself. Importantly, outliers do not take away from the existence of patterns.

## VII. Inverted Triangles

In addition to parallels, swerves, and reversals, there is another structural shape in the Qur'ān: inverted triangles. This is a way of organizing ideas in the Qur'ān: starting with the broadest idea, then gradually becoming more pointed and particular, coming to the tip. We will examine a few examples below. First is the structure of the story series in *Sūrat Maryam*. As discussed elsewhere, the story begins with the pairing of family and God, then family becomes less important and God becomes the most important. In the end, there are no longer stories, rather, there are messengers prostrating at the signs of God.[25] This can be envisioned as an inverted triangle, Figure 2.2, with family and God at the top (19:2–40), then family and God, but God is more important (19:41–57), and, finally, God and not family at the bottom (19:58).

We find this same structural shape in the beginning of *Sūrat Yūsuf*. The verses in question are the following:

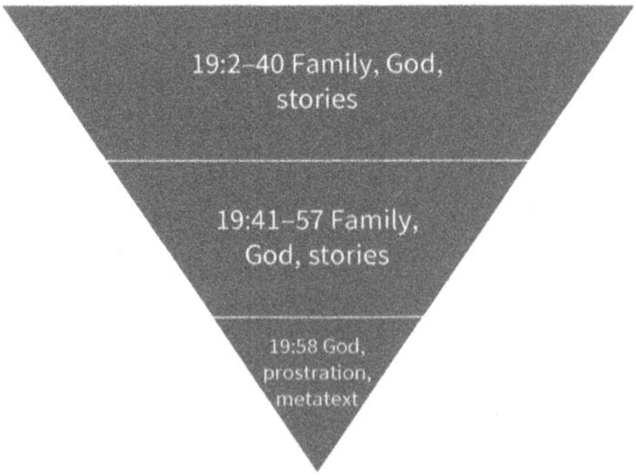


**Figure 2.2** *Sūrat Maryam* as an Inverted Triangle

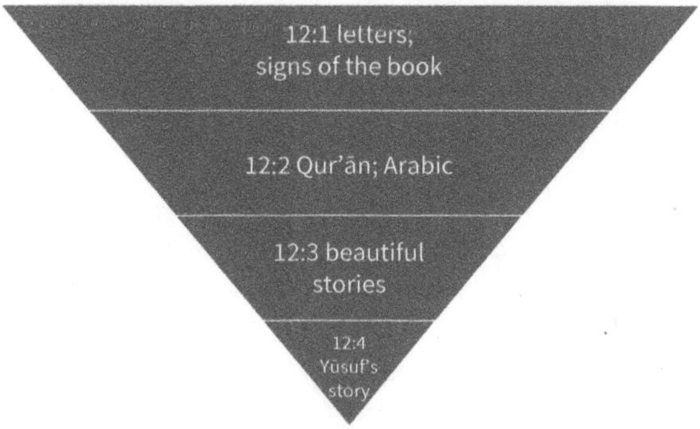


**Figure 2.3** The Introduction of *Sūrat Yūsuf* as an Inverted Triangle

12:1 Alif Lam Ra These are the verses of the Scripture that makes things clear—
2 We have sent it down as an Arabic Qur'an so that you [people] may understand.
3 We tell you [Prophet] the best of stories in revealing this Qur'an to you. Before
this you were one of those who knew nothing about them.
4 Joseph said to his father, "Father, I dreamed of eleven stars and the sun and the
moon: I saw them all bow down before me,"

Here, we start with the disconnected letters, then have mention of the signs of the book (12:1). Then we move to the more particular concept, as if in answer to the question of what book, with the answer being the Qur'ān, further modified as being in Arabic (12:2). Then the narrator mentions the most beautiful of stories (12:3) and, finally, the story of Yūsuf begins (12:4). So, we start with the most general concept: letters, then a book, then the particular book, then stories within the book, and, finally, a specific story. Again, the shape of this structure is an inverted triangle, as seen in Figure 2.3. The understanding of this structure lends us some insight into the meaning of the disconnected letters, which has proved puzzling to scholars of the Qur'ān.[26] Here, at least, the disconnected letters represent the general concept of language and the component parts of a book. This organizational structure is how the Qur'ān moves the reader or listener from thinking about the general idea of language to a particular story.

On the level of a lengthy *sūra*, there is a similar structure in *Sūrat al-Baqara*, elucidated by Nevin Reda. In Figure 2.4, we start with the broadest category of humanity (2:1–39), then the Children of Israel (2:40–123), and then the Muslim nation (2:124–286).[27] So we move from a general to a specific group. There also appears to be an element of chronology here. The organizational structure suggests either that the Muslim community is a smaller part of the

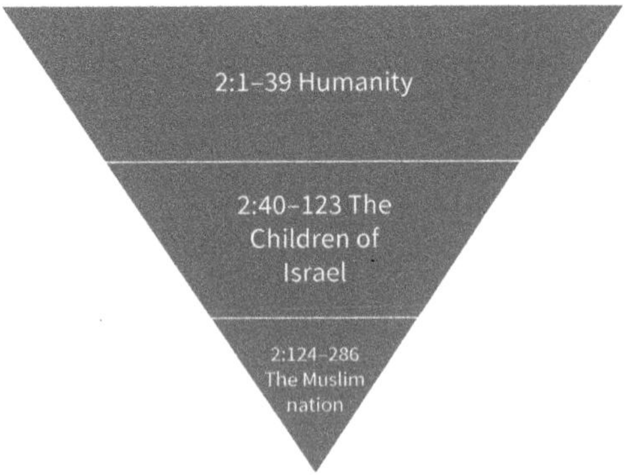


**Figure 2.4** *Sūrat al-Baqara* as an Inverted Triangle

Children of Israel, that it is an organic outgrowth from it, or a historical succession from it.

On a much smaller scale, *Sūrat al-Fātiḥa* has an inverted triangle in the names of God, as seen in Figure 2.5. First is the name Allāh (1:1 and 1:2), then *al-Raḥmān*, "the general mercy that encompasses all things" (1:1 and 1:3), then "*al-Raḥīm*, denoting the particular mercy that God bestows upon those whom He chooses" (1:1 and 1:3), and finally "*al-Mālik* pertains to His management of all affairs in the created order" (1:4).[28] Here, then, is an increasing specificity in names and also names move from a more general concept of a deity to God who is involved in the world. Again, we move from a more general concept to a specific one. First, the *sūra* establishes belief in God and

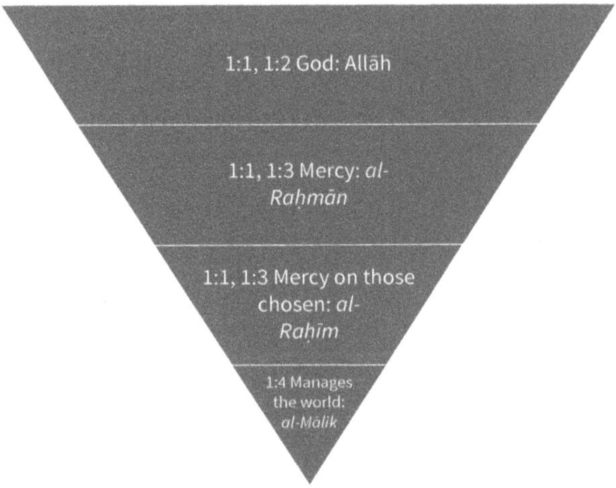


**Figure 2.5** Descriptions of God in *Sūrat al-Fātiḥa* as an Inverted Triangle

then it enlightens one about God. In fact, this is similar to how some explain the shorter *sūras* in the Qur'ān that came chronologically first (the Meccan *sūras*): first, the *sūras* establish fundamental beliefs in God, good behavior, accountability, and the Day of Judgment, then they move to the longer *sūras* with legal content. First, the Qur'ān starts with the general concept and then it moves to the particular, on a large scale (chronological order of revelation of *sūras*) and on a small scale (within *sūras*).

The structure of the inverted triangle is repeated in the Qur'ān, within and outside of stories. It elucidates an organizational logic and structure in the Qur'ān, starting with the general and moving to the specific, one time starting with a pairing of concepts and then narrowing to highlight the more important concept. Through this parallel structure, we see a logic in how the Qur'ān organizes information, which lends insight into its rhetorical style. This pattern also helps the audience understand some verses that have been puzzling, such as the disconnected letters in *Sūrat Yūsuf*. Knowing this rhetorical pattern also helps understand if, in *Sūrat al-Fātiḥa*, for example, the names of God are listed in order of priority or magnitude, or rather, in order of gradual specificity. A further direction of research would be to see if the inverted triangular structure can be found in Qur'ānic legal verses as well.

## VIII. Conclusion

It is likely that there are more parallels, swerves, reversals, triangles, and outliers in the Qur'ān. An awareness of different structural patterns will enable us to identify other examples and perhaps other structural patterns. More generally, one notices the making and breaking of patterns in the Qur'ān. These structures and patterns lend more insight into narrative and rhetorical choices of the Qur'ān. For example, the triangular structure in *Sūrat Yūsuf* helps us better understand the disconnected letters with which it begins. This structure also lends insight into Qur'ānic logic. There is an artistry, a beauty on a large, structural, and organizational scale in the Qur'ān's organizing patterns. Qur'ānic organization within *sūras* is not arbitrary or merely a compilation of related themes or stories.

Through this analysis, we see sometimes surprising connections made between thirteen Qur'ānic stories: the stories of Zakariyyā having a child, Maryam having a child, Ibrāhīm with his father, Ibrāhīm having a child, Maryam's mother, God calling Ibrāhīm an *imām*, Ibrāhīm and his son building the Ka'ba, Ibrāhīm being told to sacrifice his son, Mūsā's mother being told to throw her child into the water, and Yūsuf's being thrown into the well. We find that these stories are all connected semantically or thematically, through parallels and reversals. This draws the audience to compare and contrast the stories and the characters in them. Parallels and reversals between Mūsā and Ibrāhīm's approach to belief draw attention to the general concept of how people come to faith, as well as these specific characters and their similarities and differences. Finally, Mūsā's propensity to help people and learning whom to trust and not trust is a fascinating topic,[29] which comes to light through parallels and reversals. Although Yūsuf had to deal with betrayal, which is the breaking of trust, Mūsā is the character who deals with the trust of strangers. Why does it matter if one trusts strangers or not? Everyone is initially a stranger. How does one know whom to trust? In addition, trust is fundamental to the issue of faith. How does one know whom or what to believe? How easy is it to learn whom to trust and always make the right decision? Not so easy, according to Mūsā's story. Parallels and reversals provide a way for the Qur'ān to complicate and revisit the themes and topics it elucidates, while connections through repetition draw the audience to see the interaction of Qur'ānic verses across *sūras*.

# 3

# Repetition in the Qur'ānic Story of Mūsā

## I. Introduction

This chapter analyzes the topic of repetition in the Qur'ān, with a focus on the story of Mūsā, the Qur'ān's most frequently told story.[1] Repetition is a fraught topic within Western Qur'ānic studies scholarship. Salwa El-Awa writes about repetition in the Qur'ān:

> Those who thought that the Qur'ān contained too many unnecessary repetitions have severely criticized the language of the text on that grounds. On the other hand, those who set out to defend the text did so on the grounds that repeated topics in the Qur'ān are not repetitive in the sense that they repeat exactly the same information in each occurrence but vary in what they say about each topic each time it occurs.[2]

Similarly, in an article about *Sūrat Maryam*, Shawkat Toorawa writes, "paradoxically, repetition—or what detractors prefer to call repetitiveness—can be enlisted by both camps to undergird their argument."[3] Perhaps those who assume that repetition is a bad thing assume that something is genius when it has some element of originality, creates something new, or replaces the old.[4] Underlying the topic of repetition, some people who approach the Qur'ān wonder why its stories are not told only once, from start to end. In addition, implicit in some criticism of repetition in the Qur'ānic stories is a worry that there might be contradictions, which one then has to deal with. I will examine this issue below as well. While some scholars look at repetition as a historical byproduct of the process of the development of a text, this book does not use a historical approach. Rather, I am interested in how repetition functions in narrative. I will say briefly that even if repetition was a product of the redaction or composition of a text, if repetition was perceived as a negative literary feature, one would think that a competent redactor, author, or audience would have reacted with criticism or would have avoided repetition to begin with. This chapter will look at how repetition is used in the Qur'ānic story of Mūsā and what repetition does for Qur'ānic storytelling.

*How the Qur'ān Works*. Leyla Ozgur Alhassen, Oxford University Press. © Oxford University Press 2023.
DOI: 10.1093/oso/9780197654606.003.0003

It is worth mentioning that in some classical Arabic biographical literature and *ḥadīth* compendiums, we find multiple iterations (narrations) of the same story, and we can look at this as a parallel to repetition in Qur'ānic stories. Kecia Ali writes about the modern trend of transforming multiple iterations of *ḥadīth* into one version that reflects "the majority version," "proceed[ing] mostly forward in time from a determined starting point."[5] So what looked more like Qur'ānic stories, with multiple iterations is being transformed into a simple, linear tradition. What is lost is the challenge to deal with the multiple iterations as well as any insight that would have been gleaned in the process. Within *ḥadīth*, we also find at times someone being portrayed as asking the same question three times, and the Prophet giving the same answer three times. This use of repetition is probably a narrative technique, not a literal historical portrayal.[6]

Here, it is worth again mentioning the role of oral discourse in repetition: *ḥadīth* and the Qur'ān are and were oral and written traditions: they were recited, written down, and read. Repetition is a feature of oral literature.[7] Sandra Naddaff writes about the narrative functions of repetition in *1001 Nights*. One distinction she brings forward is that repetition may not merely derive from the oral nature of a text, but there may also be a self-consciousness in the repetition.[8] I argue that there is a narrative function to repetition in the Qur'ān, and this chapter presents and analyzes some examples of repetition in the Qur'ān and their narrative functions.

In the Qur'ān and in *tafsīr*, we can also find a discussion of repetition in the Qur'ān. In the Qur'ān, we find, for example:

> God has sent down the most beautiful of all teachings: a Scripture that is consistent and draws comparisons [*allahu nazzala aḥsana al-ḥadīthi kitāban mutashābihan mathāniya*]; that causes the skins of those in awe of their Lord to shiver. Then their skins and their hearts soften at the mention of God: such is God's guidance. He guides with it whoever He will; no one can guide those God leaves to stray (39:23).

This verse connects repetition in the Qur'ān to beauty and the emotional or spiritual resonance that the Qur'ān has on its audience. The phrase in the verse that appears to discuss repetition in the Qur'ān is *kitāban mutashābihan mathāniya*. Al-Ṭabarī gives a few explanations for this phrase; one explanation is that parts of the Qur'ān resemble other parts, there is no difference between them, and there is no contradiction.[9] Here, then, is the issue of repetition and contradiction. Other explanations are that verses of the Qur'ān resemble each other, letters resemble each other, parts of the Qur'ān verify other parts, parts of the Qur'ān lend truth to other parts, and some parts of the Qur'ān lead to other parts. Another explanation is that a verse in one *sūra* may be similar to a verse in another *sūra*.[10] These explanations are identifying repetition in the Qur'ān on the level of parts (whatever they may be), verses, and even letters. This interpretation brings to mind what we will see below in Alter, namely, that one can look at repetition on the scale of words or larger groupings of words. Throughout this book, we will indeed see multiple examples of how parts of the Qur'ān lead to other parts. Other explanations are that parts of the Qur'ān are as eloquent as others; there are recurring themes in the Qur'ān; and that the Qur'ān talks about paired concepts, such as heaven and hell, so the idea of pairs could be thematic.[11]

The analysis in this book is inspired by the lens of intratextuality, an analytical tool through which some scholars analyze repetition in the Qur'ān. In this chapter, I argue and will show that when one notices repetition of any kind in the Qur'ān, one of the first useful things to do is to turn to the context of the verses in question. After locating a verse in its context, one can look at overarching themes in its surrounding verses, as well as features such as end-rhyme and semantic echoes. This shows the importance of an intratextual approach to understanding repetition.

As seen in Appendix A, I have compiled all the stories of Mūsā in the Qur'ān into tables showing the iteration and plot summaries for each one. These include all the verses discussing Mūsā, either by name or allusion. Every verse that is part of a story is given a place in these tables. These tables were compared to other works to see if they include the same verses.

Critical to categorizing stories on Mūsā in the Qur'ān is an analysis of what constitutes a story in the Qur'ān. Stories in the Qur'ān may be either full stories, segments of stories, or story-related discourse, such as asking the audience whether they heard a specific story. One example is the introduction to the story of Mūsā in *Sūrat Ṭaha*: "Has the story of Moses come to you [Prophet]?" (20:9). While this story-related discourse is not actually narrative, I have included it in what follows.

Through my analysis, we can say that in the Qur'ān there are a total of four distinct stories about Mūsā, with forty-two iterations. The four stories have a different number of iterations per story: Mūsā and Fir'awn (twenty-four iterations), Mūsā and the book (ten iterations), Mūsā with his people (seven iterations), and Mūsā and the wise man (one iteration). With twenty-four iterations, the story of Mūsā and Fir'awn is the most-told story not only among the stories of Mūsā but also among all the stories in the Qur'ān. When looking at the next-most recounted story in the Qur'ān, one might conclude that it is Ibrāhīm with nineteen stories.[12] This total, however, includes all stories about Ibrāhīm, not just one specific story, while the story of Mūsā and Fir'awn, in particular, is told more frequently and in a variety of lengths, ranging from one to one hundred verses. The tables in Appendix A allows scholars to look at the issue of repetition in the Qur'ān; since I present the most commonly recounted story in the Qur'ān—the story of Mūsā—one would assume that repetition should certainly show itself here.

The tables in Appendix A of the stories of Mūsā in the Qur'ān are useful for exploring repetition in the story of Mūsā in the Qur'ān. When we look at these tables, we can see how much is actually repeated in the stories, and then we can read those verses and see how similar they really are. I highlight some of those similarities and differences in one particular part of the story of Mūsā—Mūsā and Fir'awn—in this chapter.

In this chapter, I begin by working from Robert Alter's and Sandra Naddaff's explanations of types of repetition and I discuss examples of them from the Qur'ān. Here, I focus on types of repetition, on a scale from small to large: root word, "motif," "theme," "sequence of actions," and "type-scene."[13] Then I discuss and give examples of what can be done with repetition, inspired again by Robert Alter. Repetition may be deployed, "aborted," or suppressed.[14] We find different manifestations of suppressed repetition, when there is focalization, characterization, and reversals. I then look at repetition and selective giving and withholding of information. Finally, I discuss repeated elements within varying length iterations of the story of Mūsā and Fir'awn in the Qur'ān. I also analyze repeated elements in introductions and conclusions to the various iterations of this story.

## II. Types of Repetition

Biblical scholar Robert Alter has analyzed repetition's narrative functions in the Bible. Although this is not a comparative study, Alter's analysis is insightful when applied to the Qur'ān, in terms of developing a method of analysis. He writes:

> One of the most imposing barriers that stands between the modern reader and the imaginative subtlety of biblical narrative is the extraordinary prominence of verbatim repetition in the Bible. Accustomed as we are to modes of narration in which elements of repetition are made to seem far less obtrusive, this habit of constantly restating material is bound to give us trouble, especially in a narrative that otherwise adheres so evidently to the strictest economy of means.[15]

Alter is explaining that readers of the Bible have difficulty when they come across repetition because it contrasts with their expectations of what a text should look like and it contrasts with other parts of the Bible, which are sparse. I would argue that readers of the Qur'ān experience a similar challenge.

When we discuss repetition, it is useful to realize that there are many forms in which repetition can occur. Alter includes a list of types of repetition found in biblical narrative, all of which can be found in the Qur'ān, and which the tables in Appendix A can help locate. His list moves from a small to a large scale. Following is a summary of Alter's list of types of repetition, to which I have incorporated Naddaff, and then added and analyzed examples for each type from the Qur'ānic stories of Mūsā.

## A. Root Word

We start with "Leitwort."[16] The semantic root of a word is used repeatedly and in a variety of ways. Similarly, Naddaff writes that we can find repetition on the level of phrases, sentences, and "patterns of language'—stemming from the Arabic "trilateral root system."[17] I analyze a number of examples of this type of repetition in the chapter on exchange encounters in this book.

Repetition of words sharing the same root letters, or repetition of the same words, are striking orally and can serve narrative effects. In the tables of the story of Mūsā in Appendix A, we see signs, *āyāt*, of God multiple times (7:106, 7:130–135, 20:23, 26:30–31, 27:13, 43:47–54, 51:39 and 79:20–23). For another example, we can turn to the scene in Mūsā's story when he sees a fire and feels drawn to it. He goes to the location and hears God speak. In one iteration, we notice an alternation of the words *min*, then *fī*, then *min* again, then we hear what God told Mūsā. The verse is as follows: "But when he reached it, a voice called out to him from the right-hand side of the valley, from a tree on the blessed ground: 'Moses, I am God, the Lord of all worlds' [*fa-lammā atāhā nūdiya min shāṭi'i al-wādi al-aymani fī al-buqʿati al-mubārakati min al-shajarati an yāmūsā innī anā allāhu rabbu al-ʿālamīn*]" (28:30). Aurally, we notice here many consonants, which make one slow down on the phrases describing the location. It builds up one's anticipation, hearing that something happened at a particular location, which is refined three times, then we are finally told what happened there. Here we see that repetition of words and consonants increases the audience's curiosity.

Another way to look at the repetition of a root word is when it is only used for one character in the Qur'ān—an exclusive repetition of a root word. We have a striking example with Mūsā in his conversation with God. God calls

Mūsā and tells him to go to Fir'awn because Fir'awn is a tyrant. God tells Mūsā that He is sending Mūsā with signs of God, and one sign is when he throws his staff. Mūsā throws his staff, and it becomes a snake. Mūsā gets scared, turns away, and initially does not turn back. The part about him not turning back occurs in two iterations with almost exact repetition. The first verse: " 'Throw down your staff,' " but when he saw it moving like a snake, he turned and fled. 'Moses, do not be afraid! The messengers need have no fear in My presence [*wa-alqi 'aṣāka fa-lammā ra'āhā tahtazzu ka-annahā jānnun wallā mudbiran wa lam yu'aqqib yā mūsā lā takhaf innī lā yakhāfu ladayya al-mursalūna*]' " (27:10). The second iteration:

> 'Throw down your staff.' When he saw his staff moving like a snake, he fled in fear and would not return. Again [he was called]: 'Moses! Draw near! Do not be afraid, for you are one of those who are safe [*wa-an alqi 'aṣāka fa-lammā ra'āhā tahtazzu ka-annahā jānnun wallā mudbiran wa lam yu'aqqib yā mūsā aqbil wa lā takhaf innaka min al-āminīna*]' (28:31).

We see many repeated words in these two verses, but my focus here is on the word *yu'aqqib*, translated as "fled" and "would not return." This form of this verb occurs only twice in the Qur'ān, in these two verses. Through this exclusive repetition, we see the depths of Mūsā's fear and sensitivity. No other messenger or Qur'ānic character is portrayed reacting to God's signs in this way. And this is in the context of him talking to God, a rare honor indeed. This also characterizes Mūsā: he fears, he feels, and shows his emotions, and this characterization is further confirmed by God telling him, with the same words twice not to fear, *lā takhaf*. So with this exclusive repeated use of this word, we see something unique about Mūsā or his situation. With this narrative technique, there is characterization and commentary on Mūsā and his story.

## B. Motif

Next in scale is repetition in an image, an appeal to the sense or an action that is present throughout a narrative. Similar to Alter, some kinds of narrative repetitions that Naddaff discusses are a motif, a character, an "action or gesture."[18] I analyze a number of examples of this type of repetition in the second and fifth chapters of this book. In the story of Mūsā, there is the action of Mūsā throwing his staff three distinct times. First, in three iterations, Mūsā throws his staff when God tells him what his mission is and that he has signs that he will take with him (20:20–21, 27:10–11, and 28:31):

20:20 He threw it down and—lo and behold!—it became a fast-moving snake.

21 He said, "Pick it up without fear: We shall turn it back into its former state."

27:10 "Throw down your staff," but when he saw it moving like a snake, he turned and fled. "Moses, do not be afraid! The messengers need have no fear in My presence,

11 and towards those who do wrong, and then replace their evil with good, I am truly most forgiving and merciful."

28:31 "Throw down your staff." When he saw his staff moving like a snake, he fled in fear and would not return. Again [he was called]: "Moses! Draw near! Do not be afraid, for you are one of those who are safe."

Then, twice, Mūsā throws his staff in front of Fir'awn and his counselors: "So Moses threw his staff and—lo and behold!—it was a snake, clear to all" (7:107) and "So Moses threw down his staff and—lo and behold!—it became a snake for everyone to see" (26:32). Finally, Fir'awn gathers his magicians and Mūsā throws his staff in front of them (7:117–119, 20:69, and 26:45).[19] So, we have the motif of the throwing of the staff in front of different audiences three times, and each time has a varied number of iterations. We can think of the first time as God showing Mūsā what his staff and consequently, he, can do, if God wills. God empowers him and makes him rethink his role in the world. Then, Mūsā shows this to Fir'awn, and surprisingly, he and God give Fir'awn a chance to prepare his magicians to try to best him in the challenge. After the final throwing, as we will see, the magicians are not able to defeat Mūsā, which makes them realize that this is indeed a miracle of God and not magic. Through the repetition of this motif, we see God making different people think about and realize God's place and their places in the world.

We can notice here that we have a grouping of three, and the chronological center is different than the outer two parts: Mūsā and the magicians come to believe that Mūsā is sent by God, which contrasts with Fir'awn in the chronological center, who does not believe. This is a pattern, with the outer parts sharing an element, people who believe, and the center point being different, someone does not believe. Surprisingly, this also follows a pattern in number of iteration: 3-2-3. This is similar to a concentric construction, a concept that Michel Cuypers writes about extensively,[20] which can be seen in Table 3.1. However, the structures Cuypers analyzes are within a *sūra*, whereas here, the pattern is across *sūras*. Perhaps this explains a structural and rhetorical difference: whereas Cuypers says the center is rhetorically privileged and a universal statement,[21] the center here does not look like that. The tables in Appendix A can be used to further explore this type of analysis, and it would

**Table 3.1** Concentric Repetition in a Motif

| Action | Number of Iterations | Consequence |
|---|---|---|
| Mūsā throws his staff in front of God | Three: 20:20–21, 27:10–11, and 28:31 | Mūsā believes |
| Mūsā throws his staff in front of Fir'awn and his counselors | Two: 7:107 and 26:32 | Fir'awn does not believe |
| Mūsā throws his staff in front of the magicians | Three: 7:117–119, 20:69, and 26:45 | Magicians believe |

certainly be worthwhile to see if other concentric constructions can be found in the Qur'ān across *sūras*, and if so, what rhetorical patterns they share.

## C. Theme

Larger in scale than root word and motif is a repetition in theme or a recurrence of a concept. I analyze a number of examples of this type of repetition in the fifth chapter of this book. In Mūsā's story there is the theme of motherhood, for example:

> 28:7 We inspired Moses' mother, saying, "Suckle him, and then, when you fear for his safety, put him in the river: do not be afraid, and do not grieve, for We shall return him to you and make him a messenger."
>
> 8 Pharaoh's household picked him up—later to become an enemy and a source of grief for them: Pharaoh, Haman, and their armies were wrongdoers—
>
> 9 and Pharaoh's wife said, "Here is a joy to behold for me and for you! Do not kill him: he may be of use to us, or we may adopt him as a son." They did not realize what they were doing.
>
> 10 The next day, Moses' mother felt a void in her heart—if We had not strengthened it to make her one of those who believe, she would have revealed everything about him—
>
> 11 and she said to his sister, "Follow him." So she watched him from a distance, without them knowing.
>
> 12 We had ordained that he would refuse to feed from wet nurses. His sister approached them and said, "Shall I tell you about a household which could bring him up for you and take good care of him?"
>
> 13 We restored him to his mother in this way, so that she might be comforted, not grieve, and know that God's promise is true, though most people do not understand.

We see the joy of Fir'awn's wife when she finds Mūsā as a baby in the water (28:9). This contrasts sharply with the portrayal of Mūsā's mother, whose heart is empty at the loss of her baby (28:10) and then is comforted by Mūsā's return to her (28:13). There is repetition in the portrayal of women with a baby, but then there is at the same time contrast when one thinks about the mother who gives up her baby out of fear (28:7) and the woman who joyfully finds and wants to adopt that baby. We can also think of her wanting, on the one hand, to protect the baby, pleading Fir'awn not to kill him (28:9), while on the other hand, she presumably does not think about from whence the baby came, who his mother is, or trying to reunite him with his mother. What we see then is one woman's joy completely oblivious of the other. In this scene there is one more woman, who is not oblivious to her mother's sadness: Mūsā's sister. She is another female caretaker in the scene, the sister who comes up with a clever way to reunite her brother with their mother, while also keeping Mūsā in Fir'awn's household and thus keeping him protected—ironically from Fir'awn himself (28:12). Because there is the portrayal of three women protecting baby Mūsā in one scene, we are able to flesh out the ways that they are similar to and contrast with each other. Here, then, repetition encourages the audience to compare the characters, actions, and situations in the story.

## D. Sequence of Actions

Next in scale is when a sequence of actions is repeated. For example, in the story of Mūsā, multiple times, we are told that Mūsā sees a fire, he goes to it, and God talks to him there (19:52, 20:10–16, 27:7–9, 28:29–30, and 79:16):

> 19:52 We called to him from the right-hand side of the mountain and brought him close to Us in secret communion;
>
> . . .
>
> 20:10 He saw a fire and said to his people, "Stay here, I can see a fire. Maybe I can bring you a flaming brand from it or find some guidance there."
>
> 11 When he came to the fire, he was called: "Moses!
>
> 12 I am your Lord. Take off your shoes: you are in the sacred valley of Tuwa.
>
> 13 I have chosen you, so listen to what is being revealed.
>
> 14 I am God; there is no god but Me, so worship Me and keep up the prayer so that you remember Me.
>
> 15 The Hour is coming--though I choose to keep it hidden--for each soul to be rewarded for its labour.

> 16 Do not let anyone who does not believe in it and follows his own desires distract you from it, and so bring you to ruin."
>
> . . .
>
> 27:7 Remember Moses said to his family, "I have seen a fire. I will bring you news from there, or a burning stick for you to warm yourselves."
>
> 8 When he reached the fire, a voice called: "Blessed is the person near this fire and those around it; may God be exalted, the Lord of all worlds.
>
> 9 Moses, I am God with the power to decide."
>
> . . .
>
> 28:29 Once Moses had fulfilled the term and was travelling with his family, he caught sight of a fire on the side of the mountain and said to his family, "Wait! I have seen a fire. I will bring you news from there, or a burning stick for you to warm yourselves."
>
> 30 But when he reached it, a voice called out to him from the right-hand side of the valley, from a tree on the blessed ground: "Moses, I am God, the Lord of all worlds."
>
> . . .
>
> 79:16 His Lord called out to him in the sacred valley of Tuwa.

The five iterations of course have similarities and differences. At the same time, although this part of the story only occurs five times in the Qur'ān, it readily comes to mind when one thinks of Mūsā. So repetition allows for brevity and even exclusion at times because it becomes part of the audience's conception of the story, whether it is repeated in every iteration or not. Repetition enables concision by playing off of evocations.

## E. Type-Scene

A scene recurs,[22] or as Naddaff explains, one event can happen repeatedly to different characters, "the same event can repeatedly happen" to one character, or "the same event can happen to different characters . . . who are replicas of one another."[23] In the story of Mūsā, we find Mūsā confronting Fir'awn, Fir'awn rejecting the message and threatening punishment, Mūsā escaping and Fir'awn himself being punished (7:106, 7:127, 7:130–137, 10:90–92, 11:99, 17:103, 20:49–55, 20:58–59, 20:77–79, 23:48, 25:36, 26:23–31, 26:52, 26:66, 28:37–42, 29:40, 40:45–46, 43:55, 44:22–31, 51:40, 54:42, 69:10, 73:16, and 79:24–25). The second chapter in this book on reversals and parallels elucidates some other examples of type-scenes from the Qur'ān more widely. According to Alter, the type-scene serves "an eminently monotheistic purpose: to reproduce in narrative the recurrent rhythm of a divinely appointed destiny in Israelite history."[24] The idea is that through the repetition of a type-scene, the Bible affirms its perspective on "Israelite history." This book and my previous scholarship explore whether there is an affirmation of Qur'ānic monotheism and prophecy in the many Qur'ānic stories in which a prophet is sent to his people, some of the people reject the message, the prophet is saved, and the disbelievers are punished. Certainly this type-scene can be a metaphor for the revelation of the Qur'ān to Prophet Muḥammad and how people respond to it.

## III. What Is Done with Repetition

### A. Deployed

Moving from thinking about different kinds of repetition and the scale on which repetition can occur, we can think about what happens to repeated elements in a text. Different kinds of repetition can be used in various ways: repetition can be deployed, "aborted," or suppressed.[25] Certainly one can find examples of all these kinds of repetition in Qur'ānic stories, and they also serve a theological purpose in the text. Below are examples of each use of repetition from the story of Mūsā. Earlier, I mentioned various examples of repetition in the story of Mūsā. I will identify various uses of repetition in four different iterations of the story of Mūsā and Fir'awn in the Qur'ān:

> 7:111 They said, "Delay him and his brother for a while, and send messengers to all the cities
> 112 to summon every learned sorcerer to you."
> 113 The sorcerers came to Pharaoh and said, "Shall we be rewarded if we win?"
> 114 and he replied, "Yes, and you will join my inner court."
> 115 So they said, "Moses, will you throw first or shall we?"
> 116 He said, "You throw," and they did, casting a spell on people's eyes, striking fear into them, and bringing about great sorcery.
> 117 Then We inspired Moses, "Throw your staff," and—lo and behold!--it devoured their fakery.
> 118 The truth was confirmed and what they had produced came to nothing:
> 119 they were defeated there and utterly humiliated.
> 120 The sorcerers fell to their knees
> 121 and said, "We believe in the Lord of all worlds,
> 122 the Lord of Moses and Aaron!"

123 but Pharaoh said, "How dare you believe in Him before I have given you permission? This is a plot you have hatched to drive the people out of this city! Soon you will see:

124 I will cut off your alternate hands and feet and then crucify you all!"

125 They said, "And so we shall return to our Lord—

126 Your only grievance against us is that we believed in the signs of our Lord when they came to us. Our Lord, pour steadfastness upon us and let us die in devotion to You."

. . .

10:79 And Pharaoh said, "Bring me every learned sorcerer."

80 When the sorcerers came, Moses said to them, "Throw down whatever you have."

81 When they did so, Moses said, "Everything you have brought is sorcery and God will show it to be false. God does not make the work of mischief-makers right;

82 He will uphold the Truth with His words, even if the evildoers hate it."

. . .

20:60 Pharaoh withdrew and gathered his strategy, then he returned.

61 Moses said to them, "Beware, do not invent lies against God or He will destroy you with His punishment. Whoever invents lies will fail."

62 So they discussed their plan among themselves, talking secretly,

63 saying, "These two men are sorcerers. Their purpose is to drive you out of your land with their sorcery and put an end to your time-honoured way of life.

64 So put together your strategy and line up for the contest. Whoever wins today is sure to prosper."

65 They said, "Moses, will you throw first or shall we?"

66 "You throw," said Moses, and--lo and behold!--through their sorcery, their ropes and staffs seemed to him to be moving.

67 Moses was inwardly alarmed,

68 but We said, "Do not be afraid, you have the upper hand.

69 Throw down what is in your right hand: it will swallow up what they have produced. They have only produced the tricks of a sorcerer, and a sorcerer will not prosper, wherever he goes."

70 [So it was, and] the sorcerers threw themselves down in submission. "We believe," they said, "in the Lord of Aaron and Moses."

71 Pharaoh said, "How dare you believe in him before I have given you permission? This must be your master, the man who taught you witchcraft. I shall certainly cut off your alternate hands and feet, then crucify you on the trunks of palm trees. You will know for certain which of us has the fiercer and more lasting punishment."

72 They said, "We shall never prefer you to the clear sign that has come to us, nor to Him who created us. So decide whatever you will: you can only decide matters of this present life—

73 we believe in our Lord, [hoping] He may forgive us our sins and the sorcery that you forced us to practise—God is better and more lasting."

74 Hell will be the reward of those who return to their Lord as evildoers: there they will stay, neither living nor dying.

75 But those who return to their Lord as believers with righteous deeds will be rewarded with the highest of ranks,

76 Gardens of lasting bliss graced with flowing streams, and there they will stay. Such is the reward of those who purify themselves.

. . .

26:36 They answered, "Delay him and his brother for a while, and send messengers to all the cities

37 to bring every accomplished sorcerer to you."

38 The sorcerers were [to be] assembled at the appointed time on a certain day

39 and the people were asked, "Are you all coming?

40 We may follow the sorcerers if they win!"

41 When the sorcerers came, they said to Pharaoh, "Shall we be rewarded if we win?"

42 and he said, "Yes, and you will join my inner court."

43 Moses said to them, "Throw down whatever you will."

44 They threw their ropes and staffs, saying, "By Pharaoh's might, we shall be victorious."

45 But Moses threw his staff and—lo and behold!—it swallowed up their trickery

46 and the sorcerers fell down on their knees,

47 exclaiming, "We believe in the Lord of all worlds,

48 the Lord of Moses and Aaron."

49 Pharaoh said, "How dare you believe in him before I have given you permission? He must be the master who taught you sorcery! Soon you will see: I will cut off your alternate hands and feet and then crucify the lot of you!"

50 "That will do us no harm," they said, "for we are sure to return to our Lord.

51 We hope that our Lord will forgive us our sins, as we were the first to believe."

Here, repetition is deployed, for example, when Fir'awn gathers the magicians (7:111–112, 10:79, 20:60, and 26:36–40). The most obvious response to repetition like this is to compare and contrast the scenes and surrounding iterations to each other.

## B. Aborted

A different use of repetition is when it is aborted, and in fact the example above also shows this in its next scene. Although Fir'awn gathers the magicians four times, the magicians declare their faith and then prostrate themselves to God in only three of the iterations (7:120–122, 20:70 and 26:46–48). We can look at this in some detail now, and specifically at how the abortion of repetition can serve the purpose of characterization. Table 3.2 focuses on Fir'awn's magicians in order to highlight similarities and differences between the iterations.

If we look at the table, we see only two elements that exist in all four iterations: Fir'awn gathers the magicians, and Mūsā tells them to commence. It is interesting to note that even in the detail of Mūsā telling them to go first, twice it is preceded by the magicians asking Mūsā who should throw first (7:115 and 20:65). In the other two iterations (10:80–82 and 26:43–44), Mūsā, unprompted, tells them to go first. Perhaps Mūsā is meant to look more bold or assertive in these iterations, or perhaps he is meant to look scared in the others. Or perhaps the magicians are made to look nervous, polite, or considerate by asking Mūsā who should go first. If we look at the table of Mūsā and Fir'awn, we see that Mūsā is scared in some verses (20:45–46, 20:67–69, 27:10–11, and 28:31). Mūsā is described as being scared in one of the iterations where the magicians ask him who should go first (20:45–46). In other words, when he is described as being scared, Mūsā does not tell the magicians unprompted to go first in the iterations.

Three of the four iterations share these events: Mūsā is scared and God comforts him (7:117–119, 20:67–69, and 26:45), the magicians throw themselves in prostration (7:120, 20:70, and 26:46), the magicians say that they believe in the Lord, the Lord of Mūsā and Hārūn (7:121–122, 20:70, and 26:47–48), and Fir'awn threatens the magicians (7:123–124, 20:71, and 26:49).

A different point of interest in terms of repetition and characterization is that in two of the iterations, the magicians ask if there is a reward for them if they are victorious and Fir'awn affirms it, and that they will become close to him (7:113–114 and 26:41–42). I analyze the *Sūrat al-Shu'arā'* verse in its larger context in Chapter 6, where we see a contrast being drawn between the magicians asking for a reward and God's messengers saying that they are not awaiting a reward from people. In the remaining two iterations, the magicians do not ask for a reward, and in one of these, they say, after professing their belief: '"we believe in our Lord, [hoping] He may forgive us our sins and the sorcery that you forced us to practise—God is better and more lasting'" (20:73). It is surprising that while they are shown asking for a reward in some iterations, in this one, they say that Fir'awn forced them

**Table 3.2** Mūsā and Fir'awn: The Magicians

| Plot Summary | Verses | | | |
|---|---|---|---|---|
| Fir'awn gathers magicians | 10:79 | 20:60 | 7:111–112 | 26:36–40 |
| Magicians ask for a reward and are promised | | | 7:113–114 | 26:41–42 |
| Mūsā warns them | | 20:61 | | |
| They debate what to do | | 20:62 | | |
| They ask who should throw first | | 20:65 | 7:115 | |
| Mūsā tells them to go first | 10:80–82 | 20:66 | 7:116 | 26:43–44 |
| Mūsā scared; God comforts | | 20:67–69 | | |
| Mūsā throws staff | | | 7:117–119 | 26:45 |
| Magicians prostrate | | 20:70 | 7:120 | 26:46 |
| Magicians say: we believe in the Lord | | | 7:121 | 26:47 |
| The Lord of Mūsā and Hārūn | | | 7:122 | 26:48 |
| Fir'awn asks the magicians how they believe | | 20:71 | 7:123 | |
| Fir'awn threatens the magicians | | | 7:123–124 | 26:49 |
| Magicians reply with faith | | 20:72–76 | 7:125–126 | 26:50–51 |

to practice magic. When we see the magicians asking for a reward, but then saying that Fir'awn compelled them to do magic, we wonder what the purpose of this discrepancy is. Perhaps this shows the varying and conflicting morals and emotions with which people can live their lives—they can be ambitious or greedy, but they can also feel forced into a situation, maybe for lack of other opportunities. Or perhaps they are looking for someone to blame for their mistakes. With this variation in iteration, there is a difference in characterization—we are not looking at flat characters, easy to judge and easy to understand. This is striking in terms of Qur'ānic narrative style. I discuss elsewhere how the Qur'ānic portrayal of characters in *Sūrat Yūsuf* prevents the audience from judging them, because, according to the Qur'ān, that is God's job.[26] Perhaps that is what we see here too. Here, we see "how substantially the same materials can be redeployed in order to make different points."[27]

## C. Suppressed

We also see iterations with verses that tell the same story and use almost the same wording, with slight variations. We can categorize these as examples of suppressed repetition, according to Alter. As discussed above, Fir'awn gathers magicians to challenge Mūsā to throw their staffs and perform something amazing. The magicians ask who should throw first using similar, but not the same, language in two verses, seen above (7:115 and 20:65). We notice that the verses begin with the same words but end differently; each match the end-rhyme of other verses in their surrounding *sūras*. Here, then, we see that suppression in repetition helps maintain end-rhyme. Here, and in other places, we see that repetition may be influenced by the context.

Elsewhere in the story, we see suppressed repetition. If we look at Table A.1 in Appendix A and Table 3.3, there are three iterations of this: Mūsā sees a fire, God asks Mūsā what is in his hand or tells him to throw what is in his hand, Mūsā throws and shows fear of what happened, and then God turns his hand white, as another sign. Four times, we see that God calls to Mūsā and tells Mūsā that He is God (19:52, 20:11–16, 27:8–9, and 28:30, all referenced above). One of the iterations is narrated by God in the first-person plural "We," but it is not a dialogue (19:52). The remaining iterations are all dialogues. There is one more iteration in which God calls to Mūsā and commands him to go to Fir'awn, but God does not introduce Himself to Mūsā (79:16–17).

So we have, then, three times when God tells Mūsā who He is. The verses are the following: "I am God; there is no god but Me [*innanī anā allahu lā ilāha illā anā*]" (20:14); "Moses, I am God with the power to decide [*innahu anā allahu al-ʿazīzu al-ḥakīm*]" (27:9); and "Moses, I am God, the Lord of all worlds [*innī anā allahu rabbu al-ʿālamīna*]" (28:30). Each one has a different version of *inna*, sometimes translated as verily, and sometimes, like here, not translated at all. All are followed by "*anā allahu*," "I am God." Then each is followed by a different modifier or description of God. In *Sūra* 27, we see the *ḥ-k-m* root three times. All of the times, it describes God. Twice, the verse with the *ḥ-k-m* root is addressed to the second person, often interpreted as Prophet Muḥammad: "You [Prophet] receive the Qur'an from One who is decisive, all knowing" (27:6) and "Truly, your Lord will decide between them in His judgment—He is the Almighty, the All Knowing" (27:78). And once is the description for God that we see here when God speaks to Mūsā (27:9). In *Sūra* 27, we have a parallel in the self-description that God tells to Mūsā and Muḥammad; both prophets receive revelation from God who characterizes Himself with *ḥ-k-m*.

In the three iterations, we see the portrayal of a dialogue in a historical event three different ways. What does it mean for God to describe Himself differently three times, for Mūsā or for the audience? We see here God's incomprehensibility, God is all these things; and at the same time, we see the limits of language, language cannot describe God completely. Perhaps we are also to think about our conception of history and reality—the Qur'ān is telling

**Table 3.3** Mūsā and Fir'awn: God Talks to Mūsā

| Plot Summary | Verses |
|---|---|
| Sees fire | 20:10, 27:7, 28:29 |
| God calls to Mūsā | 19:52, 20:11–16, 27:8–9, 28:30, 79:16 |
| God asks what's in hand, commands to throw | 20:17–19, 27:10–11, 28:31 |
| Throws, becomes a snake, don't fear | 20:20-21, 27:10–11, 28:31 |
| Hand | 20:22, 27:12, 28:32 |

us that history should not be conceived of in only one particular way. Here, then, through suppressed repetition, we see commentary on the portrayal of history, the weakness of language and the incomprehensibility and boundlessness of God. There is a contrast between the limits of human language and conceptions of history and the limitlessness of God.

## D. Suppressed: Focalization

Another way we can look at suppression of repetition in the Qur'ān is through focalization. Focalization is a term in literary analysis used to explain through whose perspective we are seeing a story. We are now going to examine different examples where there is repetition, but it is suppressed, and this allows for a difference in focalization. This change in repetition and focalization, in turn, serves a literary and theological purpose in the story. In the Qur'ānic story of Mūsā, we see that in his earlier life, Mūsā sees two people fighting. He tries to help the person that he thinks was the victim, the person from his people, and he hits the other man and accidentally kills him. I discuss this story in the previous chapter. In the Qur'ān, we see a few iterations of this scene with different focalizers and with varying degrees of detail. Twice, Mūsā mentions that he killed someone (26:14 and 28:33); Fir'awn tells Mūsā that he killed someone (26:18–22); the narrator (God) explains that Mūsā killed someone (28:15–21); and finally, God tells Mūsā that he killed someone (20:40).

We can analyze and compare these iterations by first looking at an iteration through God's focalization directed to Mūsā. Here, God is telling Mūsā his life story, and God says:

> 20:40 Your sister went out, saying, "Shall I show you someone who will nurse him?" then We returned you to your mother so that she could rejoice and not grieve. Later

you killed a man, but We saved you from distress and tried you with other tests. You stayed among the people of Midian for years, then you came here as I ordained.

41 I have chosen you for Myself.

Here, God tells Mūsā that he killed a man, but God also says He saved him. All of this is in the context of God choosing, looking after, and shaping Mūsā (20:35–41).

We can compare this to another iteration in which God as narrator tells the story, in the third person, of Mūsā killing someone. This is the most detailed telling of the story.

28:15 He entered the city, unnoticed by its people, and found two men fighting: one from his own people, the other an enemy. The one from his own people cried out to him for help against the enemy. Moses struck him with his fist and killed him. He said, "This must be Satan's work: clearly he is a misleading enemy."

16 He said, "Lord, I have wronged myself. Forgive me," so He forgave him; He is truly the Most Forgiving, the Most Merciful.

17 He said, "My Lord, because of the blessings You have bestowed upon me, I shall never support those who do evil."

18 Next morning, he was walking in the city, fearful and vigilant, when suddenly the man he had helped the day before cried out to him for help. Moses said, "You are clearly a troublemaker."

19 As he was about to attack the man who was an enemy to both of them, the man said, "Moses, are you going to kill me as you killed that person yesterday? You clearly want to be a tyrant in the land; you do not intend to put things right."

20 Then a man came running from the furthest part of the city and said, "Moses, the authorities are talking about killing you, so leave—this is my sincere advice."

21 So Moses left the city, fearful and wary, and prayed, "My Lord, save me from people who do wrong."

Here we understand that Mūsā made multiple mistakes—he trusted someone that he should not have, and possibly he hit him harder than he intended to.

There are two iterations when Mūsā mentions that he killed someone. They come in his dialogue with God. God orders Mūsā to go to Fir'awn because he is a tyrant, and Mūsā asks God for help. Mūsā is giving context for his hesitation to go to Fir'awn, as God commands. In one iteration, Mūsā says: '"besides, they have a charge against me, and I fear they may kill me"' (26:14). In the other iteration, "Moses said, 'My Lord, I killed one of their men, and I fear that they may kill me'" (28:33).

These all contrast sharply with Fir'awn telling Mūsā that he killed someone. Indeed, as Mūsā anticipated, Fir'awn tries to use this against him. Fir'awn appears to be trying to manipulate Mūsā's feelings, to make him feel guilty over what he did, and thereby make him feel like he does not deserve to be in the position to try to teach Fir'awn better actions. The verses are as follows:

> 26:18 Pharaoh said, "Did we not bring you up as a child among us? Did you not stay with us for many years?
>
> 19 And then you committed that crime of yours: you were so ungrateful."
>
> 20 Moses replied, "I was misguided when I did it
>
> 21 and I fled from you in fear; later my Lord gave me wisdom and made me one of His messengers.
>
> 22 And is this—that you have enslaved the Children of Israel—the favour with which you reproach me?"

Fir'awn, by not even daring to mention Mūsā's crime, seems to be emphasizing how terrible it is. It is ironic that Fir'awn blames Mūsā for accidentally killing someone, when Fir'awn, himself, has had many people killed on purpose (28:4), and his wife asks him not to kill a baby she finds in a box in the water (28:9). It appears that Fir'awn wants Mūsā to despair, to see himself only in his mistakes, without any potential for growth, and to therefore not see himself as a prophet and not try to change anything in his environment. Fir'awn further manipulates the events in Mūsā's life by bringing up the kindness that he did for Mūsā, raising him. Mūsā refocuses these events by acknowledging his mistake and that God guided him—God's guidance and forgiveness are what really matters. Mūsā also mentions Fir'awn's hypocrisy in emphasizing his generosity to Mūsā, although he also enslaved the Children of Israel.

There is a tremendous difference between Mūsā being told his life story by God versus by Fir'awn. In fact, this conversation is immensely generative for discussing focalization and focus. And focalizing here connects to authority and repetition. Who has the authority to retell the past—Fir'awn, Mūsā, or God? And who has the authority to shape the story? This can give us a way to see what is at stake in repetition—authority and truth. With each retelling, we are given a new way to think about a story. When the retellings are all by God, in the Qur'ān, then they are all true and meaningful. When the focalization is through Fir'awn, for example, we see how he manipulates the truth that we see in other places from God. And through the varying repetition and focalization, we see more of Fir'awn's character, that he is manipulative and hypocritical.

We see here that "the slightest strategic variations in the pattern of repetition could serve the purposes of commentary, analysis, foreshadowing, thematic assertion, with a wonderful combination of subtle understatement and dramatic force."[28] In fact, Naddaff explains that repetition always comes with difference.[29] Indeed, in the Qur'ān, while repetition may initially surprise us, when we look carefully, we see that slight variations in repetition are actually strategic elements in the narrative style—as evident in this analysis and the tables in Appendix A. In addition, one can say that the context—in terms of where the verses are located in the Qur'ān—is always different, even if the words were the exact same. But in fact, we did not actually find the exact same words in the verses that we examined for repetition. Even in the most similar ones, there are slight variations.

With the Qur'ānic stories, since they are believed to present actual historical events, one can think further about the element of history: a narrative "is intrinsically a kind of repetition, a restating, retelling, recapitulation of events or states that have existed prior to their being narratively transmuted."[30] So a story of Mūsā, even if it exists in only one iteration, such as the story in *Sūrat al-Kahf*, is a retelling told by God. What we see through repetition and history in the Qur'ān is God asserting that He is the one to interpret, shape, tell, and retell history.

## E. Suppressed: Characterization

In Alter's work there are examples of differences in characters' speech that are characteristic of them.[31] We can find some examples like this in the Qur'ān, too. In the story of Mūsā, God summons Mūsā to go to Firʿawn with God's message. Three times, Mūsā expresses his reservations, especially in regards to his speaking abilities, and asks for help. In all his expressions, we see fear. Mūsā is aware of his emotions and expresses them openly to God. We can compare this part of the story in its iterations. First, we have just a hint of the situation through God's perspective: "out of Our grace [*min raḥmatinā*] We granted him his brother Aaron as a prophet" (19:53). Here, we are not even told about any issue with speech or Mūsā's fear. The focus is on God's mercy, *raḥma*, which is an overarching word and theme in the *sūra* where we find this verse.[32] Next, in three iterations, Mūsā expresses his fear about his speech and therefore asks for God to send Hārūn with him: "so that they may understand my words" (20:28), "and I will feel stressed and tongue-tied, so send Aaron too" (26:13) and "My brother Aaron is more eloquent than I: send him with me to help me and confirm my words—I fear they may call me a liar" (28:34).

We can compare this to, sure enough, Fir'awn, who is clearly aware of Mūsā's difficulty in speech or sensitivity about it. When asking his people how they might possibly believe Mūsā, we read: "Pharaoh proclaimed to his people, 'My people, is the Kingdom of Egypt not mine? And these rivers that flow at my feet, are they not mine? Do you not see? / Am I not better than this contemptible wretch who can scarcely express himself?'" (43:51–52). We see through Fir'awn's speech his arrogance about all that he has dominance over and we see him riling up his crowd, which we also see elsewhere. Fir'awn insults Mūsā by mentioning, criticizing, and manipulating his weakness—in this case, his ineloquence. We previously discussed Fir'awn's manipulation, so this is part of the characterization of Fir'awn in his speech. We are able to make these comparisons because there are multiple iterations of this story in the Qur'ān. Here, then, we see how repetition enables characterization.

## F. Suppressed: Reversal

One type of variation in suppression of repetition is a reversal, in which "the modification of perception is achieved through the substitution, suppression, or addition of a single phrase, or through a strategic change in the order of repeated items."[33] For examples, see the previous chapter on parallels and reversals in this book. One example that we discussed above and in the previous chapter, is one mother giving up her child, the reversal of which is a woman finding the child. The irony of the situation is reflected in the language of the story, with God telling Mūsā's mother to nurse him and throw him in the water when she fears for him (28:7, referenced above). It is completely counterintuitive and ironic that this is how he will be safe. Here, through the repetition and suppression of a theme, we see a reversal, and we notice that the surrounding language also includes irony.

## G. Selective Giving and Withholding Information

Even when we have the same scene repeated in different iterations, we find selective giving and withholding information within the story. For example, although we see Mūsā in confrontational dialogue with Fir'awn a number of times, only once do we see a man who believes from among Fir'awn's people speak up and try to convince his people to believe (40:23–45). Fir'awn threatens to kill Mūsā and the sons of the believers and then:

> 40:27 Moses said, "I seek refuge with my Lord and yours from every tyrant who refuses to believe in the Day of Reckoning."
>
> 28 A secret believer from Pharaoh's people said, "How can you kill a man just for saying, 'My Lord is God'? He has brought you clear signs from your Lord—if he is a liar, on his own head be it—and if he is truthful, then at least some of what he has threatened will happen to you. God does not guide any rebellious, outrageous liar."

One wonders where this man has been in the other iterations—silent or just not mentioned—and one also wonders how he compares to the magicians in the story. Perhaps he has been present but fearful, or perhaps he is a reminder to the audience that they may have supporters even when they do not realize it. Elsewhere, I discuss how exclusive information allows the Qur'ānic audience to feel closer to the text, characters, and the narrator of the text, God.[34]

## IV. Repeated Elements

### A. Length of Iterations

There are drastic variations in lengths of iterations of the story of Mūsā and Fir'awn in the Qur'ān. In what follows, I analyze some of the shortest iterations to see what elements are contained and repeated. These iterations contain from one through four verses (17:101–104, 19:51–53, 25:35–36, 29:39–40, 51:38–40, 54:41–43, 66:11, 69:9–10, and 73:15–16). We begin with a one-verse iteration describing Fir'awn's wife: "God has also given examples of believers: Pharaoh's wife, who said, 'Lord, build me a house near You in the Garden. Save me from Pharaoh and his actions; save me from the evildoers'" (66:11). It is striking that the only one-verse iteration of this story is an exclusive allusion to Fir'awn's wife and her prayer to God for a place in paradise. Since the focus is completely on her, not on Fir'awn or Mūsā, the wife is in a privileged position, and the style reflects the content: Fir'awn's wife is distinct, and the way her story is told is also distinct.

Next comes a two-verse iteration, which focuses on comparing presumably Muḥammad to Mūsā: "We have sent a messenger to you [people] to be your witness, just as We sent a messenger to Pharaoh, / but Pharaoh disobeyed the messenger and so We inflicted a heavy punishment on him" (73:15–16). Both Muḥammad and Mūsā were messengers God sent to people. Fir'awn disobeyed and was punished; this is a warning to Muḥammad's contemporaries. The main elements of this iteration are Mūsā, Fir'awn, Muḥammad, "you"

(Muḥammad's contemporaries and/or the listener or reader of the Qur'ān), obedience to a messenger, and punishment for disobedience.

A second short iteration is "Pharaoh, too, and those before him, and the ruined cities: these people committed grave sins / and disobeyed the messenger of their Lord, so He seized them with an ever-tightening grip" (69:9–10). Unlike the previous iteration (73:15–16), Muḥammad is not mentioned here, and these verses are not addressed to the second person. Similar to the previous iteration, both include the word messenger, *rasūl*. Here, the main elements mentioned are Firʿawn and punishment. This is indicative of the fact that among all the iterations, Firʿawn's punishment is the second-most common element in the Mūsā and Firʿawn story.

Another two-verse iteration is "We gave Moses the Book and appointed his brother Aaron to help him. / We said, 'Go, both of you, to the people who have rejected Our signs.' Later We destroyed those people utterly" (25:35–36). Again, the main elements and the focus in this iteration are different than the other two. Here, for the first time, we see Hārūn. He is mentioned as being a *wazīr* for Mūsā and in a much longer iteration of this story, that is exactly how Mūsā asks for Hārūn to be his helper (20:29). Here, then, we see a key word repeated in two different iterations: a shared root word. The main elements of this iteration are Mūsā, Hārūn, the Book, God sending them to Firʿawn, and punishment.

In the last two-verse iteration (29:39–40), for the first time, we see mention of Qārūn and Hāmān:

> 29:39 [Remember] Qarun and Pharaoh and Haman: Moses brought them clear signs, but they behaved arrogantly on earth. They could not escape Us
>
> 40 and We punished each one of them for their sins: some We struck with a pebble storm; some were overcome by a sudden blast; some We made the earth swallow; and some We drowned. It was not God who wronged them; they wronged themselves.

The focus is again different, with Mūsā being sent to all of them. In the second verse, the focus is on a variety of types of punishments and the concept of people harming themselves through their wrongdoing. This mention of Qārūn and Hāmān in such a short iteration may be surprising because they do not often appear in the longer iterations of the story. Why, in a succinct iteration, are they featured? We see here that the Qur'ān is evoking their presence, our memory of them, and what we may know from elsewhere. We may say this is also an example of withholding of knowledge, and as such, one narrative function of it is to turn our attention to other parts of the Qur'ān.

I will now move on to three-verse iterations, of which there are three. In 19:51–53, Fir'awn is not mentioned by name:

> 19:51 Mention too, in the Scripture, the story of Moses. He was specially chosen, a messenger and a prophet:
> 52 We called to him from the right-hand side of the mountain and brought him close to Us in secret communion;
> 53 out of Our grace We granted him his brother Aaron as a prophet.

We see a characteristic of Mūsā, that he is *mukhlaṣ* (specially chosen), and we also see some background into how his prophethood came about—God called him at a mountain (Mount Sinai) and brought him close to him, and God gave his brother to him out of God's mercy. Mercy and God's being called the Merciful are features in this *sūra* (19), and elsewhere, when Hārūn is mentioned (25:35), it is not said that this is out of God's mercy. Readers may wonder how exactly God provided Hārūn as a help to Mūsā, and the full story comes in the next chapter of the Qur'an (20:29–36).

In the next three-verse iteration (51:38–40), compared to the other iterations, we see more detail about Fir'awn's reaction to Mūsā's message—we even see his speech:

> 51:38 There is another sign in Moses: We sent him to Pharaoh with clear authority.
> 39 Pharaoh turned away with his supporters, saying, "This is a sorcerer, or maybe a madman,"
> 40 so We seized him and his forces and threw them into the sea: he was to blame.

Then comes the last three-verse iteration (54:41–43): "The people of Pharaoh also received warnings. / They rejected all Our signs so We seized them with all Our might and power. / 'Are your disbelievers any better than these? Were you given an exemption in the Scripture?'" This selection has two similarities to 73:15–16: both do not include Mūsā's name, and both make clear comparisons between Mūsā and his people, and Muḥammad and his people.

In a four-verse iteration, we see for the first time the mention of Mūsā coming with nine signs (17:101–104):

> 17:101 In the past, We gave Moses nine clear signs—ask the Children of Israel. When Moses came to [the Egyptians], Pharaoh said to him, "Moses, I think you are bewitched."

102 He said, "You know very well that only the Lord of the heavens and earth could have sent these signs as clear proof. I think that you, Pharaoh, are doomed."
103 So he wanted to frighten them off the [dry] land, but We drowned him and those with him.
104 After his death, We told the Children of Israel, "Live in the land, and when the promise of the Hereafter is fulfilled, We shall bring you to the assembly of all people."

We also see a conversation between Mūsā and Fir'awn, including Fir'awn's accusation that Mūsā is using magic—an accusation that we see elsewhere as well. There is also for the first time mention of Banī Isrā'īl and a recounting of God's words to them.

Overall, in these short iterations, we see an introduction in all but one of them (17:101, 19:51, 25:35, 29:39, 51:38, 54:41, 69:9, and 73:15). There is Mūsā and the burning bush scene (19:52) and him asking for his brother to help him (19:53) in one iteration only. Mūsā has a dialogue with Fir'awn once (17:102). We see Fir'awn drown or punished four times (17:103, 25:36, 29:40, and 51:40). We see Mūsā with his people (17:104). And we see Fir'awn's wife once (66:11). Thus, even in the shortest iterations, there is sometimes exclusive information or details that occur only once. We also see some striking words that are repeated in other iterations, and we find some words in our iterations that reflect the larger context of the *sūra*. Overall, we see different concepts and characters mentioned in the different short iterations. This can be surprising, since one may assume that in the short iterations, they would find the main points or the main characters consistently mentioned. What we see here, then, is that all the points and characters are important, and through varying repeated elements, the text draws the audience to look more comprehensively at the Qur'ān and to compare the iterations with each other.

## B. Introductions and Conclusions

Twenty-one of the twenty-four iterations of the story of Mūsā and Fir'awn have an introduction. Three introductions include the words "Has the story of Moses come to you [Prophet]?" (20:9, 79:15, and 85:17). Sixteen introductions include mention of Mūsā and/or Fir'awn: 7:103, 10:75, 11:97, 17:101, 23:46, 28:3, 29:39, 40:24, 43:46, 44:17, 51:38, 54:41 (mentions the people of Fir'awn), 69:9, 73:15, 85:18, and 89:10. Three introductions include Hārūn (10:75, 23:45, and 25:35), and two mention Hāmān and Qārūn (29:39 and 40:24). Five introductions mention Fir'awn and his counselors, *mala'* (7:103, 10:75,

11:97, 23:46, and 43:46). Thus, although introductions are very frequent, they vary in terms of characters mentioned. These introductions are a way of framing the story, and by mentioning different people in different iterations, we see that they choose where the audience will focus. Many of the iterations (fifteen) have some kind of conclusion with the narrator's commentary, or a conclusion that moves the text to the next story or moral. This shows how the stories are reflected upon, connected to, and used within the larger context of a *sūra*. When looking at the tables, we can also note that Firʿawn is described as drowning or being punished eighteen times. Interestingly, this is more than the number of conclusions found to the story. So there does seem to be an emphasis on this element of the story.

## V. Conclusion

In this chapter, the insights drawn from scholarship on the narratological functions of repetition in the Bible and in *1001 Nights* were considered and how they might provide insights for the analysis of the Qur'ānic story of Mūsā. I used the tables in Appendix A to make some observations about repetition in the Qur'ānic story of Mūsā and Firʿawn. Even in the story that is most told in the Qur'ān—the story of Mūsā in general, and the story of Mūsā and Firʿawn in particular—there is not as much repetition as may initially be assumed. It was demonstrated, using the example of the variation in the magicians' speech, for example, that what looks like repetition actually has some important differences.

From this analysis, we can identify some assumptions that the Qur'ān seems to have about stories more generally. These assumptions include the following: a story can be told in bits and pieces. A story does not need to be told in chronological order. A story in one text can be told from a variety of narratological perspectives, or focalizers. A story can be told with an introduction and conclusion that includes different details and characters. A story does not need to include many details and can include different details, the same details, or seemingly contradictory details at different times. Dialogues that are supposed to represent the portrayal of one historic event can have different and distinct iterations. Iterations can portray the same characters in different ways. What looks like repetition can include differences when examined closely. As we see from this list, it can be useful to examine elements that we find unusual in stories; by seeing what is most unusual, it can be easier to determine our expectations and the conventions that we are expecting to see fulfilled, in contrast to the actual storytelling conventions that the Qur'ān develops and upholds.

We also saw in this chapter through the example of focalization that repetition in the Qur'ān is intimately connected to the ideas of power, storytelling, the right to tell a story, or history and truth. When Fir'awn tells a story, he tells it to rile up his audience, to assert his power, and to manipulate people and their feelings. When God tells a story, it is to guide people. When God uses repetition in the Qur'ān, it directs the audience back to the Qur'ān, by drawing one to notice, compare, and analyze.

# 4
# Repetition and the Portrayal of Time in the Story of Mūsā and Hārūn in the Qur'ān

## I. Introduction

The portrayal of time in Qur'ānic stories is an area ripe for exploration. While there exists scholarship on the portrayal of time in the Qur'ān, few scholars use narratological theories of time to analyze the portrayal and narrative uses of time in Qur'ānic stories. This chapter focuses on the portrayal of time in the Qur'ānic story of Mūsā and Hārūn in particular and uses a narratological and rhetorical lens to analyze a few iterations of the story. In this chapter, I will focus on repetition on the scale of the scene. We will see how the narrator of the Qur'ān uses the narrative to shape the reader's perceptions about time and space and to thereby reinforce theological beliefs that the Qur'ān expresses in its metanarrative. These beliefs are that God fulfills His promises, God does as God wills, and God shapes the narrative, time, and space to show that God does as God wills.

This chapter relies on Seymour Chatman's and Gerard Genette's discussions of time and discourse. The first distinction to make is between the timeline within a plot or story and the timeline in the telling of the story—in the discourse.[1] For example, the plot within a story can include the following elements: a woman wakes up, eats breakfast, and goes to work. But the way the story is told, the discourse, may not tell the story in this chronological order. Thus, we come to the issue of order: events in a story can be arranged in any order in the discourse as long as they are comprehensible.[2] In the discourse, we can see the order in different ways: flashback, analepse, and what is relevant in our case: "Flashforward (prolepse) [is] where the discourse leaps ahead, to events subsequent to intermediate events. These intermediate events must themselves be recounted at some later point, for otherwise the leap would simply constitute an ellipsis."[3] In the previous example, flashforward/prolepse is if we read that the woman wakes up and goes to work, and later we read about her

*How the Qur'ān Works*. Leyla Ozgur Alhassen, Oxford University Press. © Oxford University Press 2023.
DOI: 10.1093/oso/9780197654606.003.0004

eating breakfast. Ellipsis is when discourse time is zero; it skips some amount of story time.[4] In our example, ellipsis would be that the woman wakes up and goes to work, and we would not be told anything about her eating breakfast. We will see below one example of prolepse and a few examples of ellipsis in the stories of Mūsā and Hārūn.[5]

Although the story of Mūsā is the most frequently mentioned story in the Qur'ān, there is little scholarship about time in the story's portrayal. Mustansir Mir writes about "time jumps" in *Sūrat Yūsuf*.[6] He explains that these exist in the story because "Qur'ānic narrative usually focuses on the essence of the matter at hand, skipping details."[7] While this may be true, as we will see in this study, I argue that these time leaps serve a narrative and theological purpose and are not merely a matter of expedience.

Some scholars of the Qur'ān, such as Ahmad Obiedat and Angelika Neuwirth, give a simple linear schema of time in the Qur'ān as moving from the past to the present to the future.[8] Neuwirth argues that the idea of the Day of Judgment's closeness readjusted the preexisting cyclical conception of time to linear.[9] She describes how the Qur'ān contrasts with pre-Islamic thought, by injecting meaning into people's lives, through a belief in an afterlife.[10] Similarly, Gerhard Bowering explains that the pre-Islamic concept of *dahr* was like unavoidable fate, and the Qur'ān rejected this notion and replaced it with a linear monotheism that has people moving from birth to death and the afterlife, as determined by God.[11]

We can develop a more nuanced approach to the portrayal of time in the Qur'ān if we look at what al-Ṭabarī writes about how references to night and day before creation and in paradise are to be understood "figuratively."[12] Here, then, we have an example of a figurative approach to time in the Qur'ān. Other scholars discuss the Qur'ān's "melding and mixing times and periods," as well as its supertemporal portrayal of time.[13] Again, we see some acknowledgment of creativity in the Qur'ānic portrayal of time.

Related to time is the concept of history in the Qur'ān. Yadullah Kazmi categorizes two kinds of events in the Qur'ān: "Human Drama," which follows a "temporal logic," and "Divine Drama," which is about "primordial" events and "is subject to no such logic . . . [it] is totally alien to our historical experience and hence lies beyond the pale of our historical comprehension."[14] While this oversimplifies the issues, the distinction between the human and the divine is useful, as we will see. Perhaps most useful in Kazmi's article is his comparing history to the sea, sometimes placid and sometimes tempestuous: "the substance of history is infinitely plastic."[15] I propose we can use this analogy to describe the portrayal of time in the Qur'ān: in the Qur'ānic stories, we see time sometimes moving in a linear fashion, sometimes skipping forward and sometimes moving back, like waves rolling in and out.

Most sophisticated and convincing in his analysis is Shahzad Bashir. He argues that although modern scholarship on Islamic texts presents them as based on a linear progression of time, "Islamic materials contain complex and varied constructions of time" and include "multiple temporalities."[16] This is a "view of time as an ideological and narrative product that is forever being made and remade within Islamic perspectives."[17] Bashir explains that the way time is presented in a text can be part of how that text makes an argument. He demonstrates this by presenting three different texts and the ways that they construct time. A text can present time as "the feeling of being in a moment."[18] One text "intermix[es] time and space" and "foreground[s] Herat as a kind of metaphysical structure on which space and time can be mapped as equivalent contingent qualities."[19] In the Qur'ānic examples we discuss below, we will see how the Qur'ānic narrative foregrounds a particular element—not Mūsā, Hārūn, or God, but rather God's promise. A different text that Bashir analyzes uses the narrator as an axis: "He himself is a constant presence in the narrative through the framing and as a character within the events as they unfold."[20] This sounds like God in the Qur'ānic stories, as we will see below. Bowering also writes that time is "theocentric" in the Qur'ān and *hadīth*.[21]

Through the analysis of the portrayal of time in the story of Mūsā and Hārūn in the Qur'ān, we see not just a movement in time but also first a conversation about a time and place, and then a leap into that time and space. We will see what purpose time leaps serve for the reader and that they are reflected in the storytelling, are not just didactic, and are performative.

## II. Mūsā and Hārūn with Minimal and No Leaps in Time and Space

There are twenty verses that mention Hārūn by name in the Qur'ān.[22] Some of these verses very briefly mention Hārūn, and some will be discussed in this study. The verses that briefly mention Hārūn are 2:248, 4:163, 6:84, 19:28, 19:53, and 21:48. The verses that will be discussed are 20:30, 20:70, 20:90, 20:92, 26:13, 26:48, and 28:34. Five of the remaining iterations use the dual and mention Hārūn by name but clearly do not use time and space leaps in their portrayal of Hārūn. They are 7:103–174, 10:75–93, 23:45–49, 25:35–36, and 37:114–122. What all five of these iterations have in common is that we do not see Mūsā's request to have Hārūn as a helper and we do not see God saying He grants this request. Another way to phrase this is that in the only three iterations where Mūsā asks God to grant him Hārūn as a helper and God grants him this request, we see a folding of time and space and the appearance of Hārūn (20:1–100, 26:10–68, and 28:1–50).[23] We will discuss these examples below and will see how they serve a theological purpose of showing that because God said He would do something, God does so, and in the most expedient of ways: by causing or narrating a leap through time and space. This embodies the Qur'ānic idea that God says "be and it is" (e.g., 2:117 and 3:47). The shaping of time and space itself shows another of the theological beliefs in the Qur'ān: God is all-powerful (e.g., 3:189).

To understand the leaps in time and space in the story of Mūsā and Hārūn, we can start with an iteration that just hints at a leap of time or space. In *Sūrat al-Qaṣaṣ*, God commands Mūsā to go to Fir'awn, and Mūsā asks God to give him Hārūn as a helper on his mission: "My brother Aaron is more eloquent than I: send him with me to help me and confirm my words—I fear they may call me a liar" (28:34). God grants him his request and explains what He will do for them in the future: "God said, 'We shall strengthen you through your brother; We shall give you both power so that they cannot touch you. With Our signs you, and those who follow you, will triumph'" (28:35). Although Abdel Haleem's translation does not make it consistently clear, "We shall give you both power so that they cannot touch you. With Our signs you, and those who follow you . . ." is all in the second-person dual and could be rendered as "We shall give you both power so that they cannot touch either of you. With Our signs you two, and those who follow you two . . ." The earlier verses were clearly a dialogue between God and Mūsā, with no use of the dual. So there has been a shift from Mūsā being described with the singular to the dual. If a reader is not focused on the issue of time, space, and presence, they may overlook the importance of the dual in this verse. In this verse (28:35), Hārūn may be physically present, or the language is acknowledging his existence and his soon-to-be presence because God said He would grant Hārūn as a helper to Mūsā. We do not see Hārūn speak, and we have no further indication of his presence. The next verses only mention Mūsā. For example, we read: "But when Moses came to them with Our clear signs, they said, 'These are mere conjuring tricks; we never heard this from our forefathers'" (28:36). The fact that the translator, Abdel Haleem, does not reflect the dual in his translation perhaps indicates the subtlety of the language, or it may reflect the difficulty of translation from a language that uses the dual to a language that does not, and it shows us something that gets lost in translation.

## III. *Sūrat Ṭaha*

Aptly, Islamic studies scholar Ismail Albayrak mentions that *Sūrat Ṭaha* includes a number of words that indicate time: "Interestingly, there are a number of words which are directly related to the time such as *maw'id*, *wa'd*, *ya'idu*, *qadar*, *mīqāt* and others, which recur so often in *Sūrat Ṭā-Hā* as to indicate some kind of unifying principle."[24] The roots of the words he mentions occur nine times in *Sūrat Ṭaha* (20:40, 20:58, 20:59, 20:80, 20:86 twice, 20:87, 20:97, and 20:113) and twice in *Sūrat al-Shu'arā'* (26:38 and 26:206). This is striking, given that we see two examples of ellipsis and one example of prolepse in the story. This is reminiscent of what Sandra Naddaff, analyzing *1001 Nights*, writes: characters make a point to mention the amount of time something may take.[25] In *Sūrat Ṭaha,* we see the concept of time mentioned repeatedly.

The first example we will focus on in the story is when Mūsā sees a fire and leaves his family to go to it (20:10–11), he then is summoned by God and asks God to command his brother, Hārūn, to help him in his mission (20:29–32), promising that he and Hārūn will glorify God and be mindful of God (20:35).[26] God says He will grant Mūsā his request (20:36). After this verse, we see progressively intensifying indications that Hārūn is becoming present: Hārūn is gradually appearing in the scene. First Mūsā asks for Hārūn to help him. This is the first stage in Hārūn's appearance: he is mentioned by name (20:30). Then, God tells Mūsā, with Hārūn this time, to go to Fir'awn: "Go, you and your brother, [*idhhab anta wa-ākhūka*] with My signs, and do not weaken in remembering Me" (20:42). We have no reason to think that Hārūn was present in this scene, and yet, here he is. The command to "go" is given in the first person singular (*idhhab*), but Hārūn is added on as "and your brother."[27] Then God says, "Go, both of you, (*idhhabā*) to Pharaoh, for he has exceeded all bounds" (20:43), this time not only mentioning Hārūn but also addressing him and Mūsā directly with the second-person dual.[28] It seems that Hārūn is now present, since he is addressed directly. Finally, Hārūn is definitely present because Mūsā and Hārūn are quoted as speaking, as evidenced in the use of the dual "*qālā*," in "They said, 'Lord, we fear he will do us great harm or exceed all bounds'" (20:45). The narrative shows Hārūn's appearance and presence gradually, until he is finally completely physically present, and the next verses continue with Hārūn's complete presence. For some readers, it may be jarring to read that a person is present and not present at the same time, and yet that is how the narrator is portraying time and space in these verses—and not only is Hārūn present and not present, but he is also somewhat present. We can look at this as an example of ellipsis, in which time skips from the beginning of the dialogue of Mūsā and God to Hārūn's presence.

The Qur'ānic commentators surveyed in this study, who are readers of the text, have different responses to these verses.[29] Some make no mention of this gradual appearance, perhaps because they can explain it easily theologically (God does as He wills), but two of them do address it. Abū al-Su'ūd explains that verse 20:43 is an example of *taghlīb* and that Hārūn is actually not there. *Taghlīb* is a grammatical term to describe when a dual word is used to refer to two items that are often associated with each other by referring to the more dominant of the two items in the dual. An example of this is 'Umarān (the two 'Umārs) referring to Abū Bakr and 'Umar.[30] Abū al-Su'ūd says 20:43 and 20:45 are examples of this.[31] Abū al-Su'ūd's argument shows that the Qur'ānic portrayal of time and space here contradicts at least his understanding of these concepts, and thus he tries to reconcile them.

Sayyid Quṭb explains that in verse 20:45 Hārūn was not with Mūsā in the dialogue with God, but God folds time and place, showing Hārūn with Mūsā.[32] Quṭb thus seems more comfortable with a portrayal that defies common understandings of reality. Given the fact that God says He will grant Mūsā his request (20:36), it makes sense to see the language as showing what God says and demonstrating God's power at the same time.

Ibn al-'Arabī (d. 1240 CE/638 AH) writes about God bestowing Hārūn on Mūsā out of God's mercy (referring to 19:53), and Hārūn embodies "kindness to his brother, since his Prophethood derived from the divine Mercy, and only such [considerate] behavior was to be expected from him."[33] Going back to the idea from Shahzad Bashir, about time revolving around a particular element, I am suggesting that the portrayal of time in 20:9–56 revolves around the divine mercy that manifests in God agreeing to bestow Hārūn as a helper to Mūsā.

Through the flexible portrayal of time here, we have an example of the narrative shaping a new perception of reality for the readers—that of gradual presence—thus showing God's ability to do as He wills and God's graciousness in promptly granting Mūsā's prayer. This example of ellipsis, as well as the examples to come, is an example of performative language. Here, I refer to J. L. Austin and the idea that "to utter the sentence . . . is to do it."[34] An example often given to explain the performative is that, under the right circumstances, the statement "I now pronounce you husband and wife" actually make two people husband and wife.[35] Thus, when God says he grants Mūsā's request to give him his brother as a helper, his brother appears: the statement does what it says it is doing.

Another example of the narrator merging time and space is also present in the lengthy dialogue between Mūsā and God in *Sūrat Ṭaha*. In this dialogue, God comforts Mūsā about confronting Fir'awn: "He said, 'Do not be afraid, I am with you both, hearing and seeing everything'" (20:46). God tells them what to say to Fir'awn, and then the narrative jumps through time and space and Fir'awn responds (20:49). Given this leap in time and space, the preceding verses may suggest that God has rehearsed their lines with them, and this rehearsal is depicted as occurring at the same time as their discussion with Fir'awn (20:46–49) or it is the same scene or a somehow overlapping scene. Here, then, is another example of ellipsis in the Qur'ān. Because God said He is with them, God is, and because God is capable of doing anything, God does what God wills, even if this defies some human understandings of presence in time and place. In addition, because God commands Hārūn and Mūsā to convey a message to Fir'awn, they do so; we do not need to be told that they obey God, and because the speech is only written once, it appears as if they use the exact words that God tells them.

Once again, commentators can give us examples of various responses to these verses. Al-Tha'ālibī explains that God is with them by granting them victory and aid, an explanation that ignores the portrayal of the merging time and space.[36] Al-Ṭabarī explains that God hears what happens between Mūsā, Fir'awn, and Hārūn, or that God hears and sees the dialogue and inspires Mūsā and Hārūn in their response.[37] These theories also avoid the issue. God promises to help Mūsā and Hārūn, and God does so promptly and in a way that reshapes our perceptions of time and space. The portrayal of this fulfillment of a promise is subtle and eerie—it does not draw overt attention to itself, which is perhaps why commentators do not address it.[38] Here, we may mention one of the names or descriptions of God as being *al-muṣawwir*, the One who shapes things—so God shapes time and space.[39] The Qur'ān also describes God as the First and the Last—God is eternal and time has no power over God (verse 57:3).

This iteration of the story of Mūsā and Hārūn also includes an example of prolepse, in which the narrative skips ahead in time and then goes back. In the second dialogue of Mūsā with God, God asks Mūsā why he rushed to meet Him (20:83), and Mūsā explains, "I rushed to You, Lord, to please You" (20:84). In contrast to this, God says, "We have tested your people in your absence: the Samiri has led them astray" (20:85).[40] Mūsā returns to his people and questions them about their actions (20:86). They respond to his question, and the narration moves back in time to explain what had happened in Mūsā's absence and then moves forward to return to Mūsā's confrontation. The verses are as follows:

20:86 Moses returned to his people, angry and aggrieved. He said, "My people, did your Lord not make you a gracious promise? Was my absence too long for you? Did you want anger to fall on you from your Lord and so broke your word to me?"

87 They said, "We did not break our word to you deliberately. We were burdened with the weight of people's jewellery, so we threw it [into the fire], and the Samiri did the same,"

88 but he [used the molten jewellery to] produce an image of a calf which made a lowing sound, and they said, "This is your god and Moses' god, but he has forgotten."

89 Did they not see that [the calf] gave them no answer, that it had no power to harm or benefit them?

90 Aaron had told them, "My people, this calf is a test for you. Your true Lord is the Lord of Mercy, so follow me and obey my orders,"

91 but they replied, "We shall not give up our devotion to it until Moses returns to us."

92 Moses said, "When you realized they had gone astray, what prevented you, Aaron,

93 from coming after me? How could you disobey my orders?"

94 He said, "Son of my mother—let go of my beard and my hair!—I was afraid you would say, "You have caused division among the children of Israel and have not heeded what I said."

We see in these verses a few things: Mūsā confronts the people (20:86), they reply to him (20:87), their reply merges into a flashback showing what happened while Mūsā was away (20:88–91), we jump back to the present time with Mūsā asking Hārūn why he did not obey him (20:92–93) and Hārūn responds by asking Mūsā not to pull his beard and hair and explaining that he did not want to divide the people (20:94).[41]

Here, the way the narration moves, it seems that Mūsā is unfairly criticizing Hārūn. Maybudī explains this through the lens of friendship, the friendship between Mūsā and God:

> . . . when he [Mūsā] seized his brother by the head and pulled him severely, He [God] did not say, "Why did you do that?" . . . Within the curtain of friendship things go on that outside the curtain of friendship would all be faults, but inside the curtain of friendship
> they are tolerated.[42]

I do think God rebukes Mūsā but through narrative techniques. Referring to other verses, and relevant here, Mustansir Mir writes: "The Qur'an presents

Moses as a strong-willed but also somewhat hot-blooded individual. The impetuousness of his disposition is well brought out in certain dialogues."[43] This is apt here too. Hārūn had tried to convince the people to stop worshipping the calf, but the narrator tells the readers this (20:90–91) and then tells us how Mūsā confronts his brother (20:92–94). Albayrak points out that Hārūn says that they are being tested (20:90), and God said He tested the people (20:85). Thus, Hārūn's words confirm God's words. This can be seen as further vindicating Hārūn. Albayrak also notes that elsewhere, Mūsā uses the same verb to tell the people that they are being tested:

> God's description of the test, "We have tested them – *innā fatannā qawmaka*" is put in the mouth of Moses in 7:155: "it is only Your trial – *in hiya illā fitnatuka*." In addition Aaron's saying to the Children of Israel in 20:90, "O my people you are being tried in this – *innamā futintum bihi*" strengthens this interrelationship.[44]

It is unclear if this information is also being withheld from Mūsā, but it seems like a reasonable assumption. By withholding information of Hārūn's innocence from Mūsā, but sharing it with the readers, it appears that God the narrator is tacitly critiquing Mūsā.

Commentators do not address reasons for the ordering in the narrative discourse—the presentation of the story. In contrast to this withholding of information, Albayrak mentions that God gives Mūsā "special knowledge" by telling him that God tested the people. Albayrak writes that Sayyid Quṭb mentions this too.[45] It is interesting that they focus on what Mūsā does know—that his people were tested but do not mention what Mūsā does not know—that Hārūn is innocent. Perhaps this is an instance in which God is pointing out a character flaw in Mūsā, for, why should he assume that Hārūn is to blame?

It is not completely clear in the translation here, but it looks like Abdel Haleem, in his translation cited above, is trying to reduce the blaming of Mūsā's actions in the way he translates one of the verses. In the verse, Mūsā asks Hārūn why he did not follow him. Abdel Haleem's translation makes this look like Mūsā means physically follow. The translation is "Moses said, 'When you realized they had gone astray, what prevented you, Aaron, / from coming after me? How could you disobey my orders?' " (20:92–93). Muhammad Asad uses this interpretation and takes it a bit further, asking Hārūn what prevented him "from [abandoning them and] following me? Hast thou, then, [deliberately] disobeyed my commandment?"[46] Thus, Asad portrays Mūsā as asking Hārūn why he did not leave the disobeying people and follow Mūsā. This interpretation could make sense of the earlier flashback without blaming Mūsā.

Mūsā then is not asking why Hārūn did not follow him spiritually (which he did), but he is asking him why he did not leave the people when he found that they would not believe. Most translators do not clearly imply a physical or spiritual interpretation of the word "follow" (*tattabiʿani*) in the verse. One translator, however, does and inserts a different interpretation, showing Mūsā asking Hārūn what prevented him "from following me (and punishing them)? Dared you then disobey my biddings?"[47] Here, the idea is that Hārūn did not spiritually follow Mūsā by punishing the people.

Even if we assume that Mūsā is asking Hārūn why he did not leave the people and follow him, through Hārūn's response, we learn that Mūsā is grabbing Hārūn by his beard and hair. That this comes through the dialogue rather than first through narration surprises the reader and highlights the harshness of this behavior. Al-Ṭabarī explains that the Qur'ān does not say so, but we know that Mūsā grabbed Hārūn's head and beard.[48] Al-Ṭabarī does not explain why this is the case or how it should effect our understanding of the story or characters.

Hārūn's response seems to explain away all the interpretations discussed above. He first calls Mūsā "Son of my mother" (20:94), which brings to mind the story narrated earlier of their mother and the love she felt for Mūsā and the love God had for her (20:37–41). In addition, Salwa El-Awa suggests that calling a brother "brother" "would recall connotations of the social privileges and commitments implicit in the relationship referred to."[49] Hārūn explains that he did not want to divide the people, which may be why he was not willing to further escalate the disagreement by being more insistent, by leaving the people or by punishing them. Finally, we can add that the people's response to Hārūn in the flashback seems adamant.[50] They say: "We shall not give up our devotion to it until Moses returns to us" (20:91).[51] It does not seem likely that Hārūn could have convinced them without causing factions, as he feared. In the end, it appears that the narrator withholds information about Hārūn's past actions from Mūsā and shows the readers Mūsā's harsh and unfair treatment of Hārūn. Here, the narrator uses a flashback to show Mūsā's mistake. In other words, God is not willing to add more injustice to the injustice that Mūsā enacted upon Hārūn. Rather, God maintains justice by criticizing Mūsā's unjust treatment of Hārūn through the narrative style. This is similar to God's criticism of the Prophet Muḥammad in *Sūrat ʿAbasa* (80:1–16)—although there, the criticism is found in the content, whereas here, it is in the narrative style. God is just (e.g., 2:281, 3:18, and 41:46) and God commands people to be just (4:58, 5:8 and 16:90), even if it is against oneself, one's parents or relatives (4:135 and 6:152). So although Mūsā is God's prophet, God stands for justice by highlighting Mūsā's injustice and highlighting that Hārūn did in fact make good decisions in a difficult situation.

Whitney Bodman mentions the unusual ordering of Adam's story later in the *sūra* (20:115–121). He writes, "clearly narrative order is not important here."[52] What I am arguing is that "narrative order" can be discussed on the level of the discourse and the story, and the way that order and time are used and portrayed serves the purpose of showing God's justice and God's fulfilling His promises. What we see in the instances of the narrator merging time and space—the prolepse and ellipsis—in *Sūrat Ṭaha* are narrative choices that shape a concept of the world: one in which God is just, God is supreme, God keeps His promise to people, and God can do whatever God wills—in narrative portrayal and in the world. These examples also convey God's involvement in people's lives: God is literally with people. All the examples are also subtle enough that the reader has to think and ask questions in order to notice them.

## IV. *Sūrat al-Shu'arā'*

When looking at the Qur'ānic story of Mūsā and Hārūn, we are looking at multiple iterations of the same story. Here it is useful to look at the scholarship of Sandra Naddaff, who writes about repetition and time in her work on the *1001 Nights*. Naddaff writes that when there is repetition in a story, the reader already knows the events, so they are not significant; what is significant is "the undertaking of the act, the rite of (often narrative) passage that is signified in the accomplishment of the act."[53] So novelty of an act is not important, but the act itself is. Furthermore, Naddaff writes that "any act worth performing once is worth performing over and over again."[54] She writes about repetition as being on a vertical axis, with time on a horizontal axis.[55] However, "no action, no matter how carefully imitated, can ever exactly repeat its precursor," so there will always be differences in the repetition because it is at a different time.[56] Interesting, also, is the idea that "repetition has no significant meaning without the temporal dimension."[57] So repetition should be analyzed with an eye toward time—both the portrayal of time within the story, and the interaction of time and the reading/listening(s) of the text. Some scholarship of the Qur'ān simplistically and sometimes dismissively mentions the patterns in the stories, or the repetition within them while disregarding the way that time is portrayed within the stories. Perhaps key in the Qur'ānic context and its messages is that repetition makes a text timeless, it brings it to an eternal state.[58] Repetition "draw[s] the eye of the viewer away from the things of this world toward the perception of a design that potentially repeats itself into the realm of the divine."[59] That repetition brings a text closer to the eternal is incredibly generative for the Qur'ān.

Now we can focus on another iteration of the Qur'ānic story of Mūsā and Hārūn. The portrayal of time in *Sūrat al-Shuʿarāʾ* (26:10–68) is similar to the portrayal of time in *Sūrat Ṭaha*. In particular, we see ellipsis in both chapters, with Hārūn and God appearing on the scene. It is striking that we see repetition both in the story and in the discourse.

> 26:10 Your Lord called to Moses: "Go to those wrongdoers,
> 11 the people of Pharaoh. Will they not take heed?"
> 12 Moses said, "My Lord, I fear they will call me a liar,
> 13 and I will feel stressed and tongue-tied, so send Aaron too;
> 14 besides, they have a charge against me, and I fear they may kill me."
> 15 God said, "No [they will not]. Go, both of you, with Our signs--We shall be with you, listening.
> 16 Go, both of you, to Pharaoh and say, 'We bring a message from the Lord of all worlds:
> 17 let the Children of Israel leave with us.' "
> 18 Pharaoh said, "Did we not bring you up as a child among us? Did you not stay with us for many years?
> 19 And then you committed that crime of yours: you were so ungrateful."
> 20 Moses replied, "I was misguided when I did it
> 21 and I fled from you in fear; later my Lord gave me wisdom and made me one of His messengers.
> 22 And is this--that you have enslaved the Children of Israel--the favour with which you reproach me?"

First, God calls Mūsā and tells him to go to Firʿawn (26:10–11). Mūsā expresses his fear (26:12) and then asks for Hārūn to help him (26:13). God, without using any words to directly say that He is granting Mūsā's prayer, commands both Mūsā and Hārūn with the dual, as in the previous iteration, "Go, both of you" (*fa-dhhabā*, 26:15). The next verse continues to use the dual to command both Mūsā and Hārūn: "Go, both of you, to Pharaoh and say, 'We bring a message from the Lord of all worlds' " (26:16). Again, as if they were rehearsing their lines with God, we leap in time and space and both Mūsā and Hārūn are speaking to Firʿawn: "let the Children of Israel leave with us"

(26:17, *ma'anā*). Next, we see Fir'awn's response, which he addresses directly to Mūsā: "Pharaoh said, 'Did we not bring you up as a child among us? Did you not stay with us for many years? / And then you committed that crime of yours: you were so ungrateful'" (26:18–19). Here, Fir'awn only addresses Mūsā, in the singular, and he moves the conversation back to the past, when Mūsā was raised amongst Fir'awn's household. So he moves us back in space and time. This is incredibly important in their relationship, which we explore throughout this book: Fir'awn is manipulative and wants Mūsā to see himself only as his past vulnerability and mistakes—an adopted child and a person who killed someone.

Interestingly, when Fir'awn replies using the singular to address Mūsā, this is the turning point that switches most of the rest of the story to an interaction between Fir'awn and Mūsā without Hārūn being mentioned. Mūsā acknowledges his misdeed, of course in the singular (26:20). Fir'awn asks the people around him if they hear what their messenger (in the singular) is saying (26:27). They discuss God's existence, and then Mūsā alone performs his miracles (26:30–35). This contrasts with the earlier verse in which God commands both Mūsā and Hārūn to go with God's signs to Fir'awn: "God said, 'No [they will not]. Go, both of you, with Our signs--We shall be with you, listening'" (26:15).

Mūsā and his brother are both mentioned later in a few verses. In the first, people mention both of them: "They answered, 'Delay him and his brother for a while, and send messengers to all the cities'" (26:36). The magicians later mention "the Lord of Moses and Aaron" (26:48). Also, Mūsā and his people are referred to as a group people, "a puny band," which we may assume includes Hārūn, but he is not explicitly mentioned (26:54). These references do not make it clear that Hārūn is present at the time that he is mentioned (26:54–55).[60] In another reference, we notice the narrator mentioning Mūsā only: "Then We revealed Our will to Moses, 'Leave with My servants by night, for you will be pursued!'" (26:52).[61] Thus, in contrast to the *Sūrat Ṭaha* iteration, Hārūn first appears, but then he disappears. His disappearance is quite subtle and seems to be triggered by Fir'awn's not mentioning him. It is as if Fir'awn is trying to usurp the grammatical nuances and the discourse of the text, as well as God's power.

Similar to the *Sūrat Ṭaha* iteration, Mūsā says God is with him, and we indeed see God as a character, actively participating in the scene. First, Mūsā says to his people that God is with them: "Moses said, 'No, my Lord is with me: He will guide me'" (26:62). Then, we repeatedly see God with Mūsā, by inspiring him and acting in the story, "and We revealed to Moses: 'Strike the sea with your staff.' It parted—each side like a mighty mountain— / and We brought the others to that place: / We saved Moses and all his companions, and drowned the rest" (26:63–66).

In this iteration of the story of Mūsā and Hārūn, we have seen some examples of ellipsis, which include a leap in time and place. We have also seen that after Hārūn appeared on the scene, his presence was greatly de-emphasized—perhaps symbolically showing Fir'awn's usurpation of control within the story and in the discourse. In addition, we saw that God appeared actively in the scene, when Mūsā said God is with them.

## V. Conclusion

In this study, we can think about God in God's various roles as a character, narrator, and implied author of Qur'ānic stories. Wayne Booth writes that "the purposes of the individual work should dictate the standards by which it is judged."[62] One obvious purpose of the Qur'ān is to establish people's beliefs in God. Thus, the techniques that the Qur'ān and its stories use should affirm this belief. The methods that the narrator uses in the Qur'ān should further that belief, and they do. When the narrator merges time and space, God shows that God can do as God wills, and the reader comes to new perceptions of reality when reading the stories in question.

The examples of time and space merging in this study are portrayed with such subtlety that a reader can miss them if she is not reading carefully. God the narrator merges time and space, confirming God the creator's role as creator: God created everything, and God can do as God wills. Thus, God can merge time and space if God wills. The examples of ellipsis and prolepse that we saw in this study show theological beliefs in the Qur'ān are not just didactic, they are also reflected in the storytelling. What we saw in the examples throughout this study is that time and space are also part of God's creation, subject to God's will and promise. In the repetition of the Mūsā and Hārūn story where Mūsā asks God to grant him Hārūn as a helper and God grants him this request, we see a folding of time and space with the appearance of Hārūn (20:1–100, 26:10–68, and 28:1–50). In the example of the flashback that shows Mūsā unfairly blaming Hārūn, God stands for justice by showing that Hārūn was in the right. Repetition shows us the various portrayals of time and that God manipulates time and space as God wills to fulfill His promise and to enact justice; thus, God is the central factor in time and its portrayal in the Qur'ān.

Inspired by Naddaff, we analyzed the relationship between time and repetition, and that perhaps as a result of the patterns that repetition shows the audience, repetition brings the audience to an appreciation of the divine. Things move and happen in ways that God knows, wills or wants. Prophets and people come and go, but God remains: "Everyone on earth perishes / all that remains is the Face of your Lord, full of majesty, bestowing honour" (55:26–27).

# 5

# Echoing Phrases, Words, and Actions in Qur'ānic Stories

## Exchange Encounters, Fasting, Feasting, and Faith

## I. Introduction

Much scholarship of Qur'ānic stories revolves around their biblical parallels and possible sources.[1] Some see Qur'ānic stories as bits and pieces that were taken from other places and assembled in the Qur'ān, often with allusions that alone remind the reader of the story at hand.[2] For some, it is a given that the Qur'ān is a hodgepodge with no or little literary merit, despite the developed scholarship on Qur'ānic literary style within Arabic scholarship.[3] Some claim that there is no Qur'ānic narrative, with the exception of *Sūrat Yūsuf*.[4] As Walid Saleh writes:

> Insightful and erudite as it might have been, the citing-of-parallels approach, the hallmark of early Quranic higher criticism, has become a barrier to a proper understanding of the function of biblical stories in the Qur'ān. . . . The Qur'ān was . . . never seen as able to present a coherent vision of its own, rather than a refracted image of what its "original" sources were.[5]

In this chapter, I use a narratological approach to analyze the "coherent vision" of Qur'ānic stories on fasting and feasting by focusing on echoing phrases, words, and actions in order to explore how Qur'ānic stories interact with each other in a "web of design."[6]

In his "Sodom as Nexus: The Web of Design in Biblical Narrative," Robert Alter examines various motifs to understand the story of Abraham in Genesis 17 and its connection to the story of Lot, while demonstrating that the stories of the Bible are not atomistic and they fit together.[7] He concludes by emphasizing the importance of going beyond admiring "the artistry of biblical narrative within the limits of an episode . . . to see how the episode is purposefully woven into larger patterns of motifs, symbols, and themes, keywords, key

*How the Qur'ān Works*. Leyla Ozgur Alhassen, Oxford University Press. © Oxford University Press 2023.
DOI: 10.1093/oso/9780197654606.003.0005

phrases and plots."[8] His perspective of the stories and how they are linked together is one that can be useful in studies of Qur'ānic stories, as not only do Qur'ānic narratives exist, but they are woven together, with metanarrative, to reinforce theological beliefs.

Throughout the Qur'ān, we see fasting (*ṣiyām*) as referring to abstaining from food, drink, and sexual intercourse during Ramaḍān as well as other times of the year. However, when we look in the Qur'ān for narrative portrayals of fasting, we find only two stories that include fasting, both of which appear to be stories of fasting from speech rather than fasting from food and drink. These are in the stories of Maryam and Zakariyyā. For Zakariyyā, fasting from speech is a sign that he is to have a child in old age (3:41 and 19:10). Maryam is told not to speak to anyone, and she obeys (19:26–30). She is told to say she is undertaking a fast from speaking, "*ṣawm*"—a hapax in the Qur'ān (19:26). Zakariyyā's fast from speech is referred to as neither *ṣiyām* nor *ṣawm*, but the action seems to be the same as Maryam's, as we will see below. In the Qur'ānic portrayals of fasting, there are references to abstinence from food and drink as well as abstinence from speech. In this study I explore how and to what extent Maryam's and Zakariyyā's fasts connect to the other fasts in the Qur'ān and then to stories of feasting in the Qur'ān. By exploring representations of fasting and feasting in Qur'ānic stories, a more complete picture of both repetition and narrative in the Qur'ān can be drawn.

When we examine the stories of fasting in the Qur'ān, we find that they are exchange encounters, featuring offering and sacrifice.[9] Suzanne Pinckney Stetkevych explores the idea of a ritual exchange in the *qaṣīdah* and in the Qur'ānic story of Sulaymān. There, we see that someone who has sinned works to be reincorporated into the favor of his "L/lord" by "submission," "a declaration of allegiance," the bestowal of a gift, and then the receiving of a gift.[10] We do not find all of the same elements in what follows, but we certainly find something being given and something being received.

When we move from stories of fasting to stories of feasting, we find that they are also exchange encounters. Throughout these stories in the Qur'ān, the motifs of annunciation, fasting, food, children, and sacrifice of various forms are repeated. The basic form of the exchange encounter can be seen in the stories of Zakariyyā and Maryam, in which they are to fast (to make a sacrifice) in exchange for a child. From there, the stories have variations through which we see that asking for things from God is not a problem; the issue is how one asks, which is a reflection of one's belief. All of this, I will show, is connected to the metanarrative verse 2:186. Throughout this study, I will demonstrate that the various exchange encounters in the Qur'ān unite the Qur'ānic stories on fasting and feasting, and they are united both thematically and stylistically.

## II. Zakariyyā's Fast (3:41 and 19:10)

Zakariyyā is mentioned in three stories in the Qur'ān (3:37–42, 19:1–11, and 21:89–90). The first two instances mention his fasting from speech. In one story, Zakariyyā prays to God to give him good offspring (3:38). He is told that he will be blessed with a child (3:39), to which he responds with surprise, asking how he can have a child when he is old and his wife is barren. The response is that God does as God wills (3:40). The next verse is the crux of our focus on Zakariyyā: "He said, 'My Lord, give me a sign.' 'Your sign,' [the angel] said, 'is that you will not communicate with anyone for three days, except by gestures. Remember your Lord often; celebrate His glory in the evening and at dawn.'" (3:41). In these verses, Zakariyyā is told he will not speak to people.

Many of the surveyed commentators explain why Zakariyyā asks for a sign. It seems that they want to show that Zakariyyā asks for this not because his faith is weak but because he simply wants some clarification about the situation. The fact that they are concerned with his faith can be seen to indicate that the story has brought issues of faith to their minds; the issue of faith comes up in other examples that I discuss below. For example, the commentators known as al-Jalālayn clarify that Zakariyyā wants a sign that his wife is pregnant.[11] Al-Tha'ālibī mentions that some commentators explain that Zakariyyā does not doubt that he will be granted a child, but he wants to know the timing of the pregnancy. Al-Tha'ālibī specifies that Zakariyyā wants to know how his wife's constitution will be changed and how he and his wife can have a child now that they are old.[12] Al-Ṭabarī explains that Zakariyyā asks for the sign so that he knows this is not a whisper from Satan.[13] Abū al-Su'ūd mentions that a weak explanation for Zakariyyā's asking for a sign is that he is surprised because he made his prayer sixty years before he got the news of its acceptance, and he forgot about it.[14]

At this point, it is useful to turn to the other iteration of Zakariyyā's story that mentions his abstaining from speech (19:1–11). This story has many similarities to 3:37–42. It begins with Zakariyyā's prayer for a child, even though he is old and his wife is barren (19:3–6). He is told that he will have a child, and he asks in surprise how this could be (19:7–8). The response is that this is easy for God (19:9). Then, once again, Zakariyyā asks for a sign and is told that his sign is that he will not talk to people for three days: "He said, 'Give me a sign, Lord.' He said, 'Your sign is that you will not speak to anyone for three full [days and] nights' " (19:10). He then goes to his people, and he signals to them to praise God day and night (19:11).

Sayyid Quṭb writes that this sign suits Zakariyyā's emotional state. He is unable to talk with people, and thus will be cut off from them, but will be connected with God instead.[15] Similarly focusing on the connection between God and Zakariyyā, al-Ghazālī explains that this fast was to be "a token of gratitude to God."[16]

Again, some of the surveyed commentators discuss the reasons for Zakariyyā asking for a sign. For example, Ibn Kathīr explains that Zakariyyā wants to have comfort in his heart, and that this is like Ibrāhīm when he asks to see the dead brought to life (2:260; I discuss this story later in this chapter).[17] *Tafsīr al-Jalālayn* explains that Zakariyyā wants a sign that his wife is pregnant.[18] Abū al-Su'ūd explains that Zakariyyā wants to know the time of conception.[19] Al-Ṭabarī writes that Zakariyyā was unsure and wondered if Satan was trying to deceive him; he wanted a sign to comfort his heart, and he wanted a sign that this was from God.[20] According to Quṭb, Zakariyyā wants to know how God will provide the child. He also wants reassurance.[21] There is also some discussion on whether Zakariyyā willingly or unwillingly stops speaking. However, the sacrifice is present either way. This story can be usefully interpreted as an exchange encounter, in which Zakariyyā receives a child in exchange for sacrificing his speech.[22]

## III. Maryam's Fast (19:26–30)

Maryam is mentioned in five stories in the Qur'ān (3:42–48, 19:16–29, 21:91–92, 23:50. and 66:12). In only one of these instances, she is told to fast from speaking, and unlike in Zakariyyā's stories, the word *ṣawm* is present (19:26). In this verse, Maryam is in labor and in pain. She expresses her desperation, and someone comforts her and says: "so eat, drink, be glad, and say to anyone you may see: 'I have vowed to the Lord of Mercy to abstain from conversation, and I will not talk to anyone today' " (*fa-kulī wa-shrabī wa-qarrī 'aynan fa-immā tarayinna min al-bashari aḥadan fa-qūlī innī nadhartū li-l-raḥmāni ṣawman fa-lan ukallima al-yawma insiyya*; 19:26).[23] In terms of the exchange encounter, we see in this and Zakariyyā's stories the element of children, and then they give up speech. A contrast in the stories is that Zakariyyā is told not to speak when he is first given news of the child; Maryam is told not to speak when she will encounter people with her newborn.

Important in terms of the exchange encounter is that both Maryam and Zakariyyā ask God how this could happen, even though they may be addressed by someone else. Although Zakariyyā is addressed by a being without a name, he asks God for clarification (19:8) and for a sign (19:10). In another iteration, Zakariyyā (3:40–41) and Maryam (3:47) again address "my Lord." Mustansir Mir explains: "Mary receives from the angels the news of the birth of a son, but, being thoroughly perturbed, she addresses her question to God Himself, as if only God could answer such a question."[24] My explanation is that Maryam and Zakariyyā are portrayed addressing God directly because they know that this is God's will and a result of God's power.[25] I will further explore the use of the word "*rabbi*" in its larger Qur'ānic context below. It is also worth mentioning here that Hosn Abboud aptly explains that "*al-rabb*" always appears in the dialogue between the protagonists and their Lord, which is a more intimate form of address, whereas the word "Allāh" "always appears in the debate or in the polemic."[26]

## IV. Fasting and Asking for Things from God (2:186)

Now, I will shift our focus to a non-narrative verse that does not mention fasting but comes in between verses discussing fasting, and it is directly related to the issue of asking God for things (2:186). I include it with the surrounding verses:

> 2:185 It was in the month of Ramadan that the Qur'an was revealed as guidance for mankind, clear messages giving guidance and distinguishing between right and wrong. So any one of you who sees in that month should fast, and anyone who is ill or on a journey should make up for the lost days by fasting on other days later. God wants ease for you, not hardship. He wants you to complete the prescribed period and to glorify Him for having guided you, so that you may be thankful.
>
> 186 [Prophet], if My servants ask you about Me, I am near. I respond to those who call Me, so let them respond to Me, and believe in Me, so that they may be guided [*wa-idhā sa'alaka ʿibādī ʿannī fa-innī qarībun ujību daʿwata al-dāʿi idhā daʿāni fa-lyastajībū lī wa-lyu'minū bī laʿallahum yarshudūn*].
>
> 187 You [believers] are permitted to lie with your wives during the night of the fast: they are [close] as garments to you, as you are to them. God was aware that you were betraying yourselves, so He turned to you in mercy and pardoned you: now you can lie with them—seek what God has ordained for you—eat and drink until the white thread of dawn becomes distinct from the black. Then fast until nightfall. Do not lie with them during the nights of your devotional retreat in the mosques: these are the bounds set by God, so do not go near them. In this way God makes His messages clear to people, that they may guard themselves against doing wrong.

188 Do not eat up [*wa-lā ta'kulū*] your property wrongfully, nor use it to bribe judges, intending sinfully and knowingly to eat up [*li-ta'kulū*] parts of other people's property.

In verse 2:185, we first see Ramaḍān and the idea of fasting. Then in verse 2:186 God says He is near. We may say verse 2:187 looks like feasting, telling people that they can have sexual intercourse, eat, and drink at night in Ramaḍān. Finally, verse 2:188, uses word play to tell people not to unjustly eat, "*ta'kulū*" possessions; the root for eating, *'-k-l*, occurs twice in this verse. In terms of Qur'ānic literary style, it is noteworthy to see word play in a legal verse and that it connects one legal injunction with another. This verse also shows the importance of a good translation: if the translation did not reflect eating, verse 2:188 would seem completely disconnected from the previous verses. In these verses, we move from fasting (2:185), to God's nearness (2:186), to feasting (2:187), and then to fasting again (2:188). What becomes clear here is that fasting and feasting are really about what is appropriate in what situation.

I am interested in understanding how a verse about supplicating to God, God's answering people's prayers, and God's nearness might connect to fasting in the Qur'ānic portrayal. To answer these questions, I will start with a look at commentary on the verse and then move to a broader discussion of the verse in the context of the Qur'ānic narrative portrayal of fasting. Among commentators, al-Jalālayn, al-Thaʿālibī, and al-Ṭabarī explain that people asked the Prophet if God is near, so they can whisper to Him, or if God is far, so they should ask for things at a regular volume.[27] They are giving some historical context to this verse. In modern discussion on verse 2:186, Fathi Osman writes that this verse tells readers "how close God is to the human being . . . [and] is closely related to the spiritual atmosphere of fasting and self-restraint."[28]

Neuwirth explains that this verse is addressing the Prophet, and he is told to tell believers that God is near. She also writes that "this verse does not smoothly connect with its immediate context, but strikingly switches" its addressees.[29] Abdel Haleem explains the shift from you to I by identifying verse 2:186 as using *iltifāt* and dynamism. He explains that the verse does not tell the Prophet to tell people that God is near (elsewhere in the Qur'ān, God tells the Prophet what to say to people); rather, "God Himself answers directly and immediately."[30]

It is noteworthy that God refers to Himself in verse 2:186 with the first-person singular, thus forming an intimate and direct grammatical connection with God's servants.[31] Connecting it with the story of Zakariyyā, Zakariyyā is referred to as God's "servant" (*ʿabd*, 19:2), and the verse about God responding to His "servants" uses the same word in the plural (*ʿibād*, 2:186).

Neuwirth looks outside of the Qur'ān to show how the verse about asking God for things connects with the verses about fasting. She writes that this verse is a reference to Psalm 20:9 and to Talmudic liturgical practices, which connect this verse to the fasting verses, all of which, she says, connect to the Yom Kippur fasting.[32]

In contrast, this chapter shows, by looking within the Qur'ān, how the verses connect to each other. In Figure 5.1, we see how all the verses on fasting in the Qur'ān interact. It is useful to note that the verses interplay in both directions. As seen in Figure 5.1, in Zakariyyā's story and his fast, Zakariyyā prays quietly or secretly to have a child and is told he will have one. When he is surprised, he asks how this could happen and he asks for a sign. The sign is for him to abstain from speaking, though it is not clear why this fasting is a sign. Zakariyyā's fasting from speech is reminiscent of Maryam's fast, since they are both told to abstain from speaking after being told of the coming

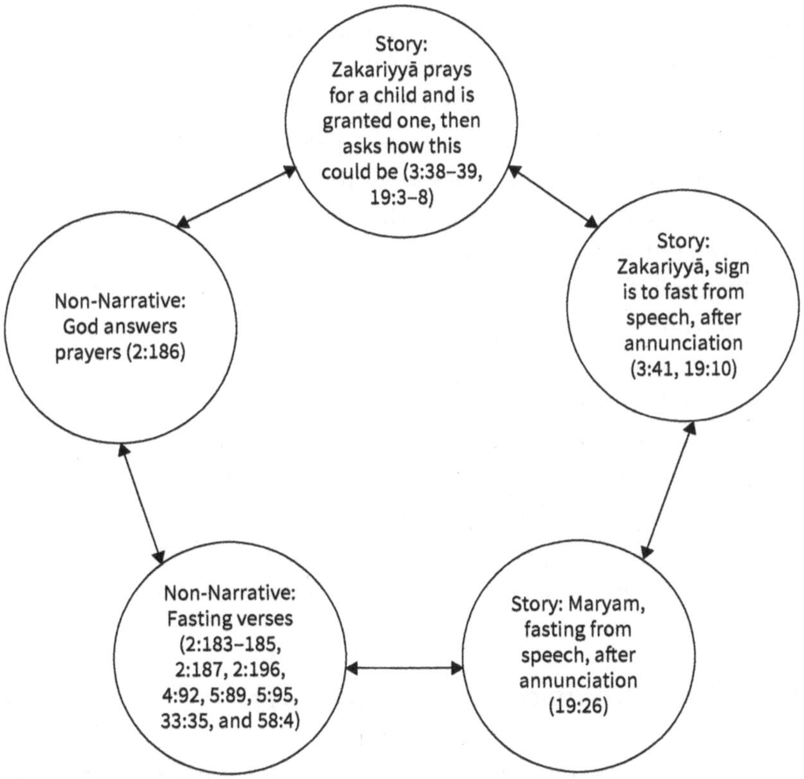


**Figure 5.1** The Intratextuality of Verses About Fasting in the Qur'ān

miraculous birth of a child. In addition, their stories are the only ones to include fasting from speech in the Qur'ān. While Zakariyyā's fast is not called "*ṣawm*," essentially it is like Maryam's fast from speech, and her fast is called "*ṣawm*." Thus, Zakariyyā's story leads to Maryam's in an intratextual manner. From there, we move to the set of verses that actually discuss fasting, in particular, 2:183–188. Implanted in a discussion on fasting in Ramaḍān is the verse about God answering prayers (2:186). This verse can be seen as an answer to Zakariyyā's question about how he could have a child, both verses linked with the same root letters in the words *'abd* (19:2) and *'ibād* (2:186). They are also linked by the fact that Zakariyyā asks God how this could happen, and the response in 2:186 is from God in the first-person singular. Interestingly, commentary indirectly adds an additional connection in the idea of the volume of the prayer, as mentioned earlier. Zakariyyā's prayer is a quiet one (19:3), and God hears prayers at any volume. Zakariyyā can have a child because he prayed to God for this, and God answers His servants' prayers.[33] The connection between Zakariyyā's supplication and God's description of responding to people's supplications can be explored in the root *d-'-w*, found in Zakariyyā's supplication (3:38 and 19:4) and verse 2:186.

It is effectively as if Zakariyyā hears the answer that the Qur'ānic audience hears, that God answers the prayers of the one who asks. Because the audience knows this, it is as if the characters do too. In fact, although Zakariyyā initially asks how this could happen and asks for a sign, he does not ask further, once he is told that God does as God wills and that his sign is to fast. Thus, we see a connection between the fasts from speech depicted in the stories to the Qur'ānic verses on the fast from food and drink in Ramaḍān. We can then move from the Ramaḍān fast to other fasts in the Qur'ān, since they are all from food and drink; the verses about fasting in the Qur'ān are in fact connected to each other, linguistically, thematically, and narratologically. The stories of Maryam and Zakariyyā, their fasts and their prayers are all connected to believers' fasts and their supplications to God. Looking at the relevant verses from an intratextual perspective, the Qur'ānic text moves from one story to another story to non-narrative legal verses. It thus presents an intermixing and a conversation across seven *sūras*, an interplay that revolves around echoing words and phrases, repeated actions, context, and motifs.

## V. Maryam's Provisions (3:35 and 3:37)

From Maryam's story of fasting, we can move to the opposite, feasting, as her story also includes a scene involving food. During her upbringing, whenever

Zakariyyā would come to see her in the temple, he would find her with provisions (assumed to be food). Zakariyyā asks where the provisions come from and Maryam responds: "They are from God: God provides limitlessly for whoever He will" (3:37). As far as Zakariyyā knows, he is Maryam's provider of food, so he must be surprised at how she is obtaining food from elsewhere. Neuwirth points out the irony that Zakariyyā "has been put in charge of Mary, yet his care turns out to be unnecessary."[34] Carl Ernst similarly explains, "it appears that men are unnecessary to this chiefly feminine narrative."[35]

In terms of the exchange encounter of giving up food or speech and receiving a child, this scene is a variation. We need to move back a few verses to see who is giving up what, and we find Maryam's mother dedicating her to God. The story begins with the prayer of Maryam's mother: "Imran's wife said, 'Lord, I have dedicated what is growing in my womb entirely to You; so accept this from me. You are the One who hears and knows all'" (3:35). God accepts the baby: "Her Lord graciously accepted her and made her grow in goodness" (3:37). God accepts her with goodness (*ḥasanin*), and not only makes her grow, but also makes her grow with goodness (*ḥasanan*) (3:37). We are then told that Zakariyyā took care of Maryam, and then we are told of Maryam's provisions from God (3:37). Here the exchange encounter has changed so that we see the mother giving her child to God, and in return, the child receives provisions from God. Another element in the exchange encounter is present: the direct address to God, in Maryam's mother's prayer to God, "*rabbi*" (3:35). Thus, in Maryam's feast, we have a reversal on the exchange: the child is symbolically exchanged for food, but probably as a reflection of God's generosity, the child receives the food.[36]

## VI. Providing a Feast: Ibrāhīm and His Guests (11:69–76)

Next in the exchange encounter is a story that maintains the elements of offering food and getting a child: in the Qur'ānic story of Ibrāhīm and his wife, angels come to Ibrāhīm and his family, and he offers them a roasted calf to eat (11:69–76). When they do not eat, he becomes worried; they tell him not to worry, they came for the people of Lūṭ, then they inform him and his wife that they are to have a child. What we see, then, is that Ibrāhīm offers food, and in return, receives a child. In this story, the elements of a child and sacrificing food are present. While we do not see Ibrāhīm asking God about having a child, his wife expresses her shock at having a child (11:72), and then Ibrāhīm pleads to God for Lūṭ's people (11:74). Zakariyyā's child is a surprise because of his and his wife's age (19:4–8), and Ibrāhīm's wife expresses surprise for the same reason. Elsewhere, Ibrāhīm thanks God for his children and describes God as hearing all supplications, *la-sami' al-du'ā'* (14:39), which is also how Zakariyyā describes God in his prayer (*sami' al-du'ā'* 3:38). We thus see a connection between Zakariyyā's supplication (3:38 and 19:4), God's description of responding to people's supplications (2:186), and Ibrāhīm (14:39), through the root *d-'-w*. As discussed in Chapter 2, the response to Maryam's surprise at the news of having a baby (19:21) closely echoes the response to Ibrāhīm's wife (51:30), both answers use the word *rabb*, explaining that this is what your Lord says.

One may wonder why Ibrāhīm is frightened, and if it is because the visitors who are actually angels refuse to eat. Is eating considered a part of human nature, so if one abstains, one is not human? Or perhaps, going with the theme of sacrifice, if one's offering is not accepted, it is worrisome? Many of the surveyed commentators explain Ibrāhīm's fear by writing that when a guest is offered food, if the guest does not eat, the host thinks the guest is there for bad and not for good.[37] Another iteration of the story mentions Ibrāhīm being scared of the angels but does not mention them abstaining from food (15:51–53). We can understand Ibrāhīm's fear through the exchange encounter: this is, in fact, an incomplete exchange. Because the angels did not partake of the food offered to them, later, Ibrāhīm is asked to sacrifice his child. However, they are both spared this fate (37:83–113).

## VII. Fasting from Water (2:249–251)

Next is another variation on the exchange encounter: now we see a sacrifice of water (rather than food), as a test and to belong with God's messenger (rather than to receive a child). In the story of Ṭālūt (2:249–251), Ṭālūt tells his people that they are to be tested by God and they should not drink more than a handful from the river that they will cross:

> 2:249 When Talut set out with his forces, he said to them, "God will test you with a river. Anyone who drinks from it will not belong with me, but anyone who refrains from tasting it will belong with me; if he scoops up just one handful [he will be excused]." But they all drank [deep] from it, except for a few. When he crossed it with those who had kept faith, they said, "We have no strength today against Goliath and his warriors." But those who knew that they were going to meet their

Lord said, "How often a small force has defeated a large army with God's permission! God is with those who are steadfast."

250 And when they met Goliath and his warriors, they said, "Our Lord, pour patience on us, make us stand firm, and help us against the disbelievers,"

251 and so with God's permission they defeated them. David killed Goliath, and God gave him sovereignty and wisdom and taught him what He pleased. If God did not drive some back by means of others the earth would be completely corrupt, but God is bountiful to all.

Their fast from water is a sacrifice they make to pass their test, to be on the side of God and God's messenger, to develop their patience, and for God to answer their prayer to be victorious in battle (2:249–251).

Among modern scholarship on this story, Walid Saleh emphasizes the surprising request for an army to abstain from drinking water before a battle and that such a request would resonate with desert-dwelling people who understand the importance of water for sustaining life:[38]

It was not hunger that the Qur'ān chose to depict in the episode of Saul, which the ethos of the desert made sure to make an element one should overcome, but thirst, a state which can only evoke death, shrieking owls in deserted ruins, and graves thirsty for revenge. Nothing apparently, not even the great fear of the desert thirst, should turn the hearts from trusting God.[39]

In terms of the theme of fasting and feasting in the Qur'ān, we now see a fast from water in exchange for belonging to Ṭālūt's community, to pass a test and for prayers for victory to be accepted. We also see a prayer made and addressed directly to God and made by multiple people: "Our Lord," "*rabbanā*" (2:250).

## VIII. Consuming a Feast: The Table (5:112–115)

In the final instance of an exchange encounter with food in a Qur'ānic story discussed in this chapter, we see 'Īsā's disciples ask him if his Lord can send them a feast (5:112). They are told that they will receive it, but they are warned too (5:115).

5:111 and how I inspired [*wa idh awḥaytu ilā*] the disciples to believe in Me and My messengers—they said, "We believe and bear witness that we devote ourselves [to God]."

112 When the disciples said, "Jesus, son of Mary, can your Lord send down a feast to us from heaven?" he said, "Beware of God if you are true believers."

113 They said, "We wish to eat from it; to have our hearts reassured; to know that you have told us the truth; and to be witnesses of it."

114 Jesus, son of Mary, said, "Lord, send down to us a feast from heaven so that we can have a festival—the first and last of us—and a sign from You. Provide for us: You are the best provider."

115 God said, "I will send it down to you, but anyone who disbelieves after this will be punished with a punishment that I will not inflict on anyone else in the world."

In this story, there is a reversal on the stories of Maryam and Zakariyyā's stories. Instead of giving up food, speech, or a child, people request food. They do not pray to God directly, but they ask 'Īsā to ask God for them. This is especially surprising because God inspires them with faith (with the root *w-ḥ-y*), they profess their faith (5:111), and yet, they then ask to see a miracle from God, and they ask for it indirectly. In exchange, they are told to have faith, and that if they do not, they will be punished with a punishment more severe than anyone has endured.

We can see a summary of the exchange encounters and this reversal in Table 5.1. We start with the basic exchange encounter of Zakariyyā, who asks for and receives a child, and then Maryam's is a slight variation because she does not actually ask to have a child. Then the pattern is set and there are more and

**Table 5.1** Exchange Encounters in Qur'ānic Stories

| Verses | Sacrifices something | Receives something | Direct address to God |
|---|---|---|---|
| Zakariyyā's fast (3:41 and 19:10) | 3:41, 19:10 (sacrifices speech) | 3:9, 19:7–8, 19:19 (receives a child) | 19:8, 19:10 |
| Maryam's fast (19:26–30) | 19:26 (sacrifices speech) | 19:19 (receives a child) | 3:47 |
| Maryam's provisions (3:35 and 3:37) | 3:35 (mother sacrifices child) | 3:37 (child receives provisions) | 3:35 |
| Ibrāhīm and his guests (11:69–76) | 11:69 (offers food) | 11:71 (receives a child) | 11:74 |
| Fasting from water (2:249–251) | 2:249 (sacrifice water) | 2:249-251 (receive belonging, victory) | 2:250 |
| Consuming a feast: the table (5:112–115) | 5:114 (have faith) | 5:112–113 (request feast) | 5:112 (indirect), 5:114 |

intensifying variations. This is part of Qur'ānic narrative style, as discussed in Chapter 2. All the exchange encounters include a direct appeal to God, which is fundamental, as we will see below.

Turning our focus to the story of 'Īsā's people, there are a number of issues that come to light from this story and are discussed in the surveyed commentaries. First is a matter of the wording of the disciples' request, "can your Lord send down a feast to us" (*hal yastaṭiy'u rabbuka an yunazzila 'alaynā mā'idatan*, 5:112). For example, al-Ṭabarī explains that some say that this means can you ask your God; it does not express doubt that God has the power to do this. Al-Ṭabarī explains that a different opinion, with which he agrees, is that they are asking if God will answer 'Īsā's prayer, but they do not doubt that God has this ability.[40] Al-Tha'ālibī shares this perspective.[41] Al-Zamakhsharī differs sharply. Although he agrees that they ask 'Īsā to ask God, he says this reflects their doubts, and that these are not the words of true believers; hence 'Īsā's reply to them, to "Beware of God if you are true believers" (5:112).[42] Abū'l-Su'ūd explains that some say they did not believe, and some say they believed but wanted more certainty.[43]

Next come explicit explanations of why they make this request. It is not from doubt but asking for more proof,[44] to know with certainty,[45] or to acquire the knowledge that comes from witnessing something.[46] Al-Ṭabarī historically contextualizes the story by explaining that other people asked their prophets for miracles.[47] Al-Ṭabarī writes that 'Īsā's people ended up disbelieving afterward, and they were punished.[48] Some say the table came down;[49] others say the table did not come down because when they heard that God would punish them if they disbelieved, they withdrew their request.[50]

Quṭb's take on the story has some different nuances. He writes that they ask 'Īsā to ask God, as a way of acknowledging that they know that 'Īsā's miracles are from God's power, not from 'Īsā's (i.e., they do not ask 'Īsā to send them a table or feast, but they ask him to ask God).[51] 'Īsā tells them that believers do not ask for things like that;[52] he then asks for a feast from God, and the way he asks models to his people how to pray to God. For example, he affirms belief in God and addresses God as "our Lord," *rabbanā* (5:114; as opposed to "your Lord," *rabbuka*, 5:112).[53] He also explains that the threat of severe punishment for disbelief is because it is not a light matter to ask for a miracle from God.[54]

Muhammad Asad explains that the word "I will send it down" (*munazziluha*, 5:115) is a grammatical form that "implies a continued recurrence of bestowal" and that "this stress on God's ever-recurrent provision of sustenance, both physical and spiritual, explains the extreme severity of His condemnation of all who . . . deny this obvious truth; and, in addition, it implies a condemnation of any demand for a miracle as a 'proof' of God's existence."[55] Cuypers mentions something else noteworthy about the root for the word "send down" (5:112, 5:114, and 5:115): "*nazala* . . . in the Qur'ān . . . is almost synonymous with 'reveal,' "[56] which works to contrast the request of the disciples with their faith (meaning they request something be sent or revealed to them when so much has already been sent to them).[57] In addition, he mentions that the incompleteness of the account, in the question of whether the food came and if they ate from it, "is clearly deliberate—the account appears as a parable, inviting the reader-hearer to end the account himself by taking a position, that is, by believing."[58]

In this story, there is an exchange encounter in which people ask for a feast, then they are told to have faith, which we can see as a sacrifice made for their feast. They mention God in their request but indirectly: they ask 'Īsā if his God can provide them with a feast. As I will explore in more detail in the next section, the disciples show a lack of faith in their request. The evidence for this is the word they use—"*rabbuka*." Up until now, we have seen people ask from God with the first-person possessive, singular, or plural (my/our)—as reinforced in verse 2:186—or in Ibrāhīm's case, God says Ibrāhīm asked from Him. In the case of 'Īsā's people, they put some distance between themselves and God by referring to God with the second-person possessive (your Lord). This shows a lack of faith and explains why they are threatened with severe punishment.

## IX. How to Ask for Things from God

In the above story, the disciples say that they want a feast to have their hearts reassured (*taṭma'inna qulūbunā*, 5:113), using a phrase that occurs in one other Qur'ānic story (2:260).[59] In that story, Ibrāhīm, to reassure his heart, asks God to show him how He brings life to the dead. God tells him to train four birds, put parts of them on separate hilltops, and then call them and they will come:

> 2:260 And when Abraham said, "My Lord, show me how You give life to the dead" He said, "Do you not believe, then?" "Yes," said Abraham, "but just to put my heart at rest." So God said, "Take four birds and train them to come back to you. Then place them on separate hilltops, call them back, and they will come flying to you: know that God has the power to decide."

Here, the phrase that Ibrāhīm uses about comforting his heart is "*li-yaṭma'inna qalbī*." When Ibrāhīm addresses God, he says, "my Lord," *rabbi*.[60]

As with the story of the feast, commentators discuss why Ibrāhīm makes this request, and what it means about his faith. Many of the surveyed commentators say that this was to increase his certainty and to add faith to his faith.[61] Al-Ṭabarī gives context to the story: some say Ibrāhīm saw an animal that had been torn apart by a bird and an animal, so he wants to see how God would reunite parts of the animal and bring it to life.[62] Al-Thaʿālibī also writes that the majority agrees that his request is not from doubt.[63] Al-Zamakhsharī and Abū'l-Suʿūd explain that God asks Ibrāhīm if he does not believe even though God knows that Ibrāhīm is one of the strongest in faith, not for the answer, but for the sake of the listeners.[64]

Two commentators use analysis of particular words in the verse to effectively explain the issue of Ibrāhīm's faith and his request. Al-Tustarī writes that when God asks if Ibrāhīm believes and he uses the word *balā*, "yes" (2:260), this indicates that this is not a matter of doubt about his faith.[65] Furthermore, al-Tustarī compares this story to the story of ʿĪsā's people, who asked for a feast for the comfort of their hearts, but that in their case, it reflected doubt. Here, he says, the difference is that we know Ibrāhīm was a believer (*mu'min*), then he asked for comfort; the disciples wanted comfort, then they would believe (here he refers to 5:113: "They said, 'We wish to eat from it; to have our hearts reassured; to know that you have told us the truth; and to be witnesses of it'").[66] Another explanation he offers is that Ibrāhīm wanted this as a reassurance that he was God's friend (*khalīl*).[67] In addition, al-Thaʿālibī writes that Ibrāhīm's saying that he wants to see how God brings life to death (*kayf*) indicates curiosity about something that exists.[68]

In most of the previously discussed stories, someone asks for something from God—asking for things from God is not a problem, the issue is how and of whom one asks, which is actually a reflection of belief. To further develop this idea, we can turn to the words "my/our Lord" on the one hand and "your Lord" on the other hand.

Some of the verses in Qur'ānic stories that have the term "your Lord," *rabbika*, *rabbaka*, and *rabbuka*, are 2:61, 2:68–70, 5:24, 5:112, 7:134, 12:42, 12:50, and 43:49.[69] One example of the use of "your Lord" in a Qur'ānic story is as follows:

> 2:61 Remember when you said, "Moses, we cannot bear to eat only one kind of food, so pray to your Lord to bring out for us some of the earth's produce, its herbs and cucumbers, its garlic, lentils, and onions." He said, "Would you exchange better for worse? Go to Egypt and there you will find what you have asked for." They were struck with humiliation and wretchedness, and they incurred the wrath of God

> because they persistently rejected His messages and killed prophets contrary to all that is right. All this was because they disobeyed and were lawbreakers.

Abū'l-Su'ūd writes that Mūsā's people tell him to ask God for them,[70] although he does not comment if there is something wrong with this approach to prayer. Quṭb explains that they wanted something low when God wanted something high for them.[71] It is clear from the verse and commentary that there is something objectionable in their behavior. Is asking for food a problem, disregarding God's blessings or being picky and possibly ungrateful about food? Is it that Mūsā's people are asking for specific foods instead of what they have? Is it that they ask Mūsā to ask his Lord, or is it some combination of these issues?

Looking at other examples of the use of "your Lord" can help us understand part of the problem. In the story of the cow in *Sūrat al-Baqara* (2:67–71), Mūsā tells his people to slaughter a cow, and after first scoffing at the command, they ask him three separate times to ask his Lord to give more details about the cow. Quṭb writes about the use of the word "your Lord," *rabbaka*, in the story: he mentions that the people ask Mūsā to ask his God, as if He is not their God too, and as if the matter has nothing to do with them, it is just between Mūsā and his God.[72]

Mūsā's people feature in another story that includes the use of the word "your Lord," *rabbuka*: "They said, 'Moses, we will never enter while they are still there, so you and your Lord go in and fight, and we will stay here'" (5:24). The surveyed commentators write that this shows their lack of faith,[73] their rebelliousness,[74] that they have a mocking attitude,[75] and that they have no shame.[76] In addition, al-Ṭabarī attributes a story to this: before a battle, someone told Muḥammad, we do not say what Mūsā's people said, we say: you and your God go, and we go with you.[77] In Mūsā's story, their words appear problematic and mocking because they know that God will not actually come and do as they say.

The word "your Lord" *rabbaka* also occurs in the story of the People of Fir'awn (*āl Fir'awn*), who ask Mūsā to have his Lord relieve them of the plagues that are sent upon them (7:134). The context of verse 43:49 is similar, it also has the word "your Lord" *rabbaka*, and, in addition, the people address Mūsā as a magician (*sāḥir*), thus, from a Qur'ānic perspective, undermining his position as a messenger of God.

While the above stories seem to show that the use of "your Lord" signals something problematic in the speaker's faith, there are instances that complicate the matter, namely, two times when Yūsuf uses the word (12:42 and 12:50). First, Yūsuf tells a prison mate whom he thinks will be freed to tell his master (*rabbika*) about him. Al-Tustarī and al-Thaʿālibī explain that the reason Yūsuf's prison mate did not remember to tell his superior about Yūsuf and help ensure his release is because Yūsuf did not ask for help directly from God and instead asked a person; thus, he has to stay in prison longer as a punishment or lesson from God.[78] Some attribute this to a *ḥadīth*.[79] Further explanations are that Yūsuf forgot to complain to God,[80] which echoes the words his father, Yaʿqūb, uses in the same story when he says he complains to God (12:86). Al-Zamakhsharī then asks why it is wrong to ask someone for help, and he answers that it is best for a prophet to ask God (which, again, Yaʿqūb models).[81] Very similarly, Quṭb explains that Yūsuf stayed in prison longer to learn to ask God alone, and that servants of God know that God alone has all power.[82] The blaming of Yūsuf found in the commentaries is not initially obvious from the Qurʾānic story of Yūsuf. However, given the way this story interacts with the other stories we are examining—all united by the use of "*rabbika*"—the surveyed commentators appear to have some Qurʾānic basis in blaming Yūsuf.

In a second verse, Yūsuf again uses the word "*rabbika*" to refer to a person's master. In this case, a messenger of the ruler comes to Yūsuf to ask him to interpret the ruler's inscrutable dream. Then, "the king said, 'Bring him to me,' but when the messenger came to fetch Joseph, he said, 'Go back to your master [*rabbika*] and ask him about what happened to those women who cut their hands—my Lord [*rabbī*] knows all about their treachery'" (12:50). Most of the surveyed commentators explain that the word "*rabbika*" is being used to say "your master."[83] Al-Ṭabarī points out that Yūsuf uses the word "*rabb*" twice in this verse, and the second time, he uses it to refer to God.[84] Quṭb, as if building on this, helps resolve this verse along with the previous one (12:42). He explains that Yūsuf is contrasting the use of the words "your *rabb*," "your lord" with "my *rabb*," "my Lord," to make the point that the man is a messenger, *rasūl* (a word used in the verse that can also have two meanings), of his lord, and Yūsuf is a messenger of his Lord.[85] This explanation of the double meanings and word play in the verse is useful in not only explaining this verse but also in contrasting it with the previous one. In the previous verse, Yūsuf was not making a theological point, so he was in the wrong to appeal to someone else's lord; here, he uses the word to show the contrast between working for a master versus working for the Master.

The debate over one's L/lord can be seen clearly in the story of Mūsā and Firʿawn. We find in the Qurʾān: "and Pharaoh said, 'Leave me to kill Moses—let him call upon his Lord [*rabbahu*]!—for I fear he may cause you to change your religion, or spread disorder in the land.' Moses said, 'I seek refuge with my Lord and yours [*bi-rabbī wa rabbikum*] from every tyrant who refuses to believe in the Day of Reckoning'" (40:26–27). We see here Fir'awn rejecting and mocking Mūsā's appeal to his Lord, but Mūsā replies by affirming that the Lord is both his and theirs, whether they admit it or not.

The word Lord, *rabb*, occurs 975 times in the Qur'ān. This section of this chapter has focused on some examples of stories in the Qur'ān in which people use the word *rabb* with a pronoun to ask God for things. It is likely that there are outliers to the patterns discussed above; there can be other patterns as well, and some instances might be explained as people sarcastically addressing or making demands of God, whom they do not actually believe in.

There are numerous references in Qur'ānic stories to "my Lord," *rabbi*, and "our Lord," *rabbinā*, *rabbunā* and *rabbanā*; some of which are discussed earlier (2:260, 3:35–36, 3:38, 3:40–41, and 3:47).[86] What we see throughout the stories discussed here with the uses of "my/our Lord" and "your Lord" is that asking God for something is not necessarily problematic—what can be problematic is the manner of asking, and that asking in an indirect manner can indicate doubt or weakness in one's faith. While Ibrāhīm wants to see how God brings life to the dead, he asks this directly to God; meanwhile, 'Īsā's disciples ask 'Īsā to ask if his God can send them a feast, and this reflects their lack of faith (an issue that commentators debate about). Given this, Zakariyyā's asking God to grant him a child and then asking God how he can have a child is not at all problematic, and his fast is not, for example, a punishment inflicted on him because of his questions. Rather, his fasting from speech is a part of his exchange encounter. However, Yūsuf's asking someone to ask his master to help him is in fact problematic, something which most of the surveyed commentators noted without giving the reason of the specific word "your lord." Here, once again, verse 2:186 is useful: "[Prophet], if My servants ask you about Me, I am near. I respond to those who call Me, so let them respond to Me, and believe in Me, so that they may be guided." In this verse, God talks about Himself using the first-person singular, making Himself as close as He can be to those who ask of Him.

## X. Conclusion

Through an exploration of echoing phrases and actions in the Qur'ān related to fasting and feasting, it becomes clear that intratextual analysis informed by literary studies, focusing on repetition, can lend insight into the connections between Maryam's and Zakariyyā's fasts from speech and other Qur'ānic fasts and feasts, all of which can be seen as exchange encounters with giving something and receiving something. This study shows that there is a connection among fasting (even from speech), feasting, faith, and supplications in the Qur'ān. As a result of these Qur'ānic intratextual references, the narrator highlights to the reader that her hard work and attention, which the Qur'ān overtly and subtly demands, are rewarded. At the same time, these allusions signal to the reader that her knowledge is never complete: there is always something more for her to read or learn from the Qur'ān.

Beginning with Zakariyyā's fast, we see a giving of speech and a getting of a child, connected with a direct address to God. This is very similar to Maryam's fast, and thus, the two stories set up the exchange encounter in the Qur'ān. Then we have a variation, in which Maryam's mother gives her child to God and her child receives provisions. The mother directly addresses God, and we see the elements of a child and food. In an incomplete exchange encounter, Ibrāhīm offers food—which is not eaten, and receives a child—a child whom he is later commanded to sacrifice. We see the elements of a child and food, and Ibrāhīm is said to address God in his concern for Lūṭ's people. Then we come to the story of Ṭālūt and his people giving up water to receive belonging, God's support and victory. Here there is the giving of water, there is no child, but there is a request for victory and a direct appeal to God. Finally, comes the story of 'Īsā's disciples and their request for a feast, for which they are told to have faith. Here there is the element of food, but it is a request to have food; there is no child, and there is an indirect appeal to God. The exchange encounters connect the stories on fasting and feasting in the Qur'ān, thus they are united both thematically and stylistically. All these exchange encounters can be seen through the lens of the verse about appealing to God and God answering a believer's request (2:186), a verse that is situated amidst verses about fasting. Thus, the exchange encounters highlight that asking for things from God is not a problem; the issue is belief, which is reflected in the manner of asking. Through these stories, we see how Qur'ānic narratives are woven together through echoing phrases and actions, with metanarrative and legal verses, to reinforce theological beliefs. This demonstrates that a narratological analysis that focuses on repetition in Qur'ānic portrayals and semantic echoes is fundamental in establishing an understanding of Qur'ānic stories.

# 6

# Repetition in *Sūrat al-Shu'arā'*

## Prophethood, Power, and Inspiration

## I. Introduction

*Sūrat al-Shu'arā'* is comprised of an introduction, conclusion, and seven stories of prophets. This chapter analyzes repetition in the *sūra*, in the series of stories, which lends insight into its structure, and in the root letters. This analysis allows us to unpack underlying themes in the stories. We see through the analysis in this chapter how repetition occurs at various levels of scale throughout *Sūrat al-Shu'arā'* and how it is used to contrast and complicate various themes.

*Sūrat al-Shu'arā'* consists of a series of stories. Due to an introductory and concluding refrain, the structure can be explicated as seen in Table 6.1. Most of the stories include an introductory refrain, and all of them include a concluding refrain. This lends a prominent structure to the *sūra*. The stories begin with the longest, Mūsā, then the next in length and sequence is Ibrāhīm, then the rest of the stories are of similar length to each other.

The overarching theme in the *sūra* is prophecy: the *sūra* is like a social contract, modus operandi, and a setting of expectations about prophecy, mostly done through stories. Scaffolding this theme are four others. First is the theme of sources of power, inspiration, and revelation: messengers (*r-s-l*), devils (*sh-ṭ-n*), magicians (*s-ḥ-r*), poets (*sh-'-r*), and ancestors (*'-b-w*). For example, we see this in the theme of power and privilege in Mūsā's story. The next, related theme discussed in this chapter is that God sends people messengers and gives people the choice to believe or not. God punishes in the afterlife and sometimes intervenes in this life. The contrast to this is seen in Fir'awn who does not have ultimate power over people but asserts his power over them regardless. Next is the theme of messengers and their expectations from their people. Messengers of God have no control over whether people choose to believe or not, and they deliver their message as a fulfillment to God, not in expectation of reward or belief from people. The *sūra* sets the expectations that prophets have of their people (people can choose to believe or not; if they

*How the Qur'ān Works*. Leyla Ozgur Alhassen, Oxford University Press. © Oxford University Press 2023.
DOI: 10.1093/oso/9780197654606.003.0006

**Table 6.1** The Structure of *Sūrat al-Shuʿarāʾ*

| Verses | Number of Verses | People | Introductory Refrain | Concluding Refrain |
|---|---|---|---|---|
| 26:1–9 | 9 | Introduction | | 26:8–9 |
| 26:10–68 | 59 | Mūsā | | 26:67–68 |
| 26:69–104 | 36 | Ibrāhīm | | 26:103–104 |
| 26:105–122 | 18 | Nūḥ | 26:105–109 | 26:121–122 |
| 26:123–140 | 18 | Hūd | 26:123–127 | 26:139–140 |
| 26:141–159 | 19 | Ṣāliḥ | 26:141–145 | 26:158–159 |
| 26:160–175 | 16 | Lūṭ | 26:160–164 | 26:174–175 |
| 26:176–191 | 16 | Shuʿayb | 26:176–180 | 26:190–191 |
| 26:192–227 | 36 | Conclusion | | |

believe in God, they should obey God's prophets); the judgments of people that prophets can or cannot make (none); and their motivation (pleasing God). Finally, we see in the *sūra* the theme of responses to revelation and its claims: there is lying and calling others liars, insulting believers, and messengers themselves having fears. What becomes apparent through these themes is that the Qur'ān is aware that a message, magic, a prophet, and even family can be used to make claims to power; the Qur'ān makes clear what is and is not acceptable in this *sūra*.

## II. Competing Sources of Power, Inspiration, and Revelation

The first theme we will explore is of power and claims to power based on ancestry, wealth, performance of miracles, victory, revelation; inspiration from God and devils; and the people claiming inspiration: messengers, magicians, and poets. Two articles by Irfan Shahid discuss this *sūra* to decipher "Islam's attitude to poetry."[1] The rhetorical, semantic, and narratological analysis here that also looks at the entire *sūra* shows that poets are mentioned in a much larger context of competing claims to inspiration and prophecy. And, quite tellingly, multilingual Islamic literatures and cultures seemed to have figured this out, producing poetry about the Prophet Muḥammad, Ṣufi poetry, poetry to teach grammar, and many other types.

In Mūsā's story, there is a prominent theme of having, getting, maintaining, and losing power and privilege. It seems that people are trying to move a step above, while Mūsā and Hārūn are pushing them all off their pedestals, destabilizing things. We can see this through many words and phrases in the story. The various instances are explicated in Table 6.2.

The theme of messengers inspired by God, messengers who bring inspiration and revelation is represented by the *r-s-l* root in the introductory refrain to most of the stories in this *sūra*: *al-mursalīn* "messengers" and *rasūl* "messenger" (26:105, 26:107, 26:123, 26:125, 26:141, 26:143, 26:160, 26:162, 26:176, and 26:178). Mūsā's story does not include the introductory refrain, but it has the root many times. First, Mūsā asks God to send Hārūn with him to Fir'awn (*arsil*, 26:13). Then God agrees and instructs them to tell Fir'awn that they are messengers of God (*rasūl*, 26:16), and they ask him to send the Children of Israel with them (*arsil*, 26:17). Mūsā uses the command, *arsil*, twice (26:13 and 26:17); the second time is with Hārūn, too. Mūsā tells Fir'awn that God made him one of the messengers, putting himself in the context of a larger group of messengers (*al-mursalīn*, 26:21). Fir'awn tells the listeners that the messenger who was sent to them is possessed (*rasūlakum* and *ursila*, 26:27 twice). Fir'awn is using Mūsā's wording to mock him and to undermine his source of inspiration. In contrast, the *sūra* twice mentions that God inspires Mūsā, *w-ḥ-y* (26:52 and 26:63). When Fir'awn decides to gather magicians to try to best Mūsā, he sends for them (*arsala*, 26:53). So there are God's messengers; a person asking God to make another person a messenger too; God telling people to say that they are messengers of God; then Fir'awn denigrating that messenger, while calling him a messenger; and Fir'awn also rounding up his own magicians. A message and messenger can be mundane, manipulated for power—in Fir'awn's hands—or a representative of God's word.

To understand one claim of Fir'awn's to power and privilege, we can look at his discussion about his household raising Mūsā.

> 26:18 Pharaoh said, "Did we not bring you up as a child among us? Did you not stay with us for many years [*qāla alam nurabbika fīnā walīdan wa-labithta fīnā min 'umurika sinīn*]?
>
> 19 And then you committed that crime of yours: you were so ungrateful [*wa-fa'alta fa'lataka allatī fa'alta wa-anta min al-kāfirīn*]."
>
> 20 Moses replied, "I was misguided when I did it
>
> 21 and I fled from you in fear; later my Lord gave me wisdom and made me one of His messengers.
>
> 22 And is this—that you have enslaved the Children of Israel—the favour with which you reproach me?"

Fir'awn is rubbing in the fact that he raised Mūsā. Fir'awn is not Mūsā's father, but he was one of the people who raised Mūsā, or he could be saying

**Table 6.2** Struggles for Power and Privilege in Mūsā's Story in *Sūrat al-Shuʿarāʾ*

| | Instance 1 | Instance 2 | Instance 3 | Instance 4 | Instance 5 |
|---|---|---|---|---|---|
| People ask another to relinquish his power | "let the Children of Israel leave with us" (26:17) | | | | |
| People remind others of their power | "Did we not bring you up as a child among us?" (26:18) | "my Lord gave me wisdom" (26:21) | "How dare you believe in him before I have given you permission?" (26:49) | "These people are a puny band" (26:54) | "and we are a large army, on the alert" (26:56) |
| One person tells another of his misuse of power | "you have enslaved the Children of Israel" (26:22) | | | | |
| One person threatens another with power | "If you take any god other than me, I will throw you into prison" (26:29) | "Pharaoh and his people pursued them" (26:60) | | | |
| One person scares others about a potential loss of power | "He means to use his sorcery to drive you out of your land!" (26:35) | | | | |
| People talk about following others | "We may follow the sorcerers if they win!" (26:40) | | | | |
| People talk about wanting privilege | "Shall we be rewarded if we win?" (26:41) | | | | |
| One person gives privilege as a reward | "Yes, and you will join my inner court" (26:42) | | | | |
| People claim someone as a source of power | "By Pharaoh's might, we shall be victorious" (26:44) | | | | |

(*continued*)

**Table 6.2** Continued

| | Instance 1 | Instance 2 | Instance 3 | Instance 4 | Instance 5 |
|---|---|---|---|---|---|
| **People fear someone else's power** | "Moses' followers said, 'We shall definitely be caught'" (26:61) | | | | |
| **People realize the true source of power** | "and the sorcerers fell down on their knees" (26:46) | "exclaiming, 'We believe in the Lord of all worlds'" (26:47) | "That will do us no harm," they said, "for we are sure to return to our Lord" (26:50) | "Moses said, 'No, my Lord is with me: He will guide me'" (26:62). | |
| **Trying to control other's bodies** | "you have enslaved the Children of Israel" (26:22) | "I will cut off your alternate hands and feet and then crucify the lot of you!" (26:49) | Pharaoh and his people pursued them at sunrise (26:60) | | |
| **Trying to control other's faith** | But Pharaoh said [to him], "If you take any god other than me, I will throw you into prison" (26:29) | Pharaoh said, "How dare you believe in him before I have given you permission?" (26:49) | | | |
| **God empowers people** | "Leave with My servants by night" (26:52) | "and We revealed to Moses: 'Strike the sea with your staff'" (26:63) | "We saved Moses and all his companions" (26:65) | "and drowned the rest" (26:66) | |
| **God, the possessor of all power** | "your Lord alone is the Almighty, the Merciful" (26:68) | | | | |

this collectively, that his household raised Mūsā among them. Fir'awn also mentions that Mūsā stayed with them for years of his life (26:18). Mūsā was part of Fir'awn's special circle, thanks to Fir'awn, for years. Fir'awn is emphasizing his generosity and Mūsā's need to be grateful and compliant. They are not relatives by blood, so Mūsā should be even more grateful to be taken in by them. The theme of family is present here and throughout the *sūra*. The root

*'-b-w* occurs later in the dialogue between Mūsā and Firʿawn, when Firʿawn asks who the Lord is: "Moses said, 'He is your Lord and the Lord of your forefathers [*abāʾikumu al-awwalīn*]'" (26:26). So Mūsā puts Firʿawn and his ancestors in their place, relative to God. And Mūsā puts himself in his place as well—he is a messenger of God (26:21).

Mūsā is a messenger of God, and Mūsā describes God and God's message:

> 26:24 Moses replied, "He is the Lord of the heavens and earth and everything between them. If you would only have faith!"
>
> 25 Pharaoh said to those present, "Do you hear what he says?"
>
> 26 Moses said, "He is your Lord and the Lord of your forefathers."
>
> 27 Pharaoh said, "This messenger who has been sent to you is truly possessed [*la-majnūn*]."
>
> 28 Moses continued, "Lord of the East and West and everything between them. If you would only use your reason!"
>
> 29 But Pharaoh said [to him], "If you take any god other than me, I will throw you into prison"

Mūsā keeps circling back to God, *rabb*, like *dhikr* or the circling of the Kaʿba (26:24, 26:26, and 26:28). God is "the Lord of the heavens and earth and everything between them," *wa mā baynahumā* (26:24) and "Lord of the East and West and everything between them," *wa mā baynahumā* (26:28). There is parallelism and repetition here. Meanwhile, Firʿawn riles up the audience and accuses Mūsā of being possessed or crazy, *la-majnūn* (26:25 and 26:27), and finally threatens Mūsā (26:29).

We can look at the root *b-y-n* to see how the message is described as clear and then moves on to other nuances. Mūsā asks Firʿawn what he will do if he came with something clear, *bi-shay'in mubīn* (26:30), and then he throws his staff and it is a clear or manifest snake, *thuʿbānun mubīn* (26:32). Nūḥ tells his people that he is a clear warner, *nadhīrun mubīn* (26:115). Nūḥ prays for God to create an opening between him and between his people, *fa-ftaḥ baynī wa baynahum fatḥan* (26:118). Here we see the *b-y-n* and *f-t-ḥ* roots twice in succession, in an a-b-b-a pattern. In the conclusion, the narrator describes the revelation as being "in a clear Arabic tongue," *bi-lisānin ʿarabiyyin mubīn* (26:195). In contrast, in the Ibrāhīm subsection, people will realize in the afterlife that they were "clearly misguided," *ḍalālin mubīn* (26:97). Most of the occurrences of the *b-y-n* root are as the word *mubīn*, which always occurs as the last word of the verses, and thus is a rhyme word. *B-y-n* makes things clear and is a thing that is itself clear. In the use by Mūsā as a way to describe God's dominion, it also clarifies things about God. In Nūḥ's usage, when he asks

God to separate him from his people, it is a way to clarify those who believe from those who do not. So *mubīn* in this *sūra* describes the following: Mūsā's miracle; the snake, which is a miracle; a messenger; a message; and in contrast, people's misguidance. On the level of the word, we have parallels, pivots, and contrasts among a message, messengers and miracles, and people's misguidance.

Here, Mūsā uses a miracle as a way to establish his authenticity as a messenger. First, Mūsā and Fir'awn verbally spar, Fir'awn threatens to imprison Mūsā (26:22–29), Mūsā responds by asking what Fir'awn will do if he shows him something miraculous, and Fir'awn agrees to see it. Fir'awn is up for a challenge and perhaps even likes it, he is confident, or simply disbelieves Mūsā. Mūsā throws down his staff and it becomes a snake, and he extends his hand and it is white (26:32–33). Fir'awn, not skipping a beat, quickly has a theory, which he shares with the counselors around him—this is a public display, apparently: Mūsā is a sorcerer, and he is using his magic for political power to dethrone the counselors (26:34–35). This is a turning point in Fir'awn's attitude toward Mūsā. Mūsā was weak, but now he is suddenly doing something incredible. We see Fir'awn's emotions in his response: now he sees Mūsā as a threat. There is a tipping of the balance in terms of power. We can explore this through the root *'-l-m*, which Fir'awn uses to characterize Mūsā, he is a "learned [*'alīm*] sorcerer" (26:34). Mūsā is no longer a vulnerable adopted child, he is a learned magician. Knowledge can be used for power in Fir'awn's eyes, at least, if it is paired with sorcery. Fir'awn asks the counselors to suggest a course of action—he makes them see a threat to their way of life, and then he asks them to suggest a solution (26:35). They recommend sending Mūsā and Hārūn away so that they can gather their own learned, *'alīm*, sorcerers (26:36–37). They gather on a known or appointed, *ma'lūm*, day (26:38).[2]

Here we see counter to messengers is the theme of magic and magicians, expressed frequently through the root *s-ḥ-r* in Mūsā's story (26:34, 26:35, 26:37, 26:38, 26:40, 26:41, 26:46, and 26:49). A twist on this comes in the stories of Ṣāliḥ and Shu'ayb, when their people accuse them of being "bewitched," *min al-musaḥḥarīn* (26:153 and 26:185). With this repeated root, a comparison is drawn between Mūsā, Ṣāliḥ, and Shu'ayb, with Mūsā accused of being a sorcerer, while Ṣāliḥ and Shu'ayb are accused of being bewitched.

The magicians gather at the appointed time, the people are asked if they are going to attend, and they give an intriguing answer, "We may follow the sorcerers if they win" (26:38–40). The people are thinking about following the victor; perhaps, for them, victory is connected to power. The sorcerers ask if there is a reward for them if they succeed, and Fir'awn replies that they will have a position close to him (26:41–42). Fir'awn assumes that their request reflects an interest in privilege and offers it as a reward. This also lends insight into Fir'awn's initial statement to Mūsā about raising him and letting him be in his inner circle—Mūsā should have seen it as the generous gift that Fir'awn sees it as (26:18–19).

Now, we can bring in the *'-z-z* root, which describes might and power. This root occurs in the last verse of the introduction: "your Lord alone is the Almighty, the Merciful [*al-'azīzu -l-raḥīm*]" (26:9), and the exact same verse is repeated verbatim in the concluding refrain of the introduction and all the stories, except Mūsā (26:9, 26:68, 26:104, 26:122, 26:140, 26:159, 26:175, and 26:191). In a striking and contrasting way, the root is in the story of Mūsā, when the magicians throw their ropes and staffs and say, "By Pharaoh's might, we shall be victorious" (26:44). They are not. After the magicians throw their staffs and see Mūsā throw his, they realize that what he has done is actually miraculous. Although the *sūra* is framed with God telling the Prophet Muḥammad that not everyone will believe, surprisingly, the magicians do in fact end up believing. This is embodied in the *l-q-y* root, and we can zoom in to look at it in the *sūra*.[3] When the magicians have gathered, Mūsā tells them to throw, *alqū*, what they are going to throw, *mulqūn* (26:43 twice). They throw, *fa-alqaw*, their ropes and staves (26:44) and Mūsā throws, *fa-alqā*, his staff, and it defeats what the magicians have done (26:45). Then the magicians are thrown in prostration, *fa-ulqiya* (26:46). The verb is in the passive voice, they are thrown down, but by whom or by what? Maybe by their faith or by God. Instead of doing the throwing, they are being thrown. Perhaps in the way that they threw their ropes to convince people of Fir'awn's power, God throws them to show people God's power. They are tools of God or devotees. This is a foreshadowing of a word we will discuss later. We do not see the *l-q-y* root again until the conclusion to the *sūra*, where sinners are described as lending an ear to devils, *yulqūn al-sam'a*—they make their body parts tools for devils (26:223).

In this scene, there is a parallel and a contrast between the magicians in Mūsā's story and the messengers: the magicians look for *'izza* in Fir'awn yet find it in God; God is *al-'azīz*. In the conclusion, God addresses the Prophet Muḥammad and tells him to rely on *al-'azīzi -l-raḥīm* (26:217). Mūsā's story shows the magicians incorrectly attributing the root *'-z-z* to Fir'awn, while the narrator repeatedly uses it to describe God. After they believe, the magicians proclaim their faith in God, and say, "We believe in the Lord of all worlds [*rabbi l-'ālamīn*]" (26:47). They use the exact same phrase that God uses to tell Mūsā and Hārūn to go to Fir'awn and say that they are messengers of the Lord of all worlds (26:16). So Mūsā and Hārūn are so effective in their role as messengers that others use the exact same phrase used to describe them in their original mission. Fir'awn, whom they are sent to, does not say this, probably because he is trying to hold on to his power. The magicians also describe God as the Lord of Mūsā and Hārūn, so while acknowledging the existence of the Lord, they are acknowledging that the Lord sent Mūsā and Hārūn as messengers (26:48). Fir'awn comes up with a conspiracy that Mūsā must be their superior, "*la-kabīrukum*," who he taught them, '*allamakum*, magic in the first place (26:49). Here, we again see knowledge as a way to gain power.

The theme of power is complicated in contrasting the roots *q-r-b*, *q-l-b*, and *gh-l-b*. Even as root letters, these show parallels, pivots, and reversals: if we change the middle letter in *q-r-b*, we get *q-l-b*; if we change the first letter in *q-l-b*, we get *gh-l-b*. The *rā'* and *lām* have similar shapes, and the *qāf* and *ghayn* have similar rounded shapes. We can start with *q-r-b*, when Fir'awn tells the sorcerers they will be among those close to him, *al-muqarrabīn* (26:42). This root only occurs again in the conclusion, when, presumably, the Prophet is told to "Warn your nearest kinsfolk [*al-aqrabīn*]" (26:214). The *gh-l-b* root only occurs in this *sūra* in the story of Mūsā; all of its uses end the verses, and the words end with *nūn*. First, the people are asked if they will attend the challenge, and they say, "We may follow the sorcerers if they win [*al-ghālibīn*]!" (26:40). Then, "When the sorcerers came, they said to Pharaoh, 'Shall we be rewarded if we win [*al-ghālibīn*]' " (26:41). And finally, "They threw their ropes and staffs, saying, 'By Pharaoh's might, we shall be victorious [*al-ghālibūn*]' " (26:44). The magicians are not successful and instead declare their faith in God and God's messengers. Fir'awn warns them, they say this is not a problem, because they will return to God: " 'That will do us no harm,' they said, 'for we are sure to return [*munqalibūn*] to our Lord' " (26:50). *Munqalibūn* is the last word in the verse, as is *al-muqarrabīn* (26:42), and both end with a *nūn*. Ibrāhīm makes a prayer to God, describing the day "when the only one who will be saved is the one who comes before God with a heart devoted to Him [*bi-qalbin salīm*]" (26:89). Then we move to the conclusion, first that the revelation was sent down to the Prophet's heart, *'alā qalbika* (26:194), and yet the revelation "pass[es] straight through the hearts [*qulūb*] of the guilty" (26:200). Here are body parts. God says He sees you (presumably the Prophet Muḥammad) praying, and "your movements" amidst those who prostrate, *wa-taqallubaka fī al-sājidīn* (26:219). And the last verse includes, "The evildoers will find out what they will return to," *ayya munqalabin yanqalibūn* (26:227). This echoes and reflects on what the magicians tell Fir'awn, that is, they know where they will end up after death. We see hearts that receive revelation and hearts through which revelation passes. The movements of the heart are like the movements of the person in prayer. With the three roots, *q-r-b*, *q-l-b*, and *gh-l-b*, although the magicians first wanted to be victorious, *al-ghālibūn*, or close to Firʿawn, *al-muqarrabīn*, they end up instead realizing that returning to God, *munqalibūn*, is even better. The theme of having, getting, and losing power is thereby supplanted by the idea of connecting with God.

Furthermore, *q-l-b* displaces *gh-l-b*. The root *gh-l-b* is present in 26:40, 41, and 44. The root *q-l-b* is present in: 26:50, 89, 194, 200, 219, and 227. They are never present at the same time; victory is displaced by the connection to God through prayer and in the afterlife. Rather than futile preoccupations with worldly power and privilege, the message in the *sūra* is to focus on one's connection with God. This is reminiscent of another Qurʾānic verse, in which people realize that "the only refuge from God was with Him" (9:118).

We can now focus on sources of power and inspiration in the story of Ibrāhīm (26:69–104). Ibrāhīm is in this story sequence, but not in the one from *Sūrat al-Qamar*. In *Sūrat al-Shuʿarāʾ*, we see at least two swerves from the stories of Mūsā to Ibrāhīm: there is a contrast between Firʿawn as a father figure and Ibrāhīm's father, which then swerves from Ibrāhīm's relationship with his father to Ibrāhīm's relationship with God. Compared to the style in Mūsā's story, here, there is no dialogue with God. Instead, there is a dialogue between Ibrāhīm and his people (26:70–82). However, there is a closeness to God in two ways. First, Ibrāhīm repeatedly mentions the different ways that God helps him. The repetition stands out with the repetition of the suffix *–nī*, "me" (26:78–81). This then glides into a supplication from Ibrāhīm to God (26:83–87); Ibrāhīm's relationship with God is intimate and not distanced, which contrasts with how he looks at celestial bodies to come to faith, as discussed in the second chapter of this book. Interestingly, Ibrāhīm's dialogue with his people (26:70–82) merges into his supplication to God (26:83–87) and then Ibrāhīm's supplication merges into a description of Judgment Day (26:88–102). It is as if the dialogue with people moves to what is more important, a connection with God. Then, the Judgment Day section merges and overlays Ibrāhīm's speech with God's commentary. I discuss this narrative technique elsewhere as a merging and confirming of good people's speech with God's, a reward to believers.[4]

In Ibrāhīm's story, we jump pretty quickly into Ibrāhīm's relationship with his father: "Tell them the story of Abraham / when he asked his father and his people, 'What do you worship?'" (26:69–70). The theme of ancestors and descendants is present throughout Ibrāhīm's story and in the rest of the *sūra*. As mentioned earlier, in Mūsā's story, we see someone lording his fatherhood over his son, accordingly expecting allegiance or obedience; in Ibrāhīm's, a son tries to guide his father, to no avail. These two father-son stories are very different from each other, yet neither father seems to be a loving father, both fathers disbelieve in God, and both parent-child relationships are contentious. The *sūra* then pivots from the relationship between Ibrāhīm and his father to relationships with God. I write elsewhere about Ibrāhīm's story personifying the contrasts between loyalty to faith/God and loyalty to family, and we see that here, as well.[5]

We can turn to the theme of ancestors and descendants in Ibrāhīm's story, with the roots: *'-b-w, b-n-y, w-r-th, w-l-d,* and *q-d-m*. First, *'-b-w* is in Ibrāhīm's story, when Ibrāhīm asks his father, *li-abīhi*, and people about their object of worship (26:70). Ibrāhīm is unable to convince his father that it does not make sense to worship something that cannot hear, help, or harm him. Ibrāhīm's people respond that they worship what they do because that is what their ancestors did: "They replied, 'No, but this is what we saw our fathers [*abā'nā*] doing'" (26:74). Ibrāhīm pointedly responds: "Those idols you have worshipped / you and your forefathers [*abā'kum al-aqdamūn*], / are my enemies . . ." (26:75–77). Ibrāhīm asks for forgiveness for his father, *li-abī* (26:86). He prays for God to not disgrace him on Judgment Day, "the Day when neither wealth nor children [*banūn*] can help" (26:88). This is poignant because Ibrāhīm was unable to benefit his father in this world either, even though he tried. Here, then, we see no power in parents or children over the other or over their ultimate fate in the afterlife.

Ibrāhīm describes God as the one: "who created me. It is He who guides me. / He who gives me food and drink" (26:78–79). Here is the theme of senses through eating, drinking, and giving someone a drink. Ibrāhīm says that God gives him food and drink *ṭ-'-m* and *s-q-y* (26:79), which contrasts with his people serving their idols. Then: "He who will make me die and then give me life again; / and He who will, I hope, forgive my faults on the Day of Judgement" (26:81–82). The structure of verse 26:218 parallels and recalls these verses in Ibrāhīm's story (26:78, 26:79, 26:81, and 26:82). All these verses have the word *al-ladhī* in the beginning of the verse and are followed by actions that characterize God. The conclusion describes God as the one "who sees you when you stand up [for prayer]" (26:218). Interestingly, the characterizations are not the same and do not overlap. The overlaps are in the root *'-l-m* in *rabbi l-'ālamīn* before Ibrāhīm's list (26:77) and in the adjectives for God in the conclusion, *al-samī'u al-'alīm* (26:220). We have seen this root frequently throughout this *sūra*. It seems as if God the narrator here tacitly approves of Ibrāhīm's dialogue and adds to it. This is, again, the Qur'ānic narrative technique of merging words.[6] Here, we see that God does things for people.

We can find out more about God by focusing on the root *s-m-'* in the story of Mūsā and Ibrāhīm. First, God tells Mūsā to go to Fir'awn and God is listening, *mustami'ūn* (26:15). In response to Mūsā, Fir'awn mockingly asks those around him if they hear what Mūsā is saying, *a-lā tastami'ūn* (26:25). Ibrāhīm questions his people about their worshipping idols by asking them if the idols hear them, *hal yasma'ūnakum*, when they pray to them (26:72). In the conclusion, the narrator describes that the devils, *al-shayāṭīn* (26:210) do not hear the revelation, *innahum 'an al-sam'i la-ma'zūlūn* (26:212). Whereas God is the Hearing and the Knowing, *al-samī'u al-'alīm* (26:220). And then, the devils descend upon the one "who readily lends an ear to them," *yulqūn al-sam'a* (26:223). We see here the contrasts between objects of worship (idols) that do not hear and God that hears. There are those who do not hear the revelation, those who hear but are not convinced by messengers, and, finally, those who listen to devils.

There are other nuances in the concept of power in the root *'-y-y*, for signs. This root is in the concluding refrain of the stories (26:67, 26:103, 26:121, 26:139, 26:158, 26:174, and 26:190). In the introduction, this root expresses a verse of the Qur'ān (26:2), a sign from the sky (26:4), and a sign in nature—the growth of plants (26:7–8). God tells Mūsā and Hārūn to go with God's signs to Fir'awn (26:15). And then a twist on the use is in the story of Hūd, when Hūd criticizes his people for building frivolous signs, *'āyatan ta'bathūn* (26:128). Hūd warns and critiques them:

26:124 Their brother Hud said to them, "Will you not be mindful of God?
125 I am a faithful messenger sent to you:
126 be mindful of God and obey me.
127 I ask no reward of you, for my only reward is with the Lord of all worlds.
128 How can you be so vain that you set up monuments on every high place?
129 Do you build fortresses because you hope to be immortal?
130 Why do you act like tyrants whenever you attack someone?
131 Be mindful of God and obey me;
132 be mindful of Him who has provided you with everything you know—
133 He has given you livestock, sons,
134 gardens, springs—
135 for I truly fear that the torment of a grievous day will overtake you."

Another root that stands out in this story is *kh-l-d*, which does not occur elsewhere in the story or in *Sūrat al-Shu'arā'*: "Do you build fortresses because you hope to be immortal [*la'allakum takhludūn*]?" (26:129). Perhaps the people are so busy building things, hoping to become immortal, that they forget about God. This detail is absent from *Sūrat al-Qamar*. In 26:128, *'āya* is not a sign of the normal functioning of the world, a sign that should remind people of God. It is not an abnormal functioning of the world that should also remind people of God. And it is not a verse of revelation that should also remind people of God. It is, instead, a sign of their frivolity, a monument to themselves. Perhaps they seek power by being long-lasting. Ṣāliḥ's people dare him to send a sign if he is telling the truth (26:154). Finally, there is a verse in the conclusion: "Is it not proof enough for them that the learned men of the Children of Israel have recognized it?" (26:197). So *'-y-y* refers to verses of the Qur'ān; signs of God in the normal functioning of the world; signs that God may choose to send with messengers; signs in the form of punishment, which people may even ask for in challenging a messenger; and, finally, the signs that people, themselves, think that they are making, blatantly usurping God's role as maker and revealer of signs.

In this section, we have explored competing sources of power and privilege. There is political power, power to kill people, magic, miracles from God, ancestry, wealth, victory, revelation, and inspiration from devils. Messages from God are clear, and God helps people in this life. We see the throwing of things and being thrown (by God, God's miracle, or faith in God). And that true power and victory is returning to God and being rewarded with paradise.

## III. God Gives People the Choice to Believe or Not

We will now focus on the theme of God giving people the choice to believe or not, even though power is God's. We will see how this is contrasted with Fir'awn. We will also explore how God punishes in the afterlife, and God sometimes intervenes in this life, one way being by sending messengers.

First, we can look at how Fir'awn sees and presents himself to others. Surprisingly, Fir'awn uses the root *k-f-r* to describe Mūsā: "and then you committed that crime of yours: you were so ungrateful [*min al-kāfirīn*]" (26:19). Here, the translator, Abdel Haleem, and many others have translated the word as ungrateful, but it is also used for someone who does not acknowledge God and God's blessings and is thus ungrateful to God.[7] In fact, according to Toshihiko Izutsu, in the Qur'ān, *kufr* is used as the opposite of *imān* or faith.[8] Here, we might say that Fir'awn is calling Mūsā a disbeliever—in Fir'awn. Which is, indeed, perfectly consistent with Fir'awn's words in the Qur'ān, such as: "Pharaoh said, 'Counsellors, you have no other god that I know of except me'" (28:38). And it is also true: of course Mūsā denies that Fir'awn is a god or God. Interestingly, there are at least four nonrepeated roots that stand out in the story of Mūsā, and *k-f-r* is one of them (26:19).[9] *K-f-r* is not a rare root in the Qur'ān—it is, for example, repeated three times in *Sūrat al-Qamar*, even though it is a much shorter *sūra*—so it is striking to only find it once in *Sūrat al-Shu'arā'* and to describe Mūsā.

Mūsā acknowledges his crime or mistake, his fleeing in fear of Fir'awn and his people, and then God's blessing him with wisdom and making him a messenger (26:20–21). His acknowledgment of what he did is not a light matter. He uses the word "*al-ḍāllīn*" (26:20), which Ibrāhīm later uses to describe his father (26:86). This is a grave offense. Perhaps the key differentiating factor is what happened next: God gave Mūsā "wisdom and made me one of His messengers" (26:21). This contrasts with Fir'awn's criticizing Mūsā's actions in regards to Fir'awn: Mūsā's mistake matters because it matters to God, not because it matters to Fir'awn, but Fir'awn frames it as a mistake against him. Consistently, we see Fir'awn centering himself. Then Mūsā brings them back to the issue at hand: Fir'awn is enslaving people. Mūsā sarcastically asks Fir'awn about his favor, *ni'ma*, in enslaving his people: "And is this—that you have enslaved the Children of Israel—the favour with which you reproach me?" (26:22). The root, *n-'-m* later comes up when Ibrāhīm prays to be an inheritor of the Garden of Favors, *jannat al-na'īm* (26:85), then Hūd reminds his people of the livestock, *bi-an'ām*, God has granted them (26:133). Through this shared root, there is a striking contrast between what Fir'awn blesses people with (slavery)—and then expects Mūsā's loyalty—and what God blesses people with (livestock and heaven). Mūsā draws a sharp contrast between a man generously adopting a child so they become father and son and a ruler enslaving his people. This also reveals some of Fir'awn's manipulative tactics.

We see more contrasts between Fir'awn and God in the dialogue between Mūsā and Fir'awn. God tells Mūsā and Hārūn to go to Fir'awn and say, "We bring a message from the Lord of all worlds" (26:16). Fir'awn, not shying from confrontation, spits the phrase back at them, "What is this 'Lord of all worlds [*rabbu l-'ālamīn*]?'" (26:23). Clearly Fir'awn is paying attention and making note of Mūsā's and Hārūn's phrases and the concepts they present. Mūsā replies by explaining that God is the Lord [*rabb*] of the heavens and the earth and everything in between (26:24). Despite Fir'awn's objections, Mūsā persists in describing the Lord: "He is your Lord [*rabbukum*] and the Lord [*rabb*] of your forefathers" (26:26 twice). Again, regardless of Fir'awn's objections, Mūsā continues to describe the Lord [*rabb*] (26:28). Noteworthy here is the emphasis that the Lord is the Lord of Fir'awn and his predecessors, discussed above. I discuss another similar example in the previous chapter. This can be thought about in terms of the issue of how one addresses God, with *rabbana*/*rabbī* or *rabbuka*; God is all of theirs, whether they acknowledge it or not. Fir'awn replies, but interestingly, by using the word "*ilāh*": "But

Pharaoh said [to him], 'If you take any god [*ilāh*] other than me, I will throw you into prison'" (26:29). This is the only use of the *'-l-h* root in this story. The root *'-l-h* is in the introductory refrain, which is sometimes repeated after the introduction (26:108, 26:110, 26:126, 26:131, 26:144, 26:150, 26:163, and 26:179). Later, Ibrāhīm prays for God to bless him on the day when people come before God (26:89). Those in hellfire will be asked if what they worshipped other than God can save them now (26:93). They will say, by God, that they were wrong (26:97). In the conclusion, we find the root twice in one verse: "So [Prophet] do not invoke any gods beside God, or you will incur torment" (26:213), and then God mentions those who remember God frequently (26:227). So, there is a sharp contrast between Fir'awn declaring not only himself as a god but also that people will be punished if they disagree, versus people praying to God, versus people who believed in other gods finding none to save them in hell. God allows people to disbelieve in this life, but God punishes them in the afterlife; Fir'awn punishes people here, if he can.

Further exploring the theme of belief and choice, we can look at the idea of following people in the *sūra*. The root *t-b-'* is first in Mūsā's story, when the people gather and say they might follow, *nattabi'u*, the magicians if they are the victors (26:40). Later, God inspires, *w-ḥ-y*, Mūsā to flee with the people who believe in God, because they are being followed, *muttaba'ūn* (26:52), and they are indeed pursued, *fa-atba'ūhum* (26:60). Nūḥ's people complain that the "worst" people follow him, *wa-attaba'aka* (26:111). In the conclusion, the Prophet Muḥammad is told to lower his wings to those who follow him, *ittaba'aka* (26:215), and later, we are told that "those who are lost in error follow [*yattabi'uhum*] the poets" (26:224). So we see people physically following others, people spiritually following Nūḥ and Muḥammad, and people erring in following magicians and poets. Strikingly, in the example of Fir'awn and his people following Mūsā and his people, they are physically following them to try to stop them, not to spiritually follow them. Here we see that some people will follow prophets only to try to stop them.

Fir'awn questions how the magicians can believe without his first giving permission, and he threatens to cut off the hands and legs of the magicians, *y-d-y* and *r-j-l* (26:49). The dislocated body parts is a parallel to earlier in the story, when Mūsā tells God about his constricting chest, *ṣ-d-r* and his ineloquent tongue, *l-s-n* (26:13), and then God makes Mūsā's hand miraculous *y-d-y* (26:33). But there is a contrast. On the one hand, Mūsā mentions body parts while confiding his fears to God, and then God makes one miraculous; on the other hand, Fir'awn dislocates body parts. Fir'awn tries to take control of body parts that God created and controls—and in fact tries to control bodies by enslaving people. The other body part in the *sūra* is the tongue, representing language, communication, and memory. In Ibrāhīm's story, Ibrāhīm prays to have or to be remembered with a truthful tongue, *wa -ijʿal lī lisāna ṣidqin fī al-ākhirīn* (26:84). Finally, God describes the revelation as being in a clear Arabic tongue, *l-s-n* (26:195).

God speaks to Mūsā and tells him to take "My devotees,"[10] *ʿibādī*, and flee: "Then We revealed Our will to Moses, 'Leave with My servants by night, for you will be pursued!'" (26:52). While Firʿawn aims to control people and their bodies, God tells Mūsā to flee with His devotees or slaves, *bi-ʿibādī* (26:52). With the *ʿ-b-d* root being used in these very different ways, the narrator tells us that Firʿawn is not the sovereign over people, God is. Later, Ibrāhīm asks his people about what they worship: "What do you worship?," *mā taʿbudūn* (26:70), and they reply with the same verb, *naʿbūdu* (26:71). He discusses what their objects of worship, *mā kuntum taʿbudūn*, are unable to do (26:75). And when people are in hellfire, they will be asked where their objects of worship are, *mā kuntum taʿbudūn* (26:92). There is a contrast in that Firʿawn has enslaved people, whereas God gives people the choice to devote their lives to God or not. Ibrāhīm's phrase questioning his people is repeated exactly to people in hell. Here is the portrayal of people making a choice but making the wrong one. This clearly develops the idea of power discussed throughout the story. People fight for power, but power is really God's. Meanwhile, God, who has all power and control, gives people the choice to believe or not. God sends messengers to deliver a message, but people choose to follow or not, and messengers have no control over whether people choose to believe or not. They deliver their message as a fulfillment to God, not in expectation of reward or even belief from people.

We see the contrasts in people's choice and later punishment through other roots in the *sūra*. In the introduction to the *sūra*, there is: "if We had wished, We could have sent them down a sign from heaven, at which their necks would stay bowed [*fa-ẓallat aʿnāquhum*] in utter humility" (26:4). In Ibrāhīm's story, his people say, "We worship idols, and are constantly in attendance on them [*fanaẓallu lahā ʿākifīn*]" (26:71). The contrast between these verses highlights the notion that they are punishing themselves through their worship and they will bring punishment upon themselves. And finally, Shuʿayb's people are punished: "They called him a liar, and so the torment of the Day of Shadow [*yawmi al-ẓullah*] came upon them—it was the torment of a terrible day" (26:189). With the *ẓ-l-l* root, people's necks bow in humility, then people bow in service to their idols, and, finally, people are punished with the same root. The narrator is drawing a parallel between people whom God can humble, people who humble themselves through worshipping idols, and, finally, people who are punished. Here we see God's power to do as God wills, and yet, God gives people the chance to make a choice, provides guidance, and eventually punishes people who make the wrong choice.

After Mūsā and his people leave their homes (26:52), God blesses them: "We gave [such] things [*wa-awrathnāhā*] [later] to the Children of Israel [*banī isrā'īl*]" (26:59). So God intervenes in the inheritance from people to people. In this case, we presume wealth would not have passed from Fir'awn and his people to the Children of Israel, and God diverts it from the one group to the other, which connects to the theme of power and privilege. God changing the way things pass on is reminiscent of the idea of God flipping things upside down, which occurs elsewhere in the Qur'ān (e.g., 28:5–6). Further complicating the idea of inheritance, Ibrāhīm makes a lengthy supplication to God and asks to be an inheritor of, presumably, paradise: "make me one of those given [*warathati*] the Garden of Bliss" (26:85). Then, in Ibrāhīm's story, he mentions the day when wealth, *m-w-l*, and children will not benefit people (26:88). So possessions in this world are short-lived, may switch hands, and will not help people in the afterlife. The *w-r-th* root pivots off of Banī Isrā'īl's inheritance (26:59). The idea of inheritance ties ancestors with descendants, and we can see it in the root *w-r-th*. We see here that when one is on the correct side, the side of God, good things follow: "Shall the reward of good be anything but good" (55:60).

This *sūra* includes a concluding refrain that characterizes God. The refrain repeats without variation at the end of each section except the conclusion: "There truly is a sign in this, though most of them do not believe: / your Lord alone is the Almighty, the Merciful [*inna fī dhālika la-āyatan wa-mā kāna aktharuhum mu'minīn wa-inna rabbaka la-huwa al-'azīzu al-raḥīm*]" (26:8–9, 26:67–68, 26:103–104, 26:121–122, 26:139–140, 26:158–159, 26:174–175, and 26:190–191). This exact repetition of a refrain is distinct from *Sūrat al-Qamar*, as we will see in the next chapter. In the *Sūrat al-Shu'arā'* refrain, three prominent roots are *r-b-b*, *'-z-z*, and *r-ḥ-m*. We find the *r-b-b* root numerous times in the *sūra* (see Table A.6 for frequently repeated roots in the appendices). We first see it in the introduction, "your Lord [*rabbaka*] alone is the Almighty, the Merciful" (26:9), which is the concluding refrain that we see throughout the *sūra*. If we interpret this and the next verse as being addressed to Muḥammad, then we see Muḥammad as being brought into the series of messengers that are discussed. The *'-z-z* root occurs less frequently (26:9, 26:68, 26:104, 26:122, 26:140, 26:159, 26:175, 26:191, and 26:217) and is in all of the sections, including the introduction and conclusion (26:9 and 26:217). Similarly, the *r-ḥ-m* root occurs in the introduction twice, the conclusion, and all the prophetic sections in the refrain (26:5, 26:9, 26:68, 26:104, 26:122, 26:140, 26:159, 26:175, 26:191, and 26:217). The descriptors of God, "*rabbaka la-huwa al-ʿazīzu al-raḥīm*," seem to exactly summarize and contrast God with Firʿawn: God is your God, God has all power, not Firʿawn, and God is merciful, unlike Firʿawn, and actually gives people guidance and a choice to believe or not.

## IV. What Messengers Expect from People

God, who is merciful, sends messengers so that people can make the choice to believe or not. The *sūra* also discusses what messengers expect from people. There is a sharp contrast between Firʿawn's magicians, who use the root, *ʾ-j-r*, to unambiguously ask Firʿawn for a reward if they are victorious (26:41), and the messengers of God who clearly say they do not seek reward from their people, using the same root (26:109 twice, 26:127 twice, 26:145 twice, 26:164 twice, and 26:180 twice). The stories of Nūḥ, Hūd, Ṣāliḥ, Lūṭ, and Shuʿayb include exactly identical third, fourth, and fifth verses: "I am a faithful messenger sent to you [*innī lakum rasūlun amīnun*]: / be mindful of God and obey me [*fa-ittaqū allāha wa-aṭīʿūni*]. / I ask no reward of you, for my only reward is with the Lord of all worlds [*wa mā asʾalukum ʿalayhi min ajrin in ajriya illā ʿalā rabbi al-ʿālamīna*]" (26:107–109, 26:125–127, 26:143–145, 26:162–164, and 26:178–180). This is a striking amount of exact repetition. In Mūsā's story, the magicians ask if there is a reward for them if they are successful, using the *ʾ-j-r* root (26:41). There we see them wanting a reward from Firʿawn, in this world, then they realize that Mūsā is actually a messenger of God, they declare their belief in God, and they affirm this even when Firʿawn threatens them. In contrast to the magicians' initial eagerness for a reward, the messengers make clear that they are not working for a reward from the people but rather from God. These prophets and the magicians, once they believe, all refer to God as "the Lord of all worlds" (26:47). The contrast between the messengers and the magicians is clear. Actually, one may say they are in fact parallels: the messengers await a reward from God, and the magicians (initially) await a reward from Firʿawn. So the issue, then, is who one serves and represents and from whom one awaits a reward.

Messengers do not expect a reward from people, but they do expect obedience from those who believe. In a speech to his people, Nūḥ and other messengers use the roots *w-q-y* and *ṭ-w-ʿ* in very interesting ways. First is to establish belief in God (26:106), then the messenger asserts that he is a messenger of God (26:107), there is a pairing of belief in God and obeying God's messenger (26:108), then the messenger asserts that he does not want a reward from people, but rather from God (26:109), and, finally, a repetition of the verse to believe in God and obey God's messenger (26:110).

26:106 Their brother Noah said to them, "Will you not be mindful of God [*tattaqūn*]?
107 I am a faithful messenger sent to you:
108 be mindful of God and obey me [*fa-ittaqū allāha wa-aṭīʿūn*].
109 I ask no reward of you, for my only reward is with the Lord of all worlds:
110 be mindful of God and obey me [*fa-ittaqū allāha wa-aṭīʿūn*]."

26:108 and 26:110 are repeated exactly in Nūḥ's story, and this verbatim repetition is in Hūd's and Ṣāliḥ's stories as well (26:131 and 26:150). These paired verses include two verbs, and the meaning is also paired: a consequence of one's belief in God is to obey God's messenger. Two verses have the root *w-q-y* and are part of the introductory refrain that is repeated in the stories of Nūḥ (26:106 and 26:108), Hūd (26:124 and 26:126), Ṣāliḥ (26:142 and 144), Lūṭ (26:161 and 26:163), and Shuʿayb (26:177 and 26:179). Hūd encourages his people to be mindful of God, who is the source of knowledge (26:132). The remaining occurrence of the root *w-q-y* is when Shuʿayb tells his people to be mindful of God who created them and their ancestors (26:184). We see through the use of the root *w-q-y* that faith in God means one should also obey God's messenger, and two reasons to have faith in God are because God is the source of knowledge and God created people.

Messengers may tell their people specific things that they should or should not do. For example, in the story of Ṣāliḥ (26:141–159), Ṣāliḥ encourages his people to behave better and stop spreading corruption. We can look at the root *f-s-d* that occurs in this story and the story of Shuʿayb. Ṣāliḥ tells his people: "do not obey those who are given to excess / and who spread corruption [*yufsidūna*] in the land instead of doing what is right" (26:151–152). Ṣāliḥ's people are sent a camel as a sign (26:155). Ṣāliḥ tells his people that the camel and the people will each have their appointed days to drink, *yawmin maʿlūm* (26:155). In Ṣāliḥ's story, when he tells them about the camel, he says that the people and the camel will drink on alternate days, using the same phrase in Mūsā's story, when the magicians and Mūsā face off with their magic, *yawmin maʿlūmin* (26:155). Shuʿayb says to his people: "do not deprive people of what is theirs. Do not spread corruption on earth [*mufsidīn*]" (26:183).

There is a relationship between messengers and their community, expressed in various ways throughout the *sūra* with the root *q-w-m*. The root is in the introductory refrain, as the word *qawm*, in the stories of Nūḥ and Lūṭ (26:105 and 26:160). *Qawm* is in the first verse of the section on Mūsā (26:10–11) and then a different word from the same root: "their treasures and their noble dwellings [*maqām*]" is in Mūsā's story (26:58). The root is also in the beginning of Ibrāhīm's story (26:70). Nūḥ tells God that his people, *qawmī*, do not believe him (26:117). Lūṭ addresses his people as *qawm* (26:166). Shu'ayb tells his people to "weigh with correct [*al-mustaqīm*] scales" (26:182). Finally, in the conclusion is an injunction to rely on God, "who sees you when you stand up [*taqūm*] [for prayer]" (26:218). So *q-w-m* describes a group of people and connects a group to a messenger; it is where people live, it is how people should do business, and it is part of prayer. It embodies the weight of being and a position of prayer; the individual in prayer and community worshipping God together. This can be combined with the idea of bowing one's neck earlier; bowing in humility or in prayer, in this life or the next; and that the choices now have consequences in the afterlife.

## V. Responses to Revelation and Claims of Revelation

We have explored messengers' expectations from their people; now we can focus on messengers' responses to being called by God to be a messenger and people's responses to messengers. A verse early in the *sūra* mentions the extent to which the Prophet Muḥammad is saddened by his people not believing: "[Prophet], are you going to worry yourself to death because they will not believe [*la'allaka bakhi'un nafsaka allā yakūnū mu'minīn*]?" (26:3). We find the same root, *b-kh-'*, only one other place in the Qur'ān, in 18:6, with the same meaning. The verse does at least two important things at once: it is an argument for the extent to which the Prophet's intentions are genuine, and he is worried about his people, a theme that is repeated throughout the *sūra*: messengers of God are genuine in their faith and seek to do their duty to God by delivering God's message to people. At the same time, it frames the whole *sūra*; it is as if the whole *sūra* is a response to Muḥammad's worry, or a comfort to him, by showing him other messengers' struggles with their people. These two things work on different levels of the Qur'ānic audience: (1) us, the readers and listeners of the Qur'ān at all times, and (2) the Prophet Muḥammad as an audience member.[11] Prophet Muḥammad's selflessness is echoed in the introductory refrain for multiple messengers, that they are not trying to seek any reward from their people: "I am a faithful messenger sent to you: / be mindful of God and obey me. / I ask no reward of you, for my only reward is with the Lord of all worlds: / be mindful of God and obey me" (26:107–110). This is, presumably, to convince people that their intentions are to please God and to help them.

We see fear as a response to revelation in a different way, in the story of Mūsā (26:10–68). In other iterations, first Mūsā sees a fire, he goes to it, then God tells him who He is and tells him to go to Fir'awn. Here, we jump right into a dialogue, with God's command to Mūsā (26:10–11): "Your Lord [*rabbaka*] called to Moses: 'Go to those wrongdoers'" (26:10). Mūsā replies by referring to God as "My Lord [*rabbi*]," mentioning his feelings of fear (26:12) and what may be his physical manifestations of that fear—a constricted chest and a stumbling tongue (26:13). He asks God to send Hārūn with him and then mentions the crime that he previously committed and for which he fears the people may kill him (26:1–14). God says no, they will not kill him, and commands Mūsā and Hārūn to go to Fir'awn. We see Mūsā's fears in three verses in this section: twice, he tells God his fears, and once, he tells Fir'awn that he ran away in fear (26:12, 26:14, and 26:21). In this *sūra*, the *kh-w-f* root is in one other place, in the story of Hūd when Hūd tells his people that he fears that they will be punished for their wrongdoing (26:135). There is a surprising contrast between Mūsā's fears for himself, fears of what Fir'awn and his people will do to him, versus Hūd's fears for his people, fears of what God will do to them. And Prophet Muḥammad's worry for his people is also mirrored in Hūd's fear for his people (26:135). It seems that the Qur'ān is saying that one is not more prophet-like than the other and that fear is normal and can show up in different people for different reasons.

We have seen fear and worry as messengers' responses to their message; how do people respond to messengers' messages? Some people object to their messenger by critiquing the fact that the messengers are normal people like themselves. The people of Ṣāliḥ and those of Shu'ayb object that they are ordinary people like them, using the root *b-sh-r* (26:154 and 26:186).

Other people object to their messengers' followers; for example, Nūḥ's people are shown objecting to those who actually believe in him. Nūḥ encourages his people to believe, and they respond: "They answered, 'Why should we believe you when the worst sort of people [*al-ardhalūn*] follow you?'" (26:111). In fact, this root occurs in only three other places in the Qur'ān. Once is similar, in another iteration of Nūḥ's story: "But the prominent disbelievers among his people said, 'We can see that you are nothing but a mortal like ourselves, and it is clear to see that only the lowest among us [*arādhilunā*] follow you. We cannot see how you are any better than we are. In fact, we think you are a liar'" (11:27). The other two times are similar to each other, in which God as narrator describes creating people, some die young, some age, and "some are left to live on to such an age [*ardhali al-'umur*] that they forget all they once knew" (16:70 and 22:5).[12] Here, then, is repetition and distinction. The only story in the Qur'ān with the root *r-dh-l* is Nūḥ's, and both times it is lodged by Nūḥ's people as an objection to the people who follow him and is a reason for them not to follow him. This word, then, characterizes how the disbelievers in Nūḥ make judgments.

Nūḥ's response to his people's objection is worth examination. First, it includes two roots with the same letters in different orders, *'-l-m* and *'-m-l*, which feels a bit like a tongue-twister. Nūḥ's response is as follows:

> 26:112 He said, "What knowledge do I have of what they used to do [*wa mā 'ilmī bi-mā kānū ya'malūna*]?
> 113 It is for my Lord alone to bring them to account—if only you could see—
> 114 I will not drive believers away.
> 115 I am here only to give people a clear warning."

It is unclear if he disavows their prior actions, and possibly them a bit, if he is merely stating a fact, or proposing that once someone comes to faith, their previous actions are wiped clean. And perhaps the *'-l-m*/*'-m-l* tongue-twister draws attention to this answer. We will see this root combination two more times in the *sūra*. When Shu'ayb's people dare him to send a punishment upon them, he replies, "My Lord knows best what you do [*qāla rabbī a'lamu bi-mā ta'malūn*]" (26:188). These two roots are also in the last verse in the *sūra*, contrasting those who do good with those who do not and who will come to know where they will return (26:227). So, Nūḥ emphasizes his lack of knowledge in terms of judging people, Shu'ayb emphasizes God's knowledge in punishing people, and God emphasizes that oppressors, *al-ladhīna dhalamū*, will know about the final judgment. These are interesting contrasts from a lack of human knowledge—and in this case, these are messengers—to, ironically, people who have done bad having knowledge, in the afterlife. Given the larger context of the *sūra*, it does not look like Nūḥ is blaming the believers. Rather, he is making it clear that his job is merely to deliver the message. His job is not to ensure that everyone will believe, and he is not to judge them in their present, prior, or future states. God's job is to decide. This echoes what we see with the contrasting portrayals of Fir'awn and God.

In the other iteration with *r-dh-l*, where Nūḥ's people lodge a complaint about his followers (11:27), Nūḥ responds:

> 11:28 He said, "My people, think: if I did have a clear sign from my Lord, and He had given me grace of His own, though it was hidden from you, could we force you to accept it against your will?

> 29 My people, I ask no reward for it from you; my reward comes only from God. I will not drive away the faithful: they are sure to meet their Lord. I can see you are foolish.
>
> 30 My people, who could help me against God if I drove the faithful away? Will you not take heed?"

We see through Nūḥ's speech that a messenger's role is to proclaim God's message, and a messenger should not reject believers. We can recall that in the beginning of *Sūrat al-Shu'arā'*, a verse mentions Prophet Muḥammad's concern that his people will not believe. In the end of the *sūra*, God commands the Prophet Muḥammad to "lower your wing tenderly over the believers who follow you" (26:215). So a messenger should convey a message, in order to please God, should not worry about people believing or not, and should accept and embrace those who do believe.

Nūḥ's people also respond to him with a threat of violence: "So they said, 'Noah, if you do not stop this, you will be stoned'" (26:116). Nūḥ is not portrayed as replying to them, which is striking because this *sūra* contains dialogue-heavy iterations of stories. He instead makes a supplication to God—like Ibrāhīm earlier, he turns to God in supplication: "He said, 'My Lord, my people have rejected me, / so make a firm judgement between me and them [*fa-ftaḥ baynī wa baynahum fatḥan*], and save me and my believing followers'" (26:117–118). The *f-t-ḥ* root occurs twice in this verse. Interestingly, in the other iteration with the root *r-dh-l*, Nūḥ's people are not portrayed as threatening him, rather, they ask him to send down the punishment with which he has threatened them (11:32). This is both repetition and variation. Lūṭ appeals to God in a verse similar to Nūḥ's: "Lord, save me and my family from what they are doing" (26:169). Both Nūḥ and Lūṭ use the words "*najjinī*" and "*rabbi*," but they are in two verses for Nūḥ (26:117–118), and in one verse for Lūṭ (26:169). So here is repetition with variation, and a comparison is drawn between Nūḥ and Lūṭ and their stories.

Interestingly, Shu'ayb's people ask him to bring a particular punishment upon them: "'Make bits of the heavens fall down on us, if you are telling the truth.' / He said, 'My Lord [*rabbī*] knows best what you do'" (26:187–188). Ironically, this is followed with them disbelieving and being punished, so they were, in a way, right to ask to be punished: according to God, they deserve to be punished.

Throughout the *sūra*, a response from the people to messengers is to accuse them of lying. We can focus on *k-dh-b*, which indicates lying or saying that someone else is lying. We find it in every section of the *sūra*, except Ibrāhīm's (26:6, 26:12, 26:105, 26:117, 26:123, 26:139, 26:141, 26:160, 26:176, 26:186, and 26:189). After the stories of Mūsā and Ibrāhīm, the stories of Nūḥ, Hūd, Ṣāliḥ, Lūṭ, and Shuʿayb all begin with a very similar refrain. Here is the introductory refrain in Nūḥ's story:

> 26:105 The people of Noah, too, called the messengers liars [*kadhdhabat qawmu nūḥin al-mursalīna*].
> 106 Their brother Noah said to them, "Will you not be mindful of God [*idh qāla lahum akhūhum nūḥun alā tattaqūna*]?
> 107 I am a faithful messenger sent to you [*innī lakum rasūlun amīnun*]:
> 108 be mindful of God and obey me [*fa-ittaqū allāha wa-aṭīʿūni*].
> 109 I ask no reward of you, for my only reward is with the Lord of all worlds [*wa mā as'alukum ʿalayhi min ajrin in ajriya illā ʿalā rabbi al-ʿālamīna*]:
> 110 be mindful of God and obey me [*fa-ittaqū allāha wa-aṭīʿūni*]."

The stories of Nūḥ, Hūd, Ṣāliḥ, Lūṭ, and Shuʿayb all have as the first word of the first verse *kadhdhabat* or *kadhdhaba*, and the last word in the first verse is *al-mursalīna*, which makes the phrase "called the messengers liars." The names of the communities are identified in slightly different ways in these stories—the people of Nūḥ (26:105) or Lūṭ (26:160), ʿĀd (26:123), Thamūd (26:141), or *aṣḥāb al-ayka* (the forest-dwellers, 26:176). In the second verse of each section on Nūḥ, Hūd, Ṣāliḥ, Lūṭ, and Shuʿayb, each prophet is named and quoted as saying, "Will you not be mindful of God [*alā tattaqūna*]." Four of the five prophets are referred to as being his people's brother (26:106, 26:124, 26:142, and 26:161). Shuʿayb is an outlier and is not referred to as his people's brother, although everything else in the verse is the same (26:177). In the conclusion, the narrator describes the devils "*al-shayāṭīn*" as descending upon (using the same root as revelation, *n-z-l*) people: "They come down [*tanazzalu*] to every lying sinner / who readily lends an ear to them, and most of them are liars [*kādhibūn*]" (26:222–223). Clearly this is a judgment on those who have been calling God's message and messengers liars all along, but who are themselves liars and recipients of revelation from devils. This is a dialogue-heavy *sūra*; the idea of lying and calling others liars is powerful here. Communication depends on honesty. People lying breaks down communication. Communication also fails when people call someone a liar when they are actually truthful. Finally, here is a contrast between receiving revelation from God or from devils, with the root *n-z-l*.

We can contrast this to an infrequently repeated root, *ṣ-d-q*, found in Table A.7 in the appendices. First, Firʿawn challenges Mūsā to show him the amazing thing that he says he can show him, if he is really telling the truth (26:31). Ṣāliḥ's people say something similar, and in Ṣāliḥ's case, they add that he is just an ordinary person like them (26:154). As mentioned above, Shu'ayb's people also challenge him to bring punishment upon them if he is telling the truth, and they even specify the punishment (26:187). Ibrāhīm prays: "give me a good name among later generations [*wa-ij'al lī lisāna ṣidqin fī al-ākhirīn*]" (26:84). Then, in the end of Ibrāhīm's story, Ibrāhīm prays to God, and then there is a scene of hellfire:

> 26:96 There they will say to their gods, as they bicker among themselves,
> 97 "We were clearly misguided
> 98 when we made you equal with the Lord of all worlds.
> 99 It was the evildoers who led us astray,
> 100 and now we have no intercessor
> 101 and no true friend [*wa lā ṣadīqin ḥamīmin*].
> 102 If only we could live our lives again, we would be true believers!"

So disbelievers have been calling messengers liars, and then, in hell, they realize they do not have a truthful person to rely upon. Ironically, they had truthful people to rely upon when they were alive, but they rejected them and even challenged them to punish them, if they were indeed truthful.

## VI. Conclusion

This chapter focused on repetition in *Sūrat al-Shu'arā'*, in its series of stories, refrains, root letters, and themes. This analysis brings to light the various scales of repetition in the Qur'ān and how repetition is used as a narrative device for the explication and complication of themes and character development. In the next chapter, I will analyze repetition in *Sūrat al-Qamar* in detail and then compare it to *Sūrat al-Shu'arā'*.

Overall, the portrayal of Fir'awn in the *sūra* is interesting and surprising. First, Fir'awn is a formidable foe and an intelligent villain: he is up to being challenged, and he thinks quickly and comes up with explanations for surprises. He also knows how to emotionally manipulate people and use their weaknesses against them (Mūsā's guilt and the magicians' desire for power and privilege). Perhaps most surprisingly, the Qur'ān discusses Fir'awn at his level and based on his claims: Fir'awn claims to be a god, so he is parallel to and contrasted with God; the magicians are parallel to and contrasted with Mūsā. Through this, then, magic is parallel to and contrasted with inspiration from

God, and reward and punishment in this life are parallel to and contrasted with reward and punishment in the afterlife.

The *sūra* focuses on the theme of messengers: where does inspiration come from (God, versus alternate sources and to people who are not messengers); what do messengers expect from people (no reward, not even belief; messengers do not even expect the satisfaction of success); messengers of God have no control over whether people choose to believe or not; those who choose to believe should obey God and the messenger; and messengers deliver their message as a fulfillment to God, not in expectation of reward or belief from people.

# 7

# Repetition in *Sūrat al-Qamar* and a Comparison with *Sūrat al-Shu'arā'*

## I. Introduction

In this chapter, I analyze repetition in *Sūrat al-Qamar* then compare it with *Sūrat al-Shu'arā'*. I examine some of the *sūra*'s prominent features, the style, which includes the refrain, and themes, then I compare it with *Sūrat al-Shu'arā'*. Both *Sūrat al-Qamar* and *Sūrat al-Shu'arā'* include a number of Qur'ānic stories, one after another, with refrains. This allows us to compare stories and repetition within a *sūra*, and stories and repetition between *sūras*. It also provides the opportunity to compare the styles, refrains, and prominent themes within and between the *sūras*. Through echoing roots, themes, stories, and *sūras*, we will look at repetition on various scales. As a result of this analysis, we will see that sometimes the same prophets feature in a sequence of stories in different *sūras*, but their stories are told in different narratological ways and with different topics of focus. In both *sūras*, we see how repeated themes, styles, and refrains draw connection and contrast.

*Sūrat al-Najm*, *Sūrat al-Qamar*, and *Sūrat al-Raḥmān* come one after the other in the Qur'ān and have stylistic similarities. *Sūrat al-Najm* has end-rhyme with the letter *alif maqṣurā*; *Sūrat al-Qamar* uses the letter *rā'* to have end-rhyme.[1] *Sūrat al-Qamar* and *Sūrat al-Raḥmān* both have refrains. Despite this, Angelika Neuwirth incorrectly writes that other than *Sūrat al-Raḥmān*, the only *sūra* in the Qur'ān with a refrain is *Sūrat al-Mursalāt*. She writes:

> There is no text structurally comparable to *Sūrat al-Raḥmān*. The fact that a refrain is found only in one other sura, *Sūrat al-Mursalāt* (Q. 77), where it bears a different function, suggests that the refrain in *Sūrat al-Raḥmān* is a reference to a text from outside of the nascent Qur'anic community.[2]

Neuwirth has missed a number of other *sūras* with refrains: *Sūrat al-Qamar*, *Sūrat al-Shu'arā'*, *Sūrat al-Ṣāffāt*, and more.

*How the Qur'ān Works*. Leyla Ozgur Alhassen, Oxford University Press. © Oxford University Press 2023.
DOI: 10.1093/oso/9780197654606.003.0007

*Sūrat al-Qamar* includes a series of stories of five prophets. This gives us an opportunity to analyze and compare each section. As I discuss elsewhere, the Qur'ān establishes structure through end-rhyme, repeated words and phrases, and subsections.[3] We will explore some of this below. In this *sūra*, an introduction and conclusion surround a series of five stories about prophets and their people. The structure of the *sūra* is summarized in Table 7.1. The stories have an introductory refrain and a concluding refrain. Repetition draws comparison between the stories. For example, despite the pretty apparent structure of five prophets' stories one after the other, one will notice that rather than Mūsā being named, Fir'awn is (54:41). This is fascinating. Why are the people of Mūsā, Hārūn, and Fir'awn identified as the people of Fir'awn, the villain of the story? Hūd (sent to the people of 'Ād) and Ṣāliḥ (sent to the people of Thamūd) are not mentioned by name in this *sūra* either, but their people are identified by the names of their tribes, rather than the name of a villain. The stories of Nūḥ, Hūd, Ṣāliḥ, and Lūṭ do not name any villains. Through this analysis, we will come to a theory.

By examining repetition to find literary patterns, we will unearth underlying themes in *Sūrat al-Qamar*. The main theme is the relationship between the audience and the Qur'ān, developed through a dynamic style and explicated through an exploration of people claiming something is ordinary or the same old thing, and disbelieving. This is contrasted with the idea that God is the one to decide what is or is not ordinary, and God can make the ordinary into the extraordinary. This is all about God's power versus human weakness. And, finally, the Qur'ān is a bridge between God and humans, which empowers and pushes the audience to action. While the refrain instills fear, it also pushes action through the belief that the Qur'ān gives salvation and stability and connects one with God.

**Table 7.1** The Structure of *Sūrat al-Qamar*

| Verses | Number of verses | People | Refrain/Subsection | *Wa-la-qad* |
|---|---|---|---|---|
| 54:1–8 | 8 | Introduction | | 54:4 |
| 54:9–17 | 8 | Nūḥ | 54:15–17 | 54:15, 54:17 |
| 54:18–22 | 5 | Hūd | 54:21–22 | 54:22 |
| 54:23–32 | 10 | Ṣāliḥ | 54:30, 32 | 54:32 |
| 54:33–40 | 8 | Lūṭ | 54:37, 39–40 | 54:36, 54:37, 54:38, 54:40 |
| 54:41–51 | 11 | Mūsā | 54:51 | 54:41, 54:51 |
| 54:52–55 | 4 | Conclusion | | |

## II. What Is Ordinary or Extraordinary?

We can start by thinking about the underlying theme in the *sūra* that people claim something is ordinary, or the same old thing, and then choose to disbelieve. This applies to how people see messengers or miracles that God sends. Whereas the *sūra* emphasizes God is the one to decide what is worthy of being a miracle and what is not. At the same time, God can make the ordinary into the extraordinary, if God wills, as a punishment in this life, on the Day of Judgment, or in the afterlife.

We start with what we can call the introduction to the *sūra* (54:1–8):

> 54:1 The Hour draws near; the moon is split.
> 2 Yet whenever the disbelievers see a sign, they turn away and say, "Same old sorcery!"
> 3 They reject the truth and follow their own desires—everything is recorded—
> 4 although warning tales that should have restrained them have come down to them—
> 5 far-reaching wisdom—but these warnings do not help:
> 6 so [Prophet] turn away from them. On the Day the Summoner will summon them to a horrific event,
> 7 eyes downcast, they will come out of their graves like swarming locusts
> 8 rushing towards the Summoner. The disbelievers will cry, "This is a stern day!"

The *sūra* begins in media res. In the first verse, "The Hour" refers to Judgment Day, and we can interpret the moon splitting as being one of the ways that objects in nature will function abnormally on Judgment Day, a theme that is described in many places in the Qur'ān. In that case, the *sūra* begins with an apocalyptic verse, and then a general version of a story of people rejecting a message. Others explain that Prophet Muḥammad split the moon and that this is describing that incident, which in terms of narrative style, would be a dynamic mixing of times and places. And yet, when people see signs, they call it the "same old sorcery," *siḥrun mustamir* (54:2). Interestingly, this contrasts with the only other use of the same root, *s-ḥ-r*, in the *sūra*: "We released a pebble storm against them, all except the family of Lot. We saved them before dawn [*bi-saḥar*]" (54:34). The two other Qur'ānic uses of this word, in its plural, are people asking God for forgiveness in the early hours of the day (3:17 and 51:18). So, while people reject signs from God as being nothing other than old magic, God mentions saving people in the early morning hours, and people seeking forgiveness in those hours. It is as if God complicates the idea of magic here, which matches the theme throughout the *sūra*: God can decide if something is magic or not and if it should be believed or not. In contrast, people reject the signs, they follow their own whims (54:3), and although they have heard news that should have kept them in check (54:4), wisdom does them no good (54:5). For verse 54:3, Quṭb writes about the idea of people following their whims, which flutter like a heartbeat, versus God setting everything in this vast existence in its place. Everything is in its place and time.[4] So the verse contrasts the variability and fickleness of humans—their thoughts, emotions, and beliefs—to the stability of God.

And then comes: "so [Prophet] turn away from them. On the Day the Summoner will summon them to a horrific event," *fa-tawalla ʿanhum yawma yadʿu al-dāʿi ilā shay'in nukur* (54:6). Here, the imperative verb is the second-person singular and is interpreted as being addressed to Prophet Muḥammad. It may initially seem surprising that the Prophet is told to turn away from people, but if we look at the previous verses, he is being told to turn away from disbelievers. This verse adds to the dynamic style of the *sūra*, bringing in multiple layers of narration at the same time. We will see addresses to the second-person singular and addresses to the audience of the Qur'ān throughout this *sūra*. Then the verse brings in a description of Judgment Day, which continues for a few verses (54:6–8). On that day, "disbelievers will cry, 'This is a stern day!' " (54:8). There is a sharp contrast in the introduction between the apocalyptic descriptions framing the section and yet people taking signs as the "same old sorcery" (54:2).

In the introduction, we see two themes present throughout the *sūra*: time, *al-sāʿah*, and nature, represented by the moon, *al-qamar*. We can see these and other repeated themes in Table 7.2. The moon, of course, is also connected with the concept of time. Then we jump right into a general story: people receive a sign or a message and reject it. They reject the wisdom and truth from God and follow their own whims. All their deeds are recorded. The way they emerge from their graves on the Day of Judgment is compared to "swarming locusts" (54:7), another allusion to nature. Also, they are with "eyes downcast," and here we see a new theme, of the senses, in the word *abṣāruhum* (54:7). Then they realize their mistake. Here are the ideas of signs, messengers, wisdom, people rejecting the message, Judgment Day, nature, and sight. And there is a contrast between the idea of time and time ending, and people taking it as the same old thing. And what a contrast: people think nature is nothing important—and yet it is the very thing that can also destroy them if God wills.

From there, we blend into a series of stories: "Before them the people of Noah rejected the truth" (54:9). In the introduction there is a general idea of people rejecting prophets and messages, then what will happen to them on Judgment Day, and now we see that the people of Nūḥ fit the same pattern. We

**Table 7.2** Repeated Themes in *Sūrat al-Qamar*

| Verses | Time | Nature | Senses and Body Parts | God Saving People |
|---|---|---|---|---|
| 54:1–8 Introduction | *s-w-ʿ* (54:1); *y-w-m* (54:6, 8) | *q-m-r* (54:1); *j-r-d* (54:7) | *r-ʾ-y* (54:2); *b-ṣ-r* (54:7) | |
| 54:9–17 Nūḥ | | *m-w-h* (54:11, 12); *s-m-w* (54:11); *ʾ-r-ḍ* (54:12); *ʿ-y-n* (54:12); *j-n-n* (54:9) | *ʿ-y-n* (54:14) | *n-ṣ-r*: 54:10; *ḥ-m-l* (54:13); *ʿ-y-n* (54:14) |
| 54:18–22 Hūd | *y-w-m* (54:19) | *r-w-ḥ* (54:19); *n-kh-l* (54:20) | | |
| 54:23–32 Ṣāliḥ | *gh-d-w* (54:26) | *n-w-q* (54:27); *m-w-h* (54:28); *ṣ-y-ḥ* (54:31); *h-sh-m* (54:31) | *sh-r-b*: (54:28) | |
| 54:33–40 Lūṭ | *b-k-r* (54:38) | *ḥ-ṣ-b* (54:34); *ʿ-y-n* (54:37) | *ʿ-y-n* (54:37); *dh-w-q* (54:37, 39) | *n-j-w*: 54:34 |
| 54:41–51 Mūsā | *s-w-ʿ* (54:46 x 2); *w-ʿ-d* (54:46); *y-w-m* (54:48) | *al-nār* (54:48); *w-j-h* (54:48) | *dh-w-q* (54:48); *b-ṣ-r* (54:50) | *n-ṣ-r*: 54:44 |
| 54:52–55 Conclusion | | *j-n-n* (54:54); *n-h-r* (54:54) | | |

see the dynamic style of the *sūra* in its blending of the general with the particular, moving between Prophet Muḥammad's day and people, Judgment Day in the future, and then back to Nūḥ's time and people. Nūḥ's people rejected and insulted him: "Before them the people of Noah rejected the truth: they rejected Our servant, saying, 'He is mad [*majnūn*]!' Noah was rebuked" (54:9). The root *j-n-n* comes back in the end of the *sūra* in a contrasting way: "The righteous will live securely among Gardens [*jannāt*] and rivers" (54:54). Here then, is the same contrast we have already seen: people think and judge a certain way, but God shows them that they are wrong. They insult Nūḥ by saying he is crazy, but what makes him crazy in their eyes (his faith) is what gives him and people like him eternal paradise as an abode. Then comes the theme of prophets feeling defeated, and Nūḥ "called upon his Lord, 'I am defeated: help me!'" (54:10).

Perhaps counterintuitively, God's response is to flood the earth with water (54:10–11). The verse says that God opens the gates of the sky and lets the water pour, and the verse has a number of long, open *alifs*, causing sound to pour out of a reciter's mouth: *fa-fataḥnā abwāba al-samā'i bi-mā'in munhamir* (54:11). There is word play in the next few verses on the root *ʿ-y-n*, used in two of its meanings, as springs of water (54:12) and as eyes (54:14): God makes water gush forth from springs, *ʿuyunan* (54:12), and the boat that Nūḥ builds sails before God's eyes, *bi-aʿyuninā* (54:14). Even with a flood of water, everything is completely in God's control, and God carries Nūḥ (*ḥamalnāhu*, 54:13).

The theme of nature is present here in the water (54:11 and 54:12) and we will see it later in the story of Ṣāliḥ (54:28). Comparing this story to the general one in the introduction, there are the ideas of people rejecting the message and nature. Instead of punishment on Judgment Day, we see punishment on earth, through nature. Here, the narrator refers to Nūḥ as God's *ʿabd*. It may be surprising that only Nūḥ is called God's *ʿabd* in this *sūra* (54:9). While connections are forged between sections of the *sūra* through repetition, there are also some roots that are not repeated at all. This singular use makes them stand out. Also, only Nūḥ expresses the extent of his frustration by saying he feels defeated, *maghlūb* (54:10), then he asks God to make him victorious.

At the end of this section is the refrain *wa-la-qad taraknāhā āyatan fa-hal min muddakirin / fa-kayfa kāna ʿadhābī wa-nudhuri / wa-la-qad yassarnā al-qur'āna li-l-dhikri fa-hal min muddakirin*, "We have left this as a sign: will anyone take heed? / How [terrible] My punishment was and [the fulfilment of] My warnings! / We have made it easy to learn lessons from the Qur'an: will anyone take heed?" (54:15–17). Here, again, is the blending of various registers: the audience of the Qur'ān is being told to learn from the actions and consequences of previous people. Also, this is the first time in the *sūra* that the Qur'ān refers to itself. The refrain contrasts God's punishment with the Qur'ān. The Qur'ān can save people, but also, the Qur'ān gives stability, constancy, and preservation, the way that God does for the believers in the story.

The refrain then blends into a new story, connected by the occurrence of people rejecting the message and being punished: "The people of ʿAd also rejected the truth. How [terrible] My punishment was and [the fulfilment of] My warnings?" (54:18). This is essentially a story of punishment or an allusion to it—all we see of their crime is that they reject the message. Then we see their punishment (54:19–20) and the refrain (54:21–22).

Next comes the story of Ṣāliḥ (54:23–32), signaled with the same root letters as 54:18, the *k-dh-b* root, *kadhdhabat*, and *n-dh-r*, *bil-nudhur* (54:23). The people clearly say that they do not want to follow someone ordinary: "they said, 'What? A man? Why should we follow a lone man from amongst ourselves? That would be misguided; quite insane'" (54:24). Ṣāliḥ's people use the root *k-dh-b* to describe Ṣāliḥ (54:25) and *ḍ-l-l* for themselves if they were to follow him (54:24). We see here that their criteria for judgment and their actions are wrong, according to the Qur'ān; their criteria and logic is the exact opposite of what it should be. Then they are told to share water with a camel that is sent to them as a test (54:27–28), and their response is again the opposite of what it should be: "But they called their companion, who took a sword and hamstrung the camel" (54:29). There is something jarring about their bringing a companion or friend, *ṣāḥib*, to do this. Instead of encouraging each other to do good, they are encouraging each other to do bad, countering Qur'ānic morals (e.g., 3:104 and 3:110).

In this story, the *k-dh-b* root is also used differently than in any of the other uses in this *sūra*, in the word *kadhdhāb*, a variation on the repetition (54:25). In 54:25, Ṣāliḥ's people call him a liar; everywhere else in this *sūra*, the root describes disbelievers. Here is something that we sometimes see in Qur'ānic stories, that God as narrator does not hesitate to repeat the harsh, insulting, or blasphemous language that disbelievers use. This, of course, helps maintain the realism of the story. At the same time, the root is being used in contrasting ways by God on the one hand and disbelievers on the other hand. Then we return to the usage of the *k-dh-b* root in the rest of the *sūra*, when God uses the very phrase that they use and declares that they will see who the true liar is (54:26). At the end of this section is the refrain, *fa-kayfa kāna 'adhābī wa-nudhuri; wa-la-qad yassarnā al-qur'āna li-l-dhikri fa-hal min muddakir* (54:30 and 54:32). This refrain is the same as in the Hūd section, but the verses are separated, a variation on the repetition.

Then we move to the story of Lūṭ (54:33–40). This section makes a distinction to say that Lūṭ and his family were not punished, with the root *n-j-w*, which does not occur anywhere else in the *sūra* (54:34).

The last story mentions the people of Fir'awn receiving and rejecting the message (54:41–51). This story blends into an address presumably to the Prophet Muḥammad, "Are your disbelievers any better than these? Were you given an exemption in the Scripture?" (54:43).

We can now look at the role of nature throughout the *sūra*. In most of the stories, we see punishment through nature, whereas in the introduction, we see punishment on Judgment Day. Throughout the *sūra*, nature is portrayed as signs of Judgment Day (54:1 and 54:7), nature is turned into a punishment (54:11, 54:12, and 54:19), then it is a test (54:27 and 54:28), and finally, it is a reward (54:54). In Nūḥ's story, the waters gush (54:11–12), and in the same way, wind carries people away (54:19–20), there is a "blast" (54:31) and a "pebble storm" (54:34). In these examples, God transforms natural phenomena into extraordinary instances of punishment. We see throughout the *sūra* patterns of ordinary versus extraordinary: people versus messengers, signs of God and nature and the Day of Judgment. Quṭb reflects on this dichotomy by mentioning that the moon is a big sign and always there.[5] In fact, he writes, all of creation, big and small, are signs.[6] The idea is that ordinary and familiar nature should be understood as signs of God; when it is not, it might become a punishment. Ordinary and familiar nature can also be transformed into signs of or the beginning of Judgment Day. Parallel to this is that ordinary and familiar people can be transformed into messengers. This transformation is determined by God, but some people make themselves into gods and think they can judge and determine who is or is not a messenger or who deserves or does not deserve to be a messenger. What, how, and when is something transformed from ordinary and familiar to extraordinary? Because God determines it as such. People who reject signs and messengers are usurping God's role. They decide that it should be them who decides what makes something extraordinary or not.

The pattern in the *sūra* is that people do not want to follow the ordinary and are then punished with the ordinary being made extraordinary; the *sūra* starts with the ordinary being made extraordinary, as well. In other words, when one does not take signs as signs, they become punishments. The modern Muḥammad al-Ghazali writes: "Thus ordinary and familiar forces of nature, water, and air become powerful tools in the hand of God to punish and destroy the wrong-doers."[7] The contrast between everyday things being made into something extraordinary highlights God's power.

## III. God's Power Versus Human Weakness

Throughout *Sūrat al-Qamar*, there is a contrasting pattern of God's power versus human whims, opinions, and weaknesses in the face of God, God-controlled nature, and God's punishment. In the next section, we will focus on the bridge between the two, which is the stability found in the Qur'ān, and that people have a role in memorizing or preserving it. The *sūra* may initially look like it is about scaring people by telling them about punishments, which it is, but it is also about showing them their place. The *sūra* shows people their vulnerability: people are swarming locusts in the face of God's power (54:7). But it is also empowering and gives them a role: people can be a part of saving themselves by memorizing, reading, or preserving the Qur'ān in their minds, hearts, and actions.

We see the theme of God's power throughout the story, in the focus on God punishing people who reject the message. We can start by looking at the root ʿ-dh-b, which occurs frequently in *Sūrat al-Qamar*. First it is in the context of Nūḥ's story, God asks rhetorically, in the repeating refrain, "How [terrible] My punishment was and [the fulfilment of] My warnings [*fa-kayfa kāna ʿadhābī wa-nudhur*]!" (54:16), then again in the context of Hūd's story, before and after describing the punishment (54:18 and 54:21). The same refrain is repeated in Ṣāliḥ's story, after the people kill the camel (54:30). In the story of Lūṭ, there is a variation on the refrain, "Taste My [terrible] punishment and [the fulfilment of] My warnings! [*fa-dhūqū ʿadhābī wa-nudhur*]" (54:37), then it says that they were punished (54:38), then there is the refrain again with the variation (54:39). The root does not occur again in the *sūra*. The root ʿ-*dh-b* occurs in *Sūrat al-Qamar* with almost the same phrase or the repetition of a variation.

The stories of ʿĀd (54:18–22) and Firʿawn (54:41–42) do not go into detail about their sins or include their dialogue, we just see their punishment. And in the case of ʿĀd, two verses describe their punishment (54:19–20). This stylistic feature certainly adds to the theme of punishment in the *sūra*. The last story, that of Firʿawn, is short and blends into, first, a comparison with the people of Prophet Muḥammad and then punishment in the afterlife. We see here God's power and punishment, which can occur as quickly as "the blink of an eye" (54:50). And then comes another verse that plays off of the refrain and addresses the second-person plural, "We have destroyed the likes of you in the past. Will anyone take heed?" (54:51). It asks the audience, how are you different from these other people in the stories you have just encountered? It first invokes fear in the audience, but then gives them an out by asking them to take heed. Earlier, first, God suggests sarcastically that people think they have immunity from their scripture, *al-zubur* (54:43), but then they are told that, indeed, everything is recorded in their scripture, *al-zubur* (54:52). *Al-zubur* ends both verses and is the rhyme word in both. There are no exemptions, but, indeed, some people are rewarded with paradise (54:54–55). And in the last two verses of the *sūra*, for the first time, it mentions a reward, paradise.

In *Sūrat al-Qamar*, we also see human weakness in their flawed reasoning. In the stories, people who reject the messengers speak, but the messengers are not depicted speaking to their people. Nūḥ's people call him crazy (54:9); Ṣāliḥ's people say he is a man like them and he is a liar (54:24–25); and others, it is suggested, say they are a victorious group (54:44). Through this narrative technique, the audience gets to see the reasoning of disbelievers and the flaws in their reasoning. Nūḥ does speak, but he speaks to God, asking for help. It is as if God speaks for the messengers by punishing the people and warning the audience of the Qur'ān. That people already died and were punished is not the only focus or concern; the audience's choices and actions are also critical.

The theme of God's power and human weakness is embodied through the portrayal of senses and body parts in this *sūra*. There is sight, expressed through the roots *ʿ-y-n* and *b-ṣ-r*, in four of the sections in *Sūrat al-Qamar*. First, we see people with eyes downcast as they leave their graves (*b-ṣ-r*, 54:7). Then, water bursts from springs, using the root *ʿ-y-n* (54:12); we can say this is word play. The raft that saves Nūḥ floats before God's eyes, using the root *ʿ-y-n* (54:14). God blinds people's eyes as a punishment (*ʿ-y-n*, 54:37). Finally, God's will happens as fast as the blink of an eye (*b-ṣ-r*, 54:50). Through the theme of sight, there is an exploration of human fear, punishment by God, God's eyes presumably representing protection, people's eyes, punishment to the eye, punishment through the eye (the root *ʿ-y-n* for a spring), and God's power and speed. There is also the tasting of punishment, through the root *dh-w-q* (54:37, 54:39, and 54:48).

In the contrasting theme of God's power versus human weakness, Nūḥ is an interesting figure because he shows his weakness to God and asks God for help (54:10) and God gives it to him (54:11–14). We can see this through the *n-ṣ-r* root in the story of Nūḥ and Mūsā. Nūḥ says he is defeated and asks for God's help (54:10), while in the latter verse, disbelievers are characterized as saying that they support each other (54:44). Here, the portrayal of a believer feeling defeated, appealing to God and God making him victorious, is a reversal of disbelievers claiming that they are victorious, supporting each other, and then being defeated by God (54:44–45). We also see God physically saving Nūḥ from the waters by carrying him on a plank, *ḥamalnāhu* (54:13). This is God using the first-person plural, saying, "We carried him." It feels very gentle and intimate. Furthermore, Nūḥ's ship sails before God's eyes, *tajrī bi-aʿyuninā* (54:14). The level of care and intimacy increases here. Here we see *ʿ-y-n* as a body part, rather than a part of nature in a spring—which has been transformed into a punishment. So *ʿ-y-n* has moved from a blessing of nature to a punishment to a blessing again. In contrast, we see human weakness when people try to run away but cannot (54:45–46). Instead of turning to God, they try to save themselves, which is futile.

Just as God saves Nūḥ, later, God saves Lūṭ's family from punishment (54:34). This is a blessing from God, *n-ʿ-m* (54:35) to reward those who are grateful, *sh-k-r* (54:35). The theme of God saving people is expressed throughout the *sūra* with the roots *n-ṣ-r* (54:10 and 54:44), *ḥ-m-l* (54:13), *ʿ-y-n* (54:14), and *n-j-w* (54:34). We will explore the idea of the Qur'ān as a savior in the next section.

The idea of God's power manifests in the idea of stability, which we can see through the word *mustaqirr*. In the Qur'ān, the root of this word has connotations of coolness, comfort, affirming, remaining, stability, tranquility, and abode. First in the *sūra* is: "They reject the truth and follow their own desires--everything is recorded [*mustaqirr*]" (54:3). So, here is a clear contrast between people's fleeting desires and reality—everything is set and stable, or "recorded," in Abdel Haleem's translation. Later, in describing the punishment of Lūṭ's people, it says: "and early in the morning a punishment seized them that still remains [*mustaqirr*]" (54:38). In this case, the punishment, itself, is stable and lasting. We can also think about stability through the contrast of human whims and God's salvation. For the whims, we can again look at verse 54:3, and we can compare this to God saving Nūḥ: "We carried him [*ḥamalnāhu*] along on a vessel of planks and nails / that floated under Our watchful eye [*bi-aʿyuninā*], a reward for the one who had been rejected" (54:13–14). Here is God-given stability, even in the midst of chaos. Ironically, the vehicle granting stability is described as a thing of "planks and nails," which, judging by its substance alone, would not give one much confidence. The description makes this stand out, so that we realize stability is not coming from the vessel, stability is coming from God.

We can also explore Godly stability through the root *q-d-r* in the *sūra*. It occurs in the Qur'ān with the connotations of control, power, determined, measured, the All-Powerful (*al-qadīr*), the Able (*al-qādir*), and the Powerful (*al-muqtadir*). The first time it is in the *sūra* is in the flood of punishment in Nūḥ's story, when God "burst the earth with gushing springs: the waters met for a preordained purpose" (54:12). Here, the punishment is described as "preordained" in Abdel Haleem's translation. Then: "They rejected all Our signs so We seized them with all Our might and power" (54:42). And, yet, "We have created all things in due measure" (54:49). And, finally, in paradise, people are "secure in the presence of an all-powerful Sovereign [*fī maqʿadi ṣidqin ʿinda malīkin muqtadir*]' (54:55). The word *maqʿad* comes with the connotations of a foundation, position, and seat. One is not fluttering, swaying, moving, or being moved; one is not moving from one's own whims or from punishment. One is stable in God's presence.

## IV. The Qur'ān as a Bridge

Sayyid Quṭb writes about how *Sūrat al-Qamar* addresses the emotions through the mention of punishments, and it makes people fearful. When it mentions the moon's splitting and the hour coming, this should move the human heart.[8] While the refrain instills fear, it also gives hope by showing that the Qur'ān brings salvation and stability and is a means of turning to God. The Qur'ān is a bridge between people and God. This is empowering. In the *sūra*, we see that natural phenomena are all God's creation, which God can do with as God wills; the Qur'ān is also God's creation,[9] and memorizing it (as mentioned in the refrain) is a way to bring stability to one's life, as opposed to using fallible human judgment (e.g., 54:24 and 54:29) or fallible and varying whims of the heart (54:3). And God has made it easy to memorize or remember. It is fruitful to think about the idea of memorizing the Qur'ān and the root *dh-k-r* in the refrain: when someone memorizes something, they preserve it as is, so it is stable within them. The Qur'ān takes it one step further—by memorizing the Qur'ān, it also becomes a stabilizing force in one's life, so that one is not swept away by waters, winds, storms, or punishment literally or figuratively, in this life or the next.

*Sūrat al-Qamar* has a dynamic narrative style, which is critical in instilling this message. The style contrasts previous messengers, their people, and their punishments, with Prophet Muḥammad and his people, and the audience. There is direct address of the second-person singular, often understood to be the Prophet Muḥammad, and there are direct and implied addresses to the audience of the Qur'ān.

The concluding refrain shows the dynamic style: "How [terrible] My punishment was and [the fulfilment of] My warnings [*fa-kayfa kāna ʿadhābī wa-nudhur*]! / We have made it easy to learn lessons from the Qur'an: will anyone take heed?" (54:16–17, 54:21–22, 54:30, and 54:32). There is a mixing of two layers of narration: the story was told and then is talked about as a lesson from which the audience of the Qur'ān can learn.

One way that the audience is addressed in the *sūra* is in the second part of the concluding refrain: *wa-la-qad yassarnā al-qur'āna li-l-dhikri fa-hal min muddakir*. God says God made the Qur'ān easy to remember; is there anyone who remembers it? Here, there is no specific audience addressed, which gives it a sense of timelessness. A contrast is made between the audience of the Qur'ān and the people in the stories they are reading. Will the audience learn the lessons that the people in the stories rejected? The dynamic style reveals itself in the refrain by reinforcing action and choice, by asking the audience a question. It leaves it to the audience to respond. The second part of the refrain emphasizes that the Qur'ān is easy to remember, to recall, and to bring to mind. If one brings it to mind and acts accordingly, then one will not be punished. And punishment can be in this world, as in the stories, or in the afterlife, as seen in the beginning and end of the *sūra*. So this is a contrast between the Qur'ān and punishment. This verse uses the first-person plural to talk about God, *wa-la-qad yassarnā al-qur'āna*. So, God is talking about God using We. Throughout the Qur'ān, God describes God with the third-person singular, first-person singular, and first-person plural. Here the shift in the refrain is from the first-person possessive singular, *'adhābī*, to the first-person plural. The first-person singular is for punishment, and the first-person plural is about the Qur'ān. In the first verse, then, we have the first-person singular for God paired with the second-person plural, so, me and you plural. In contrast, when God talks about making the Qur'ān easy for people, it is with the first-person plural, with majesty, graciousness, and is all-encompassing. The different attributes of God seem to echo the concept of the 99 names of God. It is as if to say that the part of God that gives the Qur'ān is larger than the part that punishes. Perhaps it indicates that the attributes of God that punish are smaller or fewer than the attributes that make the Qur'ān easy.

To look at the dynamic style, we can also focus on some verses toward the end of the *sūra*:

> 54:37 they even demanded his guests from him—so We sealed their eyes—"Taste [*fa-dhūqū*] My [terrible] punishment and [the fulfilment of] My warnings!"—
> 38 and early in the morning a punishment seized them that still remains—
> 39 "Taste [*fa-dhūqū*] My [terrible] punishment and [the fulfilment of] My warnings!"
> 40 We have made it easy to learn lessons from the Qur'an: will anyone take heed?
> 41 The people of Pharaoh also received warnings.
> 42 They rejected all Our signs so We seized them with all Our might and power.
> 43 "Are your disbelievers any better than these? Were you given an exemption in the Scripture?"
> 44 Do they perhaps say, "We are a great army and we shall be victorious"?
> 45 Their forces will be routed and they will turn tail and flee.

The phrase, *fa-dhūqū*, "taste," addresses the second-person plural and occurs a few times in this selection. In verse 54:37, it is clearly part of the story; in verse 54:39, there is a merging of the story and the refrain, as if to say, you are them, lest one feel arrogant and think that they are so different from those sinners. In this selection, there is variation on the concluding refrain, which merits analysis. First: "'Taste My [terrible] punishment and [the fulfilment of] My warnings!' / We have made it easy to learn lessons from the Qur'an: will anyone take heed?" (54:39–40). In the first verse, we have *fa-dhūqū 'adhābī wa-nudhur*. It is as if God is addressing the sinners in the various stories. Then is *'adhābī*, which uses the first-person singular possessive pronoun, meaning,

"My punishment." In this part of the refrain, "Taste My [terrible] punishment and [the fulfilment of] My warnings!" (54:39), we see that it is a punishment for them and a warning for you; the audience is told to taste the warning or preview. This is prefigured earlier in the *sūra*: "We have left this as a sign: will anyone take heed?" (54:15). So, their punishment itself becomes a sign; the audience should learn from everything and change their behavior. This idea also shows itself with the second-person plural pronoun in *a-kuffārakum* (54:43) and *lakum* (54:43). In verse 54:43, an audience is being addressed, with the second-person plural. Some interpret *a-kuffārukum* as addressing Prophet Muḥammad's people, and some specify this as addressing the Quraysh. So, here, we have another layer of addressee. The verse sarcastically asks why people think they are any different than those who came before them. This is perhaps also a response to people challenging prophets to punish them: they will be punished, some time. Finally, *dhūqū* occurs again in the afterlife: "on the Day when they are dragged on their faces in Hell. 'Feel the touch of Hell'" (54:48). Here, again, is the idea of previewing something, but earlier, one is previewing in this life for the next, and from other people's mistakes, whereas, for the people in this verse, it is too late.

In the end of the *sūra*, the distinction between these two groups of people (the people in the stories and the audience) is further diminished, and the connection between them is further emphasized, with a variation on the refrain: "We have destroyed the likes of you in the past. Will anyone take heed?" (54:51). This verse stands out more in the Arabic, with the second-person plural possessive pronoun *kum* on the word *ashyā'akum*. The dynamic style is prominent here, addressing the audience in the plural, and saying that God has punished their groups, sects, or parties before.

Focusing on the refrain, we find other variations in it. For example, in the story of Ṣāliḥ, punishment comes between the two verses of the concluding refrain (54:31):

54:30 How [terrible] My punishment was and [the fulfilment of] My warnings!
31 We released a single mighty blast against them and they ended up like a fence-maker's dry sticks.
32 We have made it easy to learn lessons from the Qur'an: will anyone take heed?

Another variation is in the story of Lūṭ (54:37–40). There is a variation on the introductory refrain after that (54:41). Through these examples, we see how a refrain lends new meanings to a story. First, when there is the same refrain, but different characters and scenes, the refrain brings whatever one learns from the previous story to the new story. In this case, we see one story after another of people rejecting a message and being punished. So each telling and each refrain brings with it the previous rejection and punishment. And the refrain itself may change, which also happens here.

We find, in fact, that there are structural parallels between the refrain and the entire *sūra*. The refrain mentions punishment then the alternative: the ease of remembrance, memorizing, or reciting. The *sūra* parallels this by mentioning punishment in various forms, then reward in paradise (54:54–55). And the implication is that the consequence of connecting with and preserving the Qur'ān is reward in paradise.

## V. A Comparison of *Sūrat al-Qamar* with *Sūrat al-Shū'arā'*

We can now compare *Sūrat al-Qamar* with *Sūrat al-Shū'arā'*. In terms of style, *Sūrat al-Qamar* uses mixed layers of narration, to have a dynamic, interactive style, pushing the audience to action, while the distinctive stylistic feature in *Sūrat al-Shū'arā'* is that it is dialogue heavy. In terms of themes, *Sūrat al-Qamar* highlights that God saves and punishes people, and the audience should learn from this and hold on to the Qur'ān as their stabilizing force. The prominent theme in *Sūrat al-Shū'arā'* is prophecy, which plays out in the themes of competing claims of power and inspiration, God sending messengers and people having the choice to believe or not, the delineation of expectations between prophets and people, as well as the theme of responses to revelation.

A comparison of *Sūrat al-Qamar* and *Sūrat al-Shu'arā'* can focus on structure by comparing the length and order of the sections in each *sūra* as seen in Table 7.3. The order of the sections in *Sūrat al-Qamar* are an introduction, Nūḥ, Hūd, Ṣāliḥ, Lūṭ, Mūsā, and a conclusion. In *Sūrat al-Shu'arā'*, we have an introduction, Mūsā, Ibrāhīm, Nūḥ, Hūd, Ṣāliḥ, Lūṭ, Shu'ayb, and a conclusion. So Mūsā starts the story sequence in one *sūra* and ends it in the other; also, the stories of Ibrāhīm and Shu'ayb are in *Sūrat al-Shu'arā'* and not in *Sūrat al-Qamar*. Nūḥ, Hūd, Ṣāliḥ, and Lūṭ are present and in the same order in both *sūras*. Most of the stories that are in both *sūras* are at least twice as long in *Sūrat al-Shu'ara'*. This makes these *sūras* ripe for comparison with each other. Also interesting is that the number of verses of each story in *Sūrat al-Shu'arā'* tapers down, roughly in the shape of an inverted triangle: 59, 36, 18, 18, 19, 16, and 16. One wonders if this structure of the inverted triangle is building up to something, such as essential concepts, as we see in Chapter 2. The number of verses in the stories in *Sūrat al-Qamar* do not follow such a pattern. In both stories' series, the story of Ṣāliḥ stands out as being longer than its surrounding stories. Further research on Ṣāliḥ in other *sūras* could see if this is a consistent pattern and could try to deduce why.

We can turn to a comparison of the refrains in the two *sūras*. Both *Sūrat al-Shu'arā'* and *Sūrat al-Qamar* have introductory and concluding refrains. Unlike in *Sūrat al-Qamar*, the refrains in *Sūrat al-Shu'arā'* have no variations; they consist of the exact same words in each story. However, in two places, the first verse of the concluding refrain starts with an additional phrase (26:139 and 26:158). The refrain in *Sūrat al-Qamar* has more variations but is essentially *fa-kayfa kāna 'adhābī wa-nudhuri wa-la-qad yassarnā al-qur'āna li-l-dhikri fa-hal min muddakirin* (54:21–22). So, in *Sūrat al-Shu'arā'*, we see repetition maintained, and in *Sūrat al-Qamar*, we see repetition suppressed in the refrain. If we compare the refrains to each other, there are no echoing roots—so the refrains in these *sūras* are integral to their respective *sūras* but do not interact across these two *sūras*. In addition, the concluding refrain in *Sūrat al-Shu'arā'* is addressed to the second person, while the refrain in *Sūrat al-Qamar* is not.

Another way to compare the *sūras* is to look at the focalization in them. The focalization (narrative lens) is distinct in the two *sūras*. In *Sūrat al-Qamar*, God narrates the *sūra* usually in the first-person plural, for example, *innā*, "We" (54:27). The refrain uses the first-person singular (54:21) and the first-person plural (54:22). God describes the messengers in the third person. However, there is a change in the story of Ṣāliḥ, when God commands him to watch his people and be patient, and then to "tell them," *wa-nabbi'hum* (54:27–28). We see God address the second-person plural in the very interesting phrases discussed above: "are your disbelievers [*a-kuffārukum*]," which Abdel Haleem interprets as describing the people of Mecca (54:43), *dhūqū* (54:37, 54:39, and 54:48), and *ashyā'kum* (54:51). In *Sūrat al-Shu'arā'*, God uses the first-person plural in these verses: 26:4, 7, 52, 57, 59, 63–66, 119–120, 139, 170, 172–173, 198, 200, 204–205, and 208–209. God uses the first-person singular in one verse: 26:221. God the narrator addresses the second-person singular (often assumed to be addressing Prophet Muḥammad) in 26:3, 9, 10, 68–69, 104, 122, 140, 159, 175, 191, 194, 205, 213–219, 221, and 225. The stories describe the messengers in the third person, and unlike the Ṣāliḥ iteration in *Sūrat al-Qamar*, God never addresses the messengers in the second person. Rather, in *Sūrat al-Shu'arā'*, God the narrator narrates the stories and, within them, God and a character may speak in dialogue. Here, it is useful to mention the layers of narration within the Qur'ān, with God as narrator and as a character in the stories.[10] The variations in focalization in the two *sūras*

**Table 7.3** A Comparison of the Structure of *Sūrat al-Shu'arā'* and *Sūrat al-Qamar*

| *Sūrat al-Shu'arā'* | | | *Sūrat al-Qamar* | | |
|---|---|---|---|---|---|
| **Verses** | **Number of Verses** | **People** | **Verses** | **Number of Verses** | **People** |
| 26:1–9 | 9 | Introduction | 54:1–8 | 8 | Introduction |
| 26:10–68 | 59 | Mūsā | 54:41–51 | 11 | Mūsā |
| 26:69–104 | 36 | Ibrāhīm | --- | --- | --- |
| 26:105–122 | 18 | Nūḥ | 54:9–17 | 8 | Nūḥ |
| 26:123–140 | 18 | Hūd | 54:18–22 | 5 | Hūd |
| 26:141–159 | 19 | Ṣāliḥ | 54:23–32 | 10 | Ṣāliḥ |
| 26:160–175 | 16 | Lūṭ | 54:33–40 | 8 | Lūṭ |
| 26:176–191 | 16 | Shu'ayb | --- | --- | --- |
| 26:192–227 | 36 | Conclusion | 54:52–55 | 4 | Conclusion |

show the varied narrative techniques in the Qur'ān, what the narrator chooses to tell or not tell and how the narrator chooses to tell stories.

We can compare the same stories in the two *sūras*. As mentioned, the story of Mūsā is the first story in *Sūrat al-Shu'arā'* and is the last story in *Sūrat al-Qamar* (26:10–68 and 54:41–51). It is the longest story in both *sūras*. The two stories are told in very different ways. In fact, as we saw, what we are calling the story of Mūsā in *Sūrat al-Qamar* is introduced with Fir'awn and does not actually mention Mūsā by name at all. It is a very general telling of arrogance, punishment, and disbelief, with parts of it addressed to the second-person plural.

54:41 The people of Pharaoh also received warnings.

42 They rejected all Our signs so We seized them with all Our might and power.

43 "Are your disbelievers any better than these? Were you given an exemption in the Scripture?"

44 Do they perhaps say, "We are a great army and we shall be victorious"?

45 Their forces will be routed and they will turn tail and flee.

46 But the Hour is their appointed time—the Hour is more disastrous and more powerful:

47 truly the wicked are misguided and quite insane—

48 on the Day when they are dragged on their faces in Hell. "Feel the touch of Hell."

49 We have created all things in due measure;

50 when We ordain something it happens at once, in the blink of an eye;

51 We have destroyed the likes of you in the past. Will anyone take heed?

The concluding refrain helps us determine that all of this can be considered the story of Mūsā. There is fluidity in this last story section and in the concluding refrain. In contrast, the story of Mūsā in *Sūrat al-Shuʿarāʾ* is very detailed and follows a chronological narrative discourse. God tells Mūsā to go to Firʿawn, Mūsā asks for help, Mūsā goes to Firʿawn and talks to him, Mūsā shows him his miracles, Firʿawn gathers magicians to challenge Mūsā, Mūsā bests them, they submit in faith, God tells Mūsā to flee with his people, they do, and Firʿawn and his people follow them and then are punished. The story of Mūsā in *Sūrat al-Qamar* is really the story of Firʿawn and other disbelievers and is mostly about accountability and punishment in hellfire; the story of Mūsā in *Sūrat al-Shuʿarāʾ* is a more straightforward telling of Mūsā's interactions with Firʿawn.

The story of Ibrāhīm is only in 26:69–104. This is noteworthy because Ibrāhīm is a frequently mentioned prophet in the Qurʾān. The story of Ibrāhīm in *Sūrat al-Shuʿarāʾ* includes a lengthy dialogue between him and his people; this flows into a prayer that he makes to God, which includes him mentioning Judgment Day; and then flows into a scene of Judgment Day, in which the people of hellfire speak (26:96–102). *Sūrat al-Qamar* also portrays a scene in the afterlife (54:43–55), but it is stylistically different in that in *Sūrat al-Shuʿarāʾ* people speak and express their regret for the choices they made; in *Sūrat al-Qamar*, God speaks but people do not. People speaking in *Sūrat al-Shuʿarāʾ* is consistent with its being a dialogue-heavy *sūra*. In addition, *Sūrat al-Shuʿarāʾ* emphasizes the themes of possessions and ancestors and descendants, while *Sūrat al-Qamar* does not. In part, the story of Ibrāhīm, which is only in *Sūrat al-Shuʿarāʾ*, addresses the topic of ancestors and descendants. In *Sūrat al-Shuʿarāʾ*, for example, we see sharp contrasts between negative portrayals of parents and their children: Ibrāhīm's father is unreceptive to his son's message and even threatens him. Firʿawn, who is at least as threatening as Ibrāhīm's father, presents himself as a father-figure to Mūsā, but Mūsā replies that he enslaved Mūsā's people. The theme of ancestors and descendants is present throughout *Sūrat al-Shuʿarāʾ* but not in *Sūrat al-Qamar*. Correspondingly, some of the roots that help portray this theme are in *Sūrat al-Shuʿarāʾ* but not even once in *Sūrat al-Qamar*. These are *ʾ-b-w, b-n-y, w-r-th* and *q-d-m*. Connected with ancestors and descendants is the idea of inheritance, which God diverts from one people to another (26:57–59), and Ibrāhīm prays to inherit gardens of paradise (26:85).

The story of Nūḥ is in 26:105–122 and 54:9–17. In *Sūrat al-Shuʿarāʾ* there is a dialogue between Nūḥ and his people; we see them questioning him about the people who follow him, and we see his response. In *Sūrat al-Qamar*, we see that they call him "mad" and "rebuke" him, but that is the only thing we could consider a dialogue (54:9). In both stories, Nūḥ prays to God and says he is "defeated" and asks for "help" (54:10), but without overlapping words. In *Sūrat al-Shuʿarāʾ*, Nūḥ says: "My Lord, my people have rejected me, so make a firm judgement between me and them, and save me and my believing followers" (26:117–118). And then, his people are punished and those who believe are saved (26:119–120 and 54:11–15). Although the *Sūrat al-Qamar* version is shorter, it includes a description of the punishment, which is absent from the *Sūrat al-Shuʿarāʾ* iteration. So the *Sūrat al-Qamar* version is shorter and has a description of the punishment, and the *Sūrat al-Shuʿarāʾ* iteration has a dialogue between Nūḥ and his people.

We find the same notable differences between the stories of Hūd and Nūḥ in *Sūrat al-Qamar* and *Sūrat al-Shuʿarāʾ* (54:18–22 and 26:123–140). In *Sūrat al-Qamar*, four verses describe the punishment of Hūd's people. In *Sūrat al-Shuʿarāʾ* we instead have a lengthy dialogue between Hūd and his people. In fact, the punishment is simply tagged on to the beginning of the refrain in *Sūrat al-Shuʿarāʾ* (26:139). Hūd also mentions his fear that his people will be punished (26:135). We learn in *Sūrat al-Shuʿarāʾ* what people were doing that is considered immoral (26:128–134), something missing from *Sūrat al-Qamar*. The *Sūrat al-Qamar* iteration mentions the people's disbelief and then is entirely about punishment.

The story of Ṣāliḥ is in 26:141–159 and 54:23–32, and it does not follow the same patterns as the stories of Hūd and Nūḥ in the two *sūras*. We are told how Ṣāliḥ's people kill the camel (54:29) and how they are in turn destroyed (54:30–31). We do not hear Ṣāliḥ speak, although we hear what God tells him to say and we assume that he does (54:28).[11] The people speak for themselves, in dialogue: "they said, 'What? A man? Why should we follow a lone man from amongst ourselves? That would be misguided; quite insane!'" (54:24). It may be surprising that Ṣāliḥ does not get space to speak, but the people who reject him do. Perhaps this contrasts with us also seeing their crime and their punishment. In *Sūrat al-Shuʿarāʾ*, first are a number of verses of Ṣāliḥ's speech (26:146–52), then his people respond to him (26:153–154), he replies (26:155–156), the narrator tells us that they killed the camel (26:157), and then they are punished (26:158). We see here how repetition can have variation and how repetition is not necessarily repetitive.

The story of Lūṭ is in 26:160–175 and 54:33–40. It goes back to having the same differences between the iterations of the stories of Nūḥ and Hūd. *Sūrat al-Qamar* includes a description of the punishment itself, while *Sūrat al-Shuʿarāʾ* has a dialogue between Lūṭ and his people. In *Sūrat al-Qamar* there is also an explanation of the sin of Lūṭ's people (54:37).

The story of Shu'ayb is only in 26:176–191. It includes a dialogue between Shu'ayb and his people. It does mention the punishment that befalls the people, but this is after they dare Shu'ayb to send a punishment upon them.

Finally, we can compare the conclusions of the two *sūras*. In *Sūrat al-Qamar*, it is hard to separate the story of Mūsā from the conclusion—the story flows into the conclusion. The conclusion in *Sūrat al-Shu'arā'* discusses revelation and addresses the second-person singular, often interpreted as Prophet Muḥammad (26:194). *Sūrat al-Shu'arā'* mentions punishment (26:204–213) and that no one is punished by God without first having a warner (26:208).

Another way we can compare the *sūras* is to look at the frequently repeated root *r-s-l* in both *sūras*. To start, *r-s-l* occurs in 54:19, 54:27, 54:31, 54:34, 26:13, 26:16, 26:17, 26:21, 26:27 twice, 26:53, 26:105, 26:107, 26:123, 26:125, 26:141, 26:143, 26:160, 26:162, 26:176, and 26:178. In *Sūrat al-Qamar*, three of the four verses are clearly about a punishment that God sends to a people (54:19, 54:31, and 54:34). The remaining verse is about God sending a camel to the people as a test (54:27). The root *r-s-l* has a different focus in *Sūrat al-Shu'arā'*. There, in Mūsā's story, first Mūsā asks God to send Hārūn with him (26:13). God tells Mūsā to tell Fir'awn he is a messenger (26:16), and he does (26:21). He and Hārūn ask Fir'awn to send the Banī Isrā'īl with them (26:17). Fir'awn mocks the messenger sent to the people (26:27, twice). Finally, Fir'awn sends his people after Mūsā and his people after they run away (26:53). The remaining occurrences of the root *r-s-l* are in the introductory refrains of the stories of Nūḥ, Hūd, Ṣāliḥ, Lūṭ, and Shu'ayb, where the people did not believe their messenger, and the messenger says he is a messenger (26:105, 26:107, 26:123, 26:125, 26:141, 26:143, 26:160, 26:162, 26:176, and 26:178). So, in *Sūrat al-Qamar*, the *r-s-l* root is used mostly for punishments being sent, and in *Sūrat al-Shu'arā'*, it is used for messengers that are sent and rejected.

In all the verses except one, God is the one sending someone or something to people. In the exceptional verse, Mūsā asks Fir'awn to send the people with him. It is surprising that Fir'awn is verbally given God's role in sending people. Perhaps this is to flatter his ego or to set up a sharp contrast between Fir'awn and God, but when Fir'awn indeed does not send the people willingly, God commands Mūsā to flee with the people. God uses the word *'ibādī*, as discussed in the previous chapter, so God asserts God's supreme sovereignty over all people and things—especially over Fir'awn and the sovereignty he has usurped.

This analysis has brought to light a difference on a large scale between the two *sūras*. The content of the stories in *Sūrat al-Qamar* focuses on punishment, whereas the content of the stories in *Sūrat al-Shuʿarā'* focuses on how prophets try to convince their people and what their people say in response. Of course, there are exceptions, but they do not erase the pattern. This answers the question we posed in the beginning of the analysis of *Sūrat al-Qamar. Sūrat al-Qamar* does not include Mūsā's name, instead presenting Firʿawn's (54:41). Similarly, Hūd (sent to the people of ʿĀd) and Ṣāliḥ (sent to the people of Thamūd) are not mentioned because the focus is really on the people who rejected the prophets and their punishments. In retrospect, the verses in the introduction that say "far-reaching wisdom--but these warnings do not help: / so [Prophet] turn away from them. On the Day the Summoner will summon them to a horrific event" (54:5–6) prefigure how the stories will be narrated and what the focus of the *sūra* will be—rejection of the message and punishment.

*Sūrat al-Shuʿarā'* focuses thematically on relationships between people and messengers. *Sūrat al-Qamar* focuses on the relationship between the audience and the Qur'ān by making the audience fearful, then encouraging the audience to read, memorize, and preserve the Qur'ān. We saw that human claims to power is a prominent underlying theme in *Sūrat al-Shuʿarā'*. In *Sūrat al-Qamar*, God emphasizes God's power and human weakness. Humans think they can judge what is extraordinary or ordinary, but what they think is ordinary can become a means of their destruction.

In both *sūras*, nature is portrayed as signs of Judgment Day, nature is turned into a punishment, then it is a test, and finally, it is a reward. There are other similarities between the *sūras*. Both *sūras* play with the idea of lies and liars. The root *k-dh-b* occurs in the following verses in the *sūras*: 54:3, 54:9, 54:18, 54:23, 54:25, 54:26, 54:33, 54:42, 26:6, 26:12, 26:105, 26:117, 26:123, 26:139, 26:141, 26:160, 26:176, 26:186, 26:189, and 26:223. In *Sūrat al-Shuʿarā'*, disbelievers call messengers liars (26:6, 26:105, 26:123, 26:139, 26:141, 26:160, 26:176, 26:186, and 26:189), only to realize in hell that they do not have a truthful person to rely on. Ironically, they rejected the truthful messengers who crossed their paths in life and even challenged them to punish them. Mūsā tells God he fears his people will call him a liar (26:12); similarly, Nūḥ tells God that his people called him a liar (26:117). Finally, there is a description by God of liars (26:223). In *Sūrat al-Qamar*, first is a verse generally saying that people see signs (*āyāt*) of God and say they are lies (54:3). Then, in the introductions to the stories of Nūḥ, Hūd, Ṣāliḥ, Lūṭ, and Mūsā, we read that their people called them liars (54:9, 54:18, 54:23, 54:33, and 54:42). Mūsā's section, as mentioned earlier, is a bit unusual in that it names Firʿawn, rather than Mūsā, and mentions that the people of Firʿawn rejected God's signs (54:42). In the story of Ṣāliḥ, there are two additional uses of *k-dh-b*: his people wonder at how he has received revelation and that he must be a liar (54:25), then God says they will come to know who is actually a liar (54:26). So in both *sūras*, almost every use of the *k-dh-b* root is about people rejecting messengers or signs of God, whereas God calls those people liars (54:26) and describes liars who receive revelation from devils and contrasts them with those who trust God and pray (26:217–223).

Both *sūras* discuss misguidance or error, with the *ḍ-l-l* root. We find *ḍ-l-l* in Ṣāliḥ's and Mūsā's stories: there is a contrast between Ṣāliḥ's people saying that following a person would be an error, *ḍalāl* (54:24), and God using the same word, *ḍalāl*, to describe Fir'awn and Mūsā's people (54:47). In *Sūrat al-Shu'arā'*, Mūsā uses this root to describe himself when he accidentally killed a person (26:20), Ibrāhīm describes his father with this root, when he prays for God to forgive him (26:86). Then there is a scene in hell when disbelievers realize and say they were in error (26:97) and that other people misled them (26:99). This contrasts with Mūsā, who, fortunately, realizes his mistake in this life, rather than in the afterlife. Amongst the *ḍ-l-l* verses, the only one in which people are ironically incorrect about what would be an error is in Ṣāliḥ's story (54:24). All the other uses of *ḍ-l-l* are when God or people correctly label their own or others' actions as incorrect. Through this contrast, the Qur'ān emphasizes the flawed reasoning of Ṣāliḥ's people. In terms of reasons for not believing, in both *sūras*, people object that the prophets are ordinary people like them, using the root *b-sh-r* (26:154, 26:186, and 54:24).

As discussed in *Sūrat al-Shu'arā'*, the root *t-b-'* is first in Mūsā's story when the people consider following the magicians if they are victorious (26:40). God tells Mūsā to escape because they are being chased by Fir'awn and his people (26:52 and 26:60). Nūḥ's people insult those who follow him (26:111). In contrast, in *Sūrat al-Qamar*, Ṣāliḥ's people object to following a person like themselves (54:24). God tells Prophet Muḥammad to lower his wings to those who follow him, (26:215), and later, we are told that those who are lost follow the poets (26:224). It may look like a contradiction that Prophet Muḥammad is told to turn away from people and is told to show them compassion, but it is not. The Prophet does different things for and with different people: he turns away from disbelievers (54:6) but shows compassion to believers (26:215). In the example of Fir'awn, the people physically follow Mūsā's people because they mentally or spiritually follow Fir'awn. In *Sūrat al-Qamar*, disbelievers follow their whims (54:3). So in the two *sūras* there are people physically and/or spiritually following their own whims, magicians, poets, Nūḥ, and Muḥammad, but there are also people objecting to following a messenger because he is like themselves and presumably not an extraordinary person or because they do not like the messengers' other followers.

## VI. Conclusion

This has been a methodical analysis and comparison of stories and repetition within a *sūra* and between two *sūras*. We looked at repetition in and between the *sūras* on large and small structural scales—roots, words, refrains, themes, stories, structure, and focalization. Through this analysis, we found that the *sūras* do not overlap completely in the stories they include. Even those that overlap are told from different focalization, with a different focus, and with different narrative techniques. Both *sūras* have refrains, sometimes adhered to more closely than others with almost no overlap across *sūras*. All these details give the *sūras* different flavors, which I explore in a systematic manner.

There is some, but not overwhelming amounts of, overlap between repeated root letters across *sūras*. In both *sūras*, root letters are used in similar ways, where first a disbeliever might use a word with certain root letters, then God uses the same root in a different way to show what really is true or will happen. In terms of style, we find repetition in meaning and variation through outliers. Outliers bring contrast to themes and ideas and complicate them.

Throughout this study, we saw that different *sūras*, through narrative technique, have different foci. In *Sūrat al-Qamar*, we see that the Qur'ān can not only save people, but the Qur'ān also gives stability, constancy, and preservation, the way that God does for the believers in the story. While *Sūrat al-Qamar* has a focus on punishment and the relationship between the audience and the Qur'ān, *Sūrat al-Shu'arā'* has a focus on the relationship between people and messengers, as well as the relationship between people and power.

# 8
# Conclusion
## Connections, Narrative, and Power

We can now think about the conclusions found throughout this book. While I did not seek out stories of families in this book, many of the stories I examine do involve families—biological and through adoption, as seen in Chapter 2. Within families, we see rejection (Ibrāhīm's father) and acceptance (Firʿawn/Mūsā and al-ʿAzīz/Yūsuf). There is also parent and child separation (Mūsā and his mother, and Ibrāhīm sacrificing his child).

I explore large-scale structure and connections between thirteen scenes in Qur'ānic stories in Chapter 2. These connections bring together the themes of having children, sacrificing children, connecting to God with one's children, theft, and accusations of theft. The stories of Maryam's mother, Maryam, Zakariyyā, Ibrāhīm, Mūsā's mother, and Yūsuf are all woven together. There are parallels, reversals, swerves, and inverted triangles. This book looks at connections, interactions, and relationships between words, phrases, verses, stories, narrative, and non-narrative.

In Chapters 2 and 6, we find complicated portrayals of slavery in the stories in this book: Mūsā and Yūsuf are compared to each other, and both of their stories include slavery. We see some of the terrors of slavery in the story of Yūsuf: in the pain of his separation from his father and in the *Sūra*, we see his father's "senility" and blindness; in Yūsuf's suffering expressed in his desire for prison (instead of lack of agency over his sexual self) and in asserting his agency to choose his career once free. Firʿawn, in Mūsā's story, asserts his control over people he enslaves, only for God to turn everything upside down and give his possessions to those very same people, God's devotees.

In Chapter 3, we see the power of focalization in the Qur'ān. When Firʿawn tells Mūsā his life story, he does so to make Mūsā feel bad for being disobedient to Firʿawn, the generous adoptive father. This is completely different from when God tells Mūsā his life story. This contrast highlights focalization, authority, and repetition. Firʿawn is a usurper, through and through. He usurps God's role as master of the universe, as master of people,

*How the Qur'ān Works*. Leyla Ozgur Alhassen, Oxford University Press. © Oxford University Press 2023.
DOI: 10.1093/oso/9780197654606.003.0008

and even as master of history and narrative. Fir'awn tries to reshape history when he tells it to Mūsā, and, in observing this, we learn that repetition can be connected to authority and truth. Multiple iterations provide opportunities to think about stories in different ways and at different times in our lives. Focalization and storytelling through Fir'awn draw our attention and show us how he manipulates the truth for his own gain. This is characterization at the same time, and we see that he is manipulative, hypocritical, and a usurper. Also striking here is that the Qur'ān actually allows Fir'awn to manipulate the narrative, at least once. This shows that the Qur'ān uses the narrative to show Fir'awn's nature, trusting that the audience will understand that Fir'awn is manipulating the story.

Chapter 4 explores examples of God the narrator merging time and space, confirming God the creator's role as creator: God created everything, and God can do as God wills. The examples of ellipsis and prolepse show theological beliefs in the Qur'ān are not just didactic, but they are also reflected in the storytelling. In Chapter 4, we thought about the interactions between time and repetition, and that repetition draws the audience to reflect on the divine.

In Chapter 5, we see how exchange encounters can be seen through the lens of the verse about appealing to God and God answering a believer's request (2:186), a verse that is situated amid verses about fasting. The exchange encounters highlight that asking for things from God is not a problem; the issue is belief, which is reflected in the manner of asking. Through these stories, we see how Qur'ānic narratives are woven together through echoing phrases and actions, with metanarrative and legal verses, to reinforce theological beliefs. This demonstrates that a narratological analysis that focuses comprehensively on repetition in Qur'ānic portrayals and semantic echoes is fundamental in establishing an understanding of Qur'ānic stories. We also see how narratives and legal verses are connected in the Qur'ān—the Qur'ānic verses are not disjointed, even if previous analyses of them are.

Chapter 6 focused on repetition in *Sūrat al-Shu'arā'*, in its series of stories, refrains, root letters, and themes. This analysis brings to light the various scales of repetition in the Qur'ān and how repetition is used as a narrative device for the explication and complication of themes and character development. Perhaps most surprisingly, the Qur'ān discusses Fir'awn at his level and based on his claims: Fir'awn claims to be a god, so he is parallel to and contrasted with God; the magicians are parallel to and contrasted with Mūsā. Through this, then, magic is parallel to and contrasted with inspiration from God, and reward and punishment in this life are parallel to and contrasted with reward and punishment in the afterlife. The *sūra* focuses on the theme of messengers: where does inspiration come from (God versus inspiration coming from alternate sources to people who are not messengers); what do messengers expect from people (no reward, not even belief; messengers do not even expect the satisfaction of success); messengers of God have no control over whether people choose to believe or not; those who choose to believe should obey God and their messenger; and messengers deliver their message as a fulfillment to God, not in expectation of reward or belief from people. Throughout the *sūra*, we also see the theme of power; the Qur'ān addresses the fact that people can use claims of inspiration as a means to power.

Chapter 7 methodically analyzes and compares stories and repetition within a *sūra* and between two *sūras*. We looked at repetition in and between *Sūrat al-Shu'arā'* and *Sūrat al-Qamar*, on large and small structural scales—roots, words, refrains, themes, stories, structures, and focalization. Through this analysis, we found that the *sūras* do not overlap completely in the stories they include. Even those that overlap are told from different focalization, with a different focus, and with different narrative techniques. Both *sūras* have refrains, sometimes adhered to more closely than others, and with almost no overlap across *sūras*. All these details give the *sūras* different flavors, which I explore in a systematic manner. Throughout that chapter, we saw that different *sūras*, through narrative technique, have different foci. In *Sūrat al-Qamar*, we see that the Qur'ān can not only save people, the Qur'ān also provides stability, constancy, and preservation, the way that God does for the believers in the story. While *Sūrat al-Qamar* has a focus on punishment and the relationship between the audience and the Qur'ān, *Sūrat al-Shu'arā'* has a focus on the relationship between people and messengers, as well as the relationship between people and power.

So, throughout the book, we have the themes of families, connections, slavery, power, faith, messengers, inspiration, and one's relationship with the Qur'ān. In terms of how to read and analyze the Qur'ān, we see connections between legal and narrative verses and between theology and narrative. Analysis focused on narrative is not an accessory; it is a means to better understand the Qur'ān as a whole.

One can discuss venues for further research as a result of the analysis in this book. In Chapter 2, we saw how the structure of an inverted triangle helps us understand the disconnected letters that start *Sūrat Yusuf*. Do we see this pattern in any of the other *sūras* with disconnected letters? Does this structure help us understand other puzzling verses in the Qur'ān?

The analysis in Chapter 3 led us to find a concentric construction across *sūras*, in the story of Mūsā throwing his staff in front of different audiences. One can analyze other Qur'ānic stories to see if there are other concentric constructions across *sūras*. What other patterns—within and across *sūras*—exist that we may not notice immediately?

Chapter 5 brought us to see how the legal verses about fasting connect with the narrative portrayals of fasting—and much more. One can analyze Qur'ānic legal injunctions and stories when they seem connected and explore how they are connected. This will move us toward a holistic analysis of the Qur'ān. For example, might any of the legal verses be connected semantically with any Qur'ānic stories? Or can we find any patterns that help us understand them? In this chapter, we also saw how word play in a legal verse connects one legal injunction with another. In what other legal passages in the Qur'ān is there word play and how can it help us better understand those passages and larger underlying morals?

A completely different direction would be to look at how echoes effect Qur'ānic recitation and reception. How can Western academics better approach the Qur'ān given its oral nature?

I have long enjoyed seeing connections between things. I now realize that this book is all about connections, because that is what repetition does: it connects one thing with another. It is up to the audience to see those connections, to explore them with a sense of curiosity, and to find underlying themes and subtexts. This is how the Qur'ān adds sophistication and emotional nuances to the text.

## Appendix A: Mūsā

Looking at all the stories about Mūsā in the Qur'ān, there are four stories with forty-two iterations. A summary of the charts is in Figure A.1.

What follows are tables that include and summarize all the stories in the Qur'ān about Mūsā. When a story could be categorized under a few headings, I leaned toward one way if it included a key word from a particular story. For example, 37:114–122 tells Mūsā's story generally and could have been included in the Mūsā and Fir'awn category, however, I put it in the Mūsā and the book category, since it mentions the book, while it does not explicitly mention Fir'awn by name. Similarly, 2:49–74 could be categorized as Mūsā's people and the golden cow, with one iteration. However, the beginning of this story, 2:49–66, includes a history of Mūsā and his people, so I include it in that category. For research purposes, it may be argued that it is more useful to show how stories overlap, when they do, than to show them as independent stories. In addition, some iterations move from one story (e.g., Mūsā and Fir'awn) to another (Mūsā and his people). In these three cases, I put the relevant verses in Tables A.1 and A.3 and made note of this. I chose to repeat the same verses instead of disjointing the iterations.

Finally, there is a group of verses that are not clearly stories but do mention Mūsā. I have included those verses in a separate table, Table A.5, for reference. All of these tables can serve as a resource for scholars interested in a specific episode from Mūsā's story, type-scenes in the Qur'ān, repetition in the Qur'ān, or Qur'ānic narrative style more generally.

**Mūsā and Fir'awn (twenty-four iterations)**: 7:103–174,[1] 10:75–94, 11:96–100,[2] 14:4–8,[3] 17:101–104,[4] 19:51–53, 20:9–100,[5] 23:45–49,[6] 25:35–36, 26:10–68, 27:7–14, 28:1–50,[7] 29:39–40,[8] 40:23–48,[9] 43:46–56, 44:17–33,[10] 51:38–40,[11] 54:41–43,[12] 66:11, 69:9–10, 73:15–16, 79:15–26,[13] 85:17–22, 89:10–14.

Table A.1 looks at all the iterations about Mūsā and Fir'awn in the Qur'ān.[14] Some of these stories move into other stories. Thus, in addition to being in the Mūsā and Fir'awn table, I include 7:148–174, 14:7–8, and 20:83–100 in Table A.3 of Mūsā and his people. Also, the story of the wife of Fir'awn (66:11)

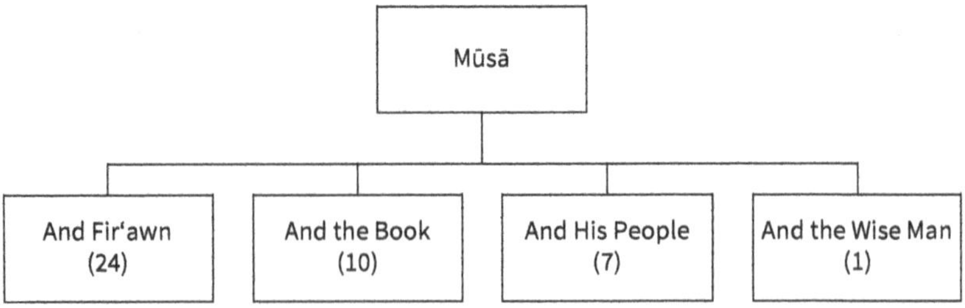


**Figure A.1** The Story of Mūsā in the Qur'ān

is included in the Mūsā and Fir'awn story, even though it does not mention Mūsā.

The total number of verses included by Robinson is less than the ones included in this study, in spite of not including 75:15–16 here. Although Robinson includes 75:15–16, I see no indication that these verses refer to Mūsā. No name is mentioned, and there is no context that makes it evident that it is Mūsā.[15]

The column on the far right of Table A.1 titled "Total" indicates the total number of times an element occurs; that is, it adds up all the iterations with that element. This is useful for research on repetition in the story. In addition, Figure A.2 is a bar graph that shows how many times each element is told. The most repeated elements are an introduction (twenty-one iterations), the element mentioning that Fir'awn was punished or drowned (eighteen iterations), a conclusion (fifteen iterations), and a command to Mūsā to tell Fir'awn about God (seven iterations).

**Mūsā and the Book (ten iterations):** 6:154, 11:110–111, 17:1–8, 21:48–50, 32:23–24, 37:114–122, 41:45, 45:16–17, 46:12, 53:36

The iterations below all mention Mūsā and a *kitāb* (a book) or *furqān* (scripture). Table A.2 does not include references to Mūsā and the *alwāḥ* (tablets; e.g., 7:145–147); those verses are included elsewhere. The columns in this table and the ones that follow are arranged by length of iteration, with the longest iteration first.

**Mūsā and his people (seven iterations):** 2:49–93,[16] 4:153–162, 5:20–26,[17] 7:148–174,[18] 14:7–8,[19] 20:83–100,[20] 61:5

There are many stories of Banī Isrā'īl in the Qur'ān. In Table A.3, I have only included the stories that mention Mūsā. These include the story of Mūsā's people and the golden calf, as well as stories of the covenant, *mīthāq*.

**Mūsā and the wise man[21] (one iteration):** 18:60–82

**Table A.1** Stories of Mūsā and Fir'awn in the Qur'ān

| Plot Element | Verses | Total |
|---|---|---|
| Narrator's introduction | 7:103, 10:75–77, 11:96–98, 14:4, 17:101, 19:51, 20:1–9, 23:45–47, 25:35, 28:1–3, 29:39, 40:23–24, 43:46, 44:17, 51:38, 54:41, 69:9, 73:15, 79:15, 85:17–20, 89:10–13 | 21 |
| Fir'awn's sins | 28:4, 40:25 | 2 |
| God sent Mūsā to oppressed | 14:5–6, 28:5–6 | 2 |
| Sees fire | 20:10, 27:7, 28:29 | 3 |
| God calls to Mūsā | 19:52, 20:11–16, 27:8–9, 28:30, 79:16 | 5 |
| God asks what's in hand, commands to throw | 20:17–19, 27:10–11, 28:31 | 3 |
| Throws, becomes a snake, don't fear | 20:20–21, 27:10–11, 28:31 | 3 |
| Hand | 20:22, 27:12, 28:32 | 3 |
| Signs | 20:23, 27:13, 43:47–54, 79:20 | 4 |
| Commands to go to Fir'awn | 20:24 and 42–44, 26:10–11, 79:17 | 3 |
| Mūsā asks for help/for his brother | 19:53, 20:25–35, 26:12–14, 28:33–34 | 4 |
| Request is granted | 20:36, 26:15, 28:35 | 3 |
| God says took care of previously | 20:37 | 1 |
| Inspired mother to throw him in the river | 20:38–39, 28:7 | 2 |
| Fir'awn's family finds Mūsā | 28:8–12 | 1 |
| Mūsā's mother is devastated | 28:10 | 1 |
| Mūsā's sister finds him; reunited with mother | 20:40, 28:11–13 | 2 |
| When he matured, God blessed him | 28:14 | 1 |
| Mūsā kills someone accidentally, runs away | 20:40, 26:14 and 18–22, 28:15–21 and 33 | 3 |
| God says made Mūsā for Himself/ chose him | 7:144, 20:41 | 2 |
| Madyan, helps women at well; marriage | 28:22–28 | 1 |
| Mūsā and Hārūn say they're scared; don't be | 20:45–46 | 1 |
| Tell Fir'awn about God | 7:104–5, 17:102, 20:47–48, 26:16–17, 28:36, 44:18–21, 79:18–19 | 7 |
| Mūsā and Fir'awn talk about God | 20:49–55, 26:23–29, 28:37–39 | 3 |
| Mūsā and Fir'awn talk about signs | 7:106, 26:30–31 | 2 |
| Throws staff | 7:107, 20:56, 26:32 | 3 |
| Hand becomes white | 7:108, 20:56, 26:33 | 3 |
| *Mala'* | 7:109, 26:34 | 2 |

*(continued)*

**Table A.1** Continued

| Plot Element | Verses | Total |
|---|---|---|
| Accuse Mūsā of trying to take over | 7:110, 10:78, 20:57 and 63–64, 26:35, 40:26 | 5 |
| Fir'awn's response to signs | 51:39, 79:21–23 | 2 |
| Mūsā's response | 40:27 | 1 |
| Believer from Fir'awn's people | 40:28–35 | 1 |
| Fir'awn challenges Mūsā | 20:58–59, 79:24 | 2 |
| Fir'awn tells Hāmān to build a tower | 28:38, 40:36–37 | 1 |
| Man who believes responds | 40:38–44 | 1 |
| Fir'awn gathers magicians | 7:111–112, 10:79, 20:60, 26:36–40 | 4 |
| Magicians ask for a reward and are promised | 7:113–4, 26:41–42 | 2 |
| Mūsā warns them | 20:61 | 1 |
| They debate what to do | 20:62 | 1 |
| They ask who should throw first | 7:115, 20:65 | 2 |
| Mūsā tells them to go first | 7:116, 10:80–82, 20:66, 26:43–44 | 4 |
| Mūsā scared; God comforts | 20:67–69 | 1 |
| Mūsā throws staff | 7:117–119, 20:69, 26:45 | 3 |
| Magicians prostrate | 7:120, 20:70, 26:46 | 3 |
| Magicians say: we believe in the Lord | 7:121, 20:70, 26:47 | 3 |
| The Lord of Mūsā and Hārūn | 7:122, 20:70, 26:48 | 3 |
| Fir'awn asks the magicians how they believe | 7:123, 20:71 | 2 |
| Fir'awn threatens the magicians | 7:123–124, 20:71, 26:49 | 3 |
| Magicians reply with faith | 7:125–126, 20:72–76, 26:50–51 | 3 |
| Fir'awn threatens people | 7:127 | 1 |
| Few people believe | 10:83 | 1 |
| God inspires Mūsā to leave secretly | 20:77, 26:52, 44:22–23 | 3 |
| Fir'awn sends people after Mūsā's people | 26:53–60 | 1 |
| Mūsā's people are scared when see water | 26:61–62 | 1 |
| Mūsā parts the sea | 26:63–65 | 1 |
| Mūsā tells people to pray/he prays | 7:128–129, 10:84–89 | 2 |
| Fir'awn's people reject signs | 7:130–135 | 1 |
| Drown in water/punished | 7:136–137, 10:90–92, 11:99, 17:103, 20:78–79, 23:48, 25:36, 26:66, 28:40–42, 29:40, 40:45–46, 43:55, 44:24–31, 51:40, 54:42, 69:10, 73:16, 79:25 | 18 |

**Table A.1** Continued

| Plot Element | Verses | Total |
|---|---|---|
| Narrator's commentary | 28:43–46 | 1 |
| Want idol | 7:138–140 | 1 |
| God saved people from Fir'awn | 7:141 | 1 |
| 40 days then meet with God | 7:142 | 1 |
| Meets with God, wants to see | 7:143, 20:83–85 | 2 |
| Tablets | 7:145–147 and 154 | 1 |
| Golden calf | 7:148, 20:87–91 | 2 |
| Regret | 7:149 | 1 |
| Mūsā returns | 7:150, 20:86 | 2 |
| Mūsā questions the people | 20:86–98 | 1 |
| Mūsā and his people | 7:151–171, 14:7–8, 17:104, 20:80–82 | 4 |
| Fir'awn's wife is an example | 66:11 | 1 |
| Conclusion | 7:172–174, 10:93–94, 11:100, 20:99–100, 23:49, 26:67–68, 27:14, 28:47–50, 40:47–55, 43:56, 44:32–33, 54:43, 79:26, 85:21–22, 89:14 | 15 |

Even though this story has only one iteration, it is represented in Table A.4 in order to show the various elements in the story; and it can be used in comparison to other tables.

## Other Verses About Mūsā

Table A.5 includes verses related to Mūsā in the Qur'ān but are not included in the previous tables because they are not stories of Mūsā.

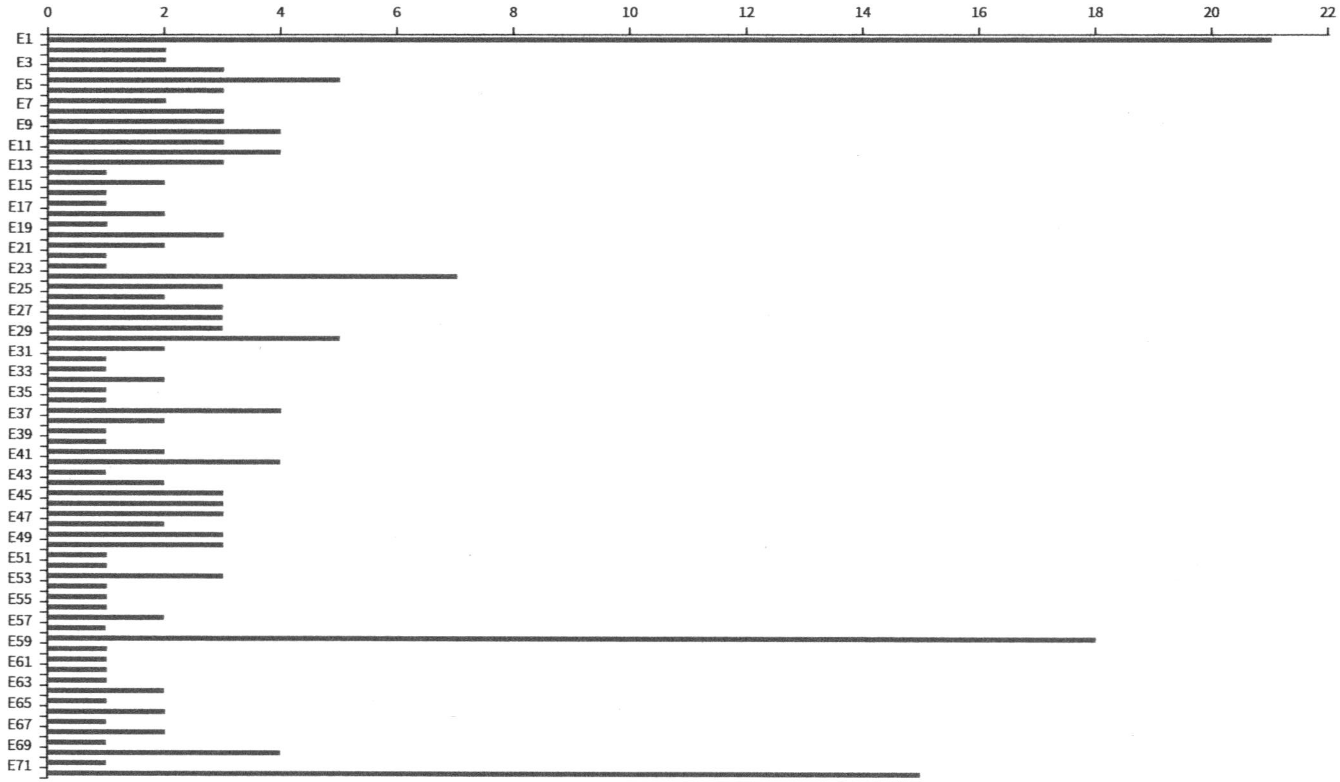


**Figure A.2** Number of Times Elements Are Repeated

**Table A.2** Stories of Mūsā and the Book in the Qur'ān

| | **37:114–122** | **17:1–8** | **21:48–50** | **11:110–111** | **32:23–24** | **45:16–17** | **46:12** | **6:154** | **41:45** | **53:36** |
|---|---|---|---|---|---|---|---|---|---|---|
| Introduction | 37:114 | 17:1 | | | | | | | | |
| God made Mūsā and Hārūn victorious | 37:115–116 | | | | | | | | | |
| Scriptures/book of Mūsā | 37:117 | 17:2 | 21:48 | 11:110 | 32:23 | 45:16 | 46:12 | 6:154 | 41:45 | 53:36 |
| There was some disagreement about it | | | | 11:110 | | 45:17 | | | 41:45 | |
| Everyone will get what they deserve | | 17:8 | | 11:111 | | 45:17 | | | | |
| You descendants of Nūḥ | | 17:3 | | | | | | | | |
| God's decree to the Children of Israel | | 17:4–7 | | | | | | | | |
| A reminder for those who fear God | | | 21:49–50 | | | | | | | |
| Conclusion | 37:118–122 | | | | 32:24 | | | | | |

**Table A.3** Stories of Mūsā and His People in the Qur'ān

| | 2:49–93 | 7:148–174 | 20:83–100 | 4:153–162 | 5:20–26 | 14:7–8 | 61:5 |
|---|---|---|---|---|---|---|---|
| God saved the people from Fir'awn | 2:49–50 | | | | | | |
| God told people to be grateful | | | | | | 14:7 | |
| Mūsā told people that God does not need their belief | | | | | | 14:8 | |
| The people worshipped the calf | 2:51, 2:92 | 7:148–152 | 20:83–91 | 4:153 | | | |
| Mūsā questions the people about the calf and punishes al-Sāmirī | | | 20:92–97 | | | | |
| God forgave them | 2:52 | 7:153 | | | | | |
| God gave Mūsā the book/tablets | 2:53, 2:78–79 | 7:154 | | | | | |
| Mūsā told his people they wronged themselves | 2:54 | | | | | | |
| The people told Mūsā they will not believe until they see God | 2:55–56 | | | | | | |
| God's blessings to the people | 2:57 | | | | 5:20 | | |
| Mūsā chose people to meet with God | | 7:155–156 | | | | | |
| Reward for those who do good | | 7:157 | | | | | |
| Those who believe in God | | 7:158 | | | | | |
| Good people in Mūsā's community | | 7:159 | | | | | |
| Told to enter the sacred land | 2:58 | 7:161 | | | 5:21 | | |
| The people refuse | 2:59 | 7:162 | | | 5:22 | | |
| Two believers told them to enter | | | | | 5:23 | | |
| The people tell Mūsā to kill the bad people in the land | | | | | 5:24 | | |
| Mūsā prays to God | | 7:151 | | | 5:25 | | |
| God said the land is forbidden to them | | | | | 5:26 | | |
| Mūsā struck a rock and 12 springs gushed forth | 2:60 | 7:160 | | | | | |
| Asked for different foods | 2:61 | | | | | | |

**Table A.3** Continued

| | 2:49–93 | 7:148–174 | 20:83–100 | 4:153–162 | 5:20–26 | 14:7–8 | 61:5 |
|---|---|---|---|---|---|---|---|
| Those who believe and do good will be rewarded | 2:62 | | | | | | |
| Made a covenant and turned away from that | 2:63–64, 2:83–84, 2:93 | | | 4:154–155 | | | |
| Those who broke the Sabbath and were punished | 2:65–66 | 7:163–166 | | | | | |
| Mūsā told the people to sacrifice a cow | 2:67 | | | | | | |
| They ask him what kind of cow and he replies | 2:68 | | | | | | |
| They ask him to clarify what color the cow is and he replies | 2:69 | | | | | | |
| They ask him to clarify further | 2:70 | | | | | | |
| He says it is a perfect cow; they tell him he is correct and slaughter it | 2:71 | | | | | | |
| They kill someone and blame each other | 2:72 | | | | | | |
| God told them to strike him with part of it | 2:73 | | | | | | |
| Even after that their hearts became as hard as rocks | 2:74 | | | | | | |
| Mūsā asks his people why they hurt him | | | | | | | 61:5 |
| Punishment and reward; those who disobey and obey | | 7:167–170 | | | | | |
| God raised the mountain above them | | 7:171 | | | | | |
| Children of Ādām testify | | 7:172 | | | | | |
| Disbelief | | 7:173 | | | | | |
| God explains the *āyāt* | | 7:174 | | | | | |
| Commentary | 2:75–77, 80–82, 85–91 | | 20:98–100 | 4:155–162 | | | |

**Table A.4** Story of Mūsā and the Wise Man in the Qur'ān

| | |
|---|---|
| Mūsā says he won't rest until he is where the seas join | 18:60 |
| Forget the spot; leave their fish there | 18:61 |
| Realize what happened | 18:62–63 |
| Turn back | 18:64 |
| Come upon a man of knowledge | 18:65 |
| Mūsā asks if he can follow and learn from him | 18:66 |
| The man says Mūsā won't be patient | 18:67–68 |
| Mūsā says he will try | 18:69 |
| The man tells Mūsā he cannot ask him questions | 18:70 |
| They embark a ship, and the man damages it; Mūsā comments | 18:71 |
| The man tells Mūsā, didn't I tell you, you wouldn't be patient? | 18:72, 18:75 |
| Mūsā asks for forgiveness | 18:73 |
| They continue and the man kills a young man; Mūsā comments | 18:74 |
| Mūsā says: if I ask you again, you don't have to continue with me | 18:76 |
| They ask some people for food and the people refuse; the man fixes a wall | 18:77 |
| The man says this is the end, but I will explain | 18:78 |
| The ship belonged to needy people and a king was capturing ships | 18:79 |
| The young boy's parents were faithful; he would have brought wickedness | 18:80 |
| We wished for God to give them something better | 18:81 |
| The wall belonged to two orphans and their treasure was beneath it | 18:82 |

**Table A.5** Verses Related to Mūsā, but Are Not Stories of Mūsā

| Reason Not Included in Tables A.1–A.4 | Verses |
|---|---|
| Mention Banū Isrā'īl only | 2:47–48* |
| Mention Mūsā, but are not stories | 2:108<br>2:136<br>3:84<br>4:164<br>6:84<br>6:91<br>11:17<br>33:69**<br>46:30<br>87:19 |
| Mention Mūsā and are stories but use him as a point of reference; they are not stories in which Mūsā is a character; he is used to identify a group of people | 2:246–248<br>28:76 |
| These verses are not clearly stories | 22:44<br>33:7<br>40:53 |

* Verses 2:49–74 are included in Table A.3.

** Al-Kallās includes 33:69 in his classification: Ṣalāh al-Dīn Khalīl al-Kallās. *Mūsā 'Alayhī al-Salām wa Qawmahu Banū Isrā'īl*. Dār ul-Bashā'ir, 2007, 19.

# Appendix B: *Sūrat al-Shu‘arā’*

Following are tables that relate to *Sūrat al-Shu‘arā’*.

**Table B.1** Frequently Repeated Root Letters in *Sūrat al-Shu‘arā’*

| Verses | *r-b-b* | *’-m-n* | *‘-l-m* | *w-q-y* | *r-s-l* | *’-l-h* | *’-y-y* | *k-dh-b* | *‘-z-z* | *s-ḥ-r* | *b-y-n* | *q-w-m* |
|---|---|---|---|---|---|---|---|---|---|---|---|---|
| 26:1–9 Introduction | 26:9 | 26:3,8 | | | | | 26:2, 4, 8 | 26:6 | 26:9 | | 26:2 | |
| 26:10–68 Mūsā | 26:10, 12, 16, 21, 23, 24, 26 x 2, 28, 47, 48, 50, 51, 62, 68 | 26:47, 49, 51, 67 | 26:16, 23, 34, 37, 38, 47, 49 | 26:11 | 26:13, 16, 17, 21, 27 x 2, 53 | 26:29 | 26:15, 67 | 26:12 | 26:44, 68 | 26:34, 35, 37, 38, 40, 41, 46, 49 | 26:24, 28, 30, 32 | 26:10, 11, 58 |
| 26:69–104 Ibrāhīm | 26:77, 83, 98, 104 | 26:102, 103 | 26:77, 98 | 26:90 | | 26:89, 93, 97 | 26:103 | | 26:104 | | 26:97 | 26:70 |
| 26:105–122 Nūḥ | 26:109, 113, 117, 122 | 26:107, 111, 114, 118, 121 | 26:109, 112 | 26:106, 108, 110 | 26:105, 107 | 26:108, 110 | 26:121 | 26:105, 117 | 26:122 | | 26:115, 118 x 2 | 26:105, 117 |
| 26:123–140 Hūd | 26:127, 140 | 26:125, 139 | 26:127, 132 | 26:124, 126, 131, 132 | 26:123, 125 | 26:126, 26:131 | 26:128, 139 | 26:123, 139 | 26:140 | | | |
| 26:141–159 Ṣāliḥ | 26:145, 159 | 26:143, 146, 158 | 26:145, 155 | 26:142, 144, 150 | 26:141, 143 | 26:144, 26:150 | 26:154, 158 | 26:141 | 26:159 | 26:153 | | |
| 26:160–175 Lūṭ | 26:164, 166, 169, 175 | 26:162, 174 | 26:164, 165 | 26:161, 163 | 26:160, 162 | 26:163 | 26:174 | 26:160 | 26:175 | | | 26:160, 166 |
| 26:176–191 Shu‘ayb | 26:180, 188, 191 | 26:178, 190 | 26:180, 188 | 26:177, 179, 184 | 26:176, 178 | 26:179 | 26:190 | 26:176, 186, 189 | 26:191 | 26:185 | | 26:182 |
| 26:192–227 Conclusion | 26:192 | 26:193, 199, 201, 215, 227 | 26:192, 197 x 2, 220, 227 | | | 26:213 x 2, 26:227 | 26:197 | 26:223 | 26:217 | | 26:195 | 26:218 |
| TOTAL | 36 | 26 | 23 | 17 | 17 | 15 | 14 | 12 | 10 | 10 | 10 | 10 |

**Table B.2** Infrequently Repeated Root Letters in *Sūrat al-Shuʿarāʾ*

| Verses | *ʿ-dh-b* | *t-b-ʿ* | *ʿ-b-d* | *ṣ-d-q* | *ḍ-l-l* | *n-ʿ-m* | *n-ṣ-r* | *n-b-ʾ* |
|---|---|---|---|---|---|---|---|---|
| 26:1–9 Introduction | | | | | 26:4 | | | 26:6 |
| 26:10–68 Mūsā | | 26:40, 52, 60 | 26:22, 52 | 26:31 | | 26:22 | | |
| 26:69–104 Ibrāhīm | | | 26:70, 71, 75, 92 | 26:84, 101 | 26:71 | 26:85 | 26:93 x 2 | 26:69 |
| 26:105–122 Nūḥ | | 26:111 | | | | | | |
| 26:123–140 Hūd | 26:135, 138 | | | | | 26:133 | | |
| 26:141–159 Ṣāliḥ | 26:156, 158 | | | 26:154 | | | | |
| 26:160–175 Lūṭ | | | | | | | | |
| 26:176–191 Shuʿayb | 26:189 x 2 | | | 26: 187 | 26:189 | | | |
| 26:192–227 Conclusion | 26:201, 204, 213 | 26:215, 224 | | | | | 26:227 | 26:221 |
| TOTAL | 9 | 6 | 6 | 5 | 3 | 3 | 3 | 3 |

# Appendix C: *Sūrat al-Qamar* and Comparisons of *Sūrat al-Shu'arā'* with *Sūrat al-Qamar*

The following are tables that relate to *Sūrat al-Qamar* and a comparison of *Sūrat al-Shu'arā'* and *Sūrat al-Qamar*.

**Table C.1** Frequently Repeated Root Letters in *Sūrat al-Qamar*

| Verses | *n-dh-r* | *k-dh-b* | *dh-k-r* | *'-dh-b* | *y-s-r* | *r-s-l* | *q-d-r* |
|---|---|---|---|---|---|---|---|
| 54:1–8 Introduction | 54:5 | 54:3 | | | | | |
| 54:9–17 Nūḥ | 54:16 | 54:9 | 54:15, 17 | 54:16 | 54:17 | | 54:12 |
| 54:18–22 Hūd | 54:18, 21 | 54:18 | 54:22 | 54:18, 21 | 54:22 | 54:19 | |
| 54:23–32 Ṣāliḥ | 54:23, 30 | 54:23, 25, 26 | 54:25, 32 | 54:30 | 54:32 | 54:27, 31 | |
| 54:33–40 Lūṭ | 54:33, 36, 37, 39 | 54:33 | 54:40 | 54:37, 38, 39 | 54:40 | 54:34 | |
| 54:41–51 Mūsā | 54:41 | 54:42 | 54:51 | | | | 54:42, 49 |
| 54:52–55 Conclusion | | | | | | | 54:55 |
| TOTAL | 11 | 8 | 7 | 7 | 4 | 4 | 4 |

**Table C.2** Infrequently Repeated Root Letters in *Sūrat al-Qamar*

| Verses | *n–ṣ–r* | *t–b–ʿ* | *q–r–r* | *z–j–r* | *n–b–ʾ* | *ḍ–l–l* | *q–w–m* | *z–b–r* | *ʾ–y–y* | *k–f–r* | *m–r–r* | *d–ʿ–w* | *ʾ–m–r* |
|---|---|---|---|---|---|---|---|---|---|---|---|---|---|
| 54:1–8 Introduction | | 54:3 | 54:3 | 54:4 | 54:4 | | | | 54:2 | 54:8 | 54:2 | 54:6, 8 | 54:3 |
| 54:9–17 Nūḥ | 54:10 | | | 54:9 | | | 54:9 | | 54:15 | 54:14 | | 54:10 | 54:12 |
| 54:18–22 Hūd | | | | | | | | | | | 54:19 | | |
| 54:23–32 Ṣāliḥ | | 54:24 | | | 54:28 | 54:24 | | | | | | | |
| 54:33–40 Lūṭ | | | 54:38 | | | | 54:33 | | | | | | |
| 54:41–51 Mūsā | 54:44 | | | | | 54:47 | | 54:43 | 54:42 | 54:43 | 54:46 | | 54:50 |
| 54:52–55 Conclusion | | | | | | | | 54:52 | | | | | |
| TOTAL | 2 | 2 | 2 | 2 | 2 | 2 | 2 | 2 | 3 | 3 | 3 | 3 | 3 |

**Table C.3** Not Repeated Root Letters in *Sūrat al-Qamar*

| Verses | *ḥ-k-m* | *ʿ-b-d* | *gh-l-b* | *ʿ-l-m* | *gh-d-w* | *f-t-n* | *ḥ-ḍ-r* | *n-j-w* | *sh-k-r* | *w-ʿ-d* | *j-r-m* | *s-ṭ-r* | *ṣ-d-q* |
|---|---|---|---|---|---|---|---|---|---|---|---|---|---|
| 54:1–8 Introduction | 54:5 | | | | | | | | | | | | |
| 54:9–17 Nūḥ | | 54:9 | 54:10 | | | | | | | | | | |
| 54:18–22 Hūd | | | | | | | | | | | | | |
| 54:23–32 Ṣāliḥ | | | | 54:26 | 54:26 | 54:27 | 54:28 | | | | | | |
| 54:33–40 Lūṭ | | | | | | | | 54:34 | 54:35 | | | | |
| 54:41–51 Mūsā | | | | | | | | | | 54:46 | 54:47 | | |
| 54:52–55 Conclusion | | | | | | | | | | | | 54:53 | 54:55 |

**Table C.4** Frequently Repeated Root Letters in *Sūrat al-Qamar* Versus *Sūrat al-Shu'arā'*

| Verses | Number of Occurrences in *Sūra* 54 (4 or more) | Number of Occurrences in *Sūra* 26 (10 or more) |
|---|---|---|
| *r-b-b* | 1 (54:10) | 36 |
| *'-m-n* | 0 | 26 |
| *'-l-m* | 1 (54:26) | 23 |
| *r-s-l* | 4 | 17 |
| *w-q-y* | 1 (54:54) | 17 |
| *'-l-h* | 0 | 15 |
| *k-dh-b* | 8 | 13 |
| *'-y-y* | 3 | 13 |
| *s-ḥ-r* | 2 (54:2, 34) | 10 |
| *b-y-n* | 2 (54:25, 28) | 10 |
| *q-w-m* | 2 (54:9, 33) | 10 |
| *'-z-z* | 1 (54:42) | 10 |
| *n-dh-r* | 11 | 5 |
| *dh-k-r* | 7 | 4 |
| *y-s-r* | 4 | 0 |
| *q-d-r* | 4 | 0 |

**Table C.5** Infrequently Repeated Root Letters in *Sūrat al-Qamar* Versus *Sūrat al-Shu'arā'*

| Verses | Number of Occurrences in *Sūra* 54 (2–3) | Number of Occurrences in *Sūra* 26 (3–9) |
|---|---|---|
| *r-ḥ-m* | 0 | 9 |
| *'-dh-b* | 7 | 9 |
| *t-b-'* | 2 | 6 |
| *'-b-d* | 1 (54:9) | 6 |
| *ṣ-d-q* | 1 (54:55) | 5 |
| *n-j-w* | 1 (54:34) | 5 (26:65, 118, 119, 169, 170) |
| *ḍ-l-l* | 2 | 4 (26:20, 86, 97, 99) |
| *kh-w-f* | 0 | 4 |
| *n-ṣ-r* | 2 | 3 |
| *n-b-'* | 2 | 3 |
| *n-'-m* | 1 (54:35) | 3 |
| *d-'-w* | 3 | 2 (26:72, 213) |
| *'-m-r* | 3 | 2 (26:35, 151) |
| *k-f-r* | 3 | 1 (26:19) |
| *m-r-r* | 3 | 0 |
| *z-b-r* | 2 | 1 (26:196) |
| *q-r-r* | 2 | 0 |
| *z-j-r* | 2 | 0 |

# Notes

## Chapter 1

1. Salwa El-Awa explains that the Qur'ānic context can refer to "textual (internal) context," meaning Qur'ānic context, or "non-textual (external) context," and can include *sunna* (prophetic traditions) or pre-Islamic poetry. This study focuses on Qur'ānic (internal) context, which I am referring to as intratextual. El-Awa, *Textual Relations in the Qur'ān*, 41–2.
2. Abdel Haleem, *Understanding the Qur'an*, 160.
3. See, e.g., Johns, "Narrative, Intertext and Allusion in the Qur'anic Presentation of Job"; Tlili, *Animals in the Qur'an*, 46; Cuypers, The Banquet, 1–26; Bodman, "The Poetics of Iblīs," 103; Abdel Haleem, *Understanding the Qur'an*, 158–9, 161, and all of Chapter 23; El-Awa, *Textual Relations in the Qur'ān*, 9, 11, 15, 41–2, 100, and 157–9; and Robinson, *Discovering the Qur'an*, see Chapter 9: "The Integrative Role of Sound and Intertextuality" and 184 for some specific examples.
4. Lybarger similarly writes in his article on Mary: "Since the story's narrative features are of focus, questions of genesis and historical influence are less important." Lybarger, "Prophetic Authority in the Qur'ānic Story of Maryam: A Literary Approach," 241.
5. Ahmed, *What Is Islam?*
6. For more on this, see Chapter 2 in this book and the chapter on *Sūrat Maryam* in Ozgur Alhassen, *Qur'ānic Stories*.
7. E.g., Sells, "Sound and Meaning in *Sūrat al-Qāri'a*."
8. Kermani, *God Is Beautiful*, 134 and 139.
9. Ong, *Orality and Literacy*, 29.
10. Ong, *Orality and Literacy*, 36–49.

## Chapter 2

1. Farrin, *Structure and Qur'anic Interpretation*; Reda, *The Al-Baqara Crescendo*; and Cuypers, *The Banquet*.
2. Bauer, "Emotion in the Qur'an."
3. Celene Ibrahim, *Women and Gender in the Qur'an* (New York: Oxford University Press, 2020), for example: 95–98 and 32–35.
4. Kennedy, *Recognition in the Arabic Narrative Tradition*, 65.
5. Ozgur Alhassen, *Qur'ānic Stories* and "A Structural Analysis of *Sūrat Maryam* Q. 19:1–58."
6. Throughout this book, I use M. A. S. Abdel Haleem's translation of the Qur'ān, unless otherwise noted. Abdel Haleem, M. A. S. *The Qur'ān: English Translation and Parallel Arabic Text* (New York: Oxford University Press, 2010).
7. al-Zamakhsharī, *al-Kashshāf*, 2:510–11.
8. Ozgur Alhassen, *Qur'ānic Stories* and Ozgur Alhassen, "A Structural Analysis of *Sūrat Maryam* Q. 19:1–58."

9. I discuss this in more detail in Ozgur Alhassen, "A Narratological Analysis of the Story of Ibrāhīm in the Qur'ān."
10. al-Tha'ālibī, *al-Jawāhir al-Ḥisān*, 2:510 and al-Maḥallī and al-Suyūṭī, *Tafsīr al-Īmamayn al-Jalālayn*, 507.
11. I discuss this in more detail in Ozgur Alhassen, "A Narratological Analysis of the Story of Ibrāhīm in the Qur'ān."
12. See, e.g., Ibrahim, "Ibn Ḥazm's Theory of Prophecy of Women," 93.
13. See Ozgur Alhassen, *Qur'ānic Stories.*
14. Saheeh International, *The Quran: Arabic Text with Corresponding English Meaning.*
15. See Ozgur Alhassen, *Qur'ānic Stories.*
16. Commentators explain that this is referring to Yūsuf and give various explanations of why the brothers say this.
17. al-Ṭabarī, *Jāmi' al-Bayān 'an Ta'wīl al-Qur'an*, 6:4561 and 4562.
18. Quṭb, *Fī Ẓilāl al-Qur'ān*, vol. 4.
19. al-Zamakhsharī, *al-Kashshāf*, 2:328.
20. For a discussion of these "signs," see Ozgur Alhassen, *Qur'ānic Stories.*
21. Ozgur Alhassen, *Qur'ānic Stories.*
22. Ozgur Alhassen, "Islam and Iconoclasm."
23. I discuss this story in more detail in Ozgur Alhassen, *Qur'ānic Stories.*
24. This discussion is also in Ozgur Alhassen, *Qur'ānic Stories.*
25. Ozgur Alhassen, *Qur'ānic Stories* and "A Structural Analysis of *Sūrat Maryam* Q. 19:1–58."
26. For more, see Ozgur Alhassen, *Qur'ānic Stories.*
27. Reda, *The Al-Baqara Crescendo*, 75.
28. Nasr et al. *The Study Quran*, 8.
29. The theme of knowing whom to trust can be found in such varied places as Jane Austen's *Pride and Prejudice.*

## Chapter 3

1. My own work on Qur'ānic stories confirms this. Sayyid Quṭb mentions this, Quṭb, *Fī Ẓilāl al-Qur'ān*, 4:2329. See also Wolf, "Moses in Christian and Islamic Tradition," 102; Khan, "The Qur'ānic View of Moses," 5; and Robinson, *Discovering the Qur'an*, 158.
2. El-Awa, "Repetition in the Qur'ān." 577. See the article for her reference.
3. Toorawa, "*Sūrat Maryam* (Q. 19)," 69, and see his footnotes numbered 75–79, pp. 77–78 for more references.
4. See, e.g., Kant, *Anthropology from a Pragmatic Point of View*; Asad, *Formations of the Secular.*
5. Ali, *The Lives of Muhammad*, 238.
6. Ali, *The Lives of Muhammad*, 231.
7. E.g., Ong, *Orality and Literacy*, 40.
8. Naddaff, *Arabesque*, 53.
9. al-Ṭabarī, *Jāmi' al-Bayān*, 9:7065.
10. al-Ṭabarī, *Jāmi' al-Bayān*, 9:7065.
11. Nasr et al., *The Study Quran*, 1124.
12. Ozgur Alhassen, "A Narratological Analysis of the Story of Ibrāhīm in the Qur'ān," 3.
13. Alter, *The Art of Biblical Narrative*, 95–6.

14. Alter, *The Art of Biblical Narrative*, 60–61.
15. Alter, *The Art of Biblical Narrative*, 88.
16. Alter, *The Art of Biblical Narrative*, 95.
17. Naddaff, *Arabesque*, 78.
18. Naddaff, *Arabesque*, 61. She refers to Suleiman, *Authoritarian Fictions: The Ideological Novel as a Literary Genre* (New York, 1983), 149–7.
19. See Section III for these verses.
20. Cuypers, *The Banquet*, e.g., 35.
21. Cuypers, *The Banquet*, 304.
22. Alter, *The Art of Biblical Narrative*, 95–6.
23. Naddaff, *Arabesque*, 61. She refers to Suleiman, *Authoritarian Fictions*, 149–7.
24. Alter, *The Art of Biblical Narrative*, 60.
25. Alter, *The Art of Biblical Narrative*, 60 and 61.
26. Ozgur Alhassen, *Qur'ānic Stories*.
27. Alter, *The Art of Biblical Narrative*, 56. For more on changes in repetition, see 97, 100, and 101.
28. Alter, *The Art of Biblical Narrative*, 91.
29. Naddaff, *Arabesque*, 54, 71.
30. Naddaff, *Arabesque*, 63.
31. Alter, *The Art of Biblical Narrative*, 98–9.
32. Toorawa, "*Sūrat Maryam* (Q. 19)."
33. Alter, *The Art of Biblical Narrative*, 100.
34. See the chapter on *Sūrat al-Qaṣaṣ* in Ozgur Alhassen, *Qur'ānic Stories*.

## Chapter 4

1. Chatman, *Story and Discourse*, 63.
2. Chatman, *Story and Discourse*, 63.
3. Chatman, *Story and Discourse*, 64.
4. Chatman, *Story and Discourse*, 68, 71.
5. Kermani mentions ellipsis in the Qur'ān, but does not give any examples: Kermani, *God Is Beautiful*, 217.
6. Mir, *Understanding the Islamic Scripture*, 144.
7. Mir, *Understanding the Islamic Scripture*, 144.
8. Obiedat, "Defining the Good in the Qur'an," 117.
9. Neuwirth, *Scripture, Poetry and the Making of a Community*, 27, 41, 392. See also 202–3.
10. Neuwirth, *Scripture, Poetry and the Making of a Community*, 27, 41, 392. See also 202–3.
11. Böwering, "The Concept of Time in Islam," 57–8.
12. Bashir, "Everlasting Doubt," 32.
13. Smith, "Deliberate Alternation of Time," 1; Kermani, *God Is Beautiful*, 172, 173.
14. Kazmi, "The Notion of History in the Qur'ān and Human Destiny," 185.
15. Kazmi, "The Notion of History in the Qur'ān and Human Destiny," 187.
16. Bashir, "On Islamic Time," 542.
17. Bashir, "On Islamic Time," 521.
18. Bashir, "On Islamic Time," 538.
19. Bashir, "On Islamic Time," 537.

20. Bashir, "On Islamic Time," 542.
21. Böwering, "The Concept of Time in Islam," 62.
22. The verses are 2:248, 4:163, 6:84, 7:122, 7:142, 10:75, 19:28, 19:53, 20:30, 20:70, 20:90, 20:92, 21:48, 23:45, 25:35, 26:13, 26:48, 28:34, 37:114, and 37:120.
23. An interesting direction for further research would be to see if there are other examples of ellipsis in the Qur'ān when God says that God will do something for someone.
24. Albayrak, "The Qur'anic Narratives of the Golden Calf Episode," 56.
25. Naddaff, *Arabesque*, 93.
26. For more on the language with which Mūsā asks for his brother's help, see Mir, *Understanding the Islamic Scripture*, 161–2.
27. This can also be translated as "with your brother."
28. Elder notices the use of the dual here: "Moses was ordered to speak in the dual to Pharaoh according to Ta Ha, but we find no mention of Aaron in Al A'raf until after Moses had performed his miracle before the court." As he mentions, this would be an interesting area for further research. Elder, "Parallel Passages in the Koran (The Story of Moses)," 258. Also, al-Kallās includes charts with verses about Mūsā, and the charts indicate how verses overlap; al-Kallās, *Mūsā 'Alayhī al-Salām wa Qawmahu Banū Isrā'īl.*
29. This is not to claim that they are representative of most readers.
30. al-Shidyaq, *Leg Over Leg*, 456, note 514.
31. al-'Amārī, *Tafsīr Abī al-Su'ūd*, 6:17–18.
32. Quṭb, *Fī Ẓilāl al-Qur'ān*, 4:2336.
33. Ibn al-'Arabi, *The Bezels of Wisdom*, 243, 244.
34. Austin, *How to Do Things with Words*, 6.
35. Ozgur Alhassen, *Qur'ānic Stories*, 17.
36. al-Tha'ālibī, *al-Jawāhir al-Ḥisān*, 2:349.
37. al-Ṭabarī, *Jāmi' al-Bayān 'an Ta'wīl al-Qur'ān*, 7:5583.
38. For more on the idea of a text drawing attention to itself, see Kermani, *God Is Beautiful*, 71.
39. Naddaff, *Arabesque*, 114 mentions *al-muṣawwir*, verse 59:24.
40. Albayrak mentions the "enigma" of al-Sāmirī's identity. Albayrak, "The Qur'anic Narratives of the Golden Calf Episode," 53. For a comparative approach to this scene, see Rubin, "Traditions in Transformation,"196–214. See also Wolf, "Moses in Christian and Islamic Tradition," 104. Wolf, with no evidence, makes unusual claims about al-Sāmirī's identity.
41. For more on Mūsā's emotional state, see Albayrak, "The Qur'anic Narratives of the Golden Calf Episode," 54. Albayrak writes (p. 57) that the response in 20:87 is echoed in 20:100–101, God's discussion of people being punished on the Day of Resurrection; Albayrak mentions this flashback (20:88–91), on p. 58, and for more on 20:92–93, see pp. 61–2. For more on 20:94, see Bodman, "The Poetics of Iblīs," 107–8.
42. Maybudī, *Kashf al-Asrār wa 'Uddat al-Abrār: Unveiling of the Mysteries and the Provision of the Pious*, 314.
43. Mustansir Mir, "Dialogue in the Qur'ān," 6, see also 7.
44. Albayrak, "The Qur'anic Narratives of the Golden Calf Episode," 52.
45. Albayrak, "The Qur'anic Narratives of the Golden Calf Episode," 52. He refers to Quṭb, *Fi ẓilāl al-Qur'ān*, 4:2347.
46. Asad, *The Message of the Qur'ān*, 4:535.
47. Amatul Rahman Omar's translation. I surveyed thirty-five translations, accessed at *Islam Awakened Qur'an Index* http://www.islamawakened.com/index.php/qur-an.
48. al-Ṭabarī, *Jāmi' al-Bayān*, 7:5627.
49. El-Awa, *Textual Relations in the Qur'ān*, 51.

50. In a way explaining this adamancy, Yazicioglu writes that al-Ghazālī, arguing against a simplistic belief in miracles, explains that "the one who believes in the prophet simply because of the 'changing of the staff into a serpent' ends up 'worshipping the golden calf.'" Yazicioglu, *Understanding the Qur'anic Miracle Stories in the Modern Age*, 40.
51. Albayrak notes a parallel between the phrasing in this verse and another in the *sūra*: "there is a striking similarity between Q.20:91, 'they said: we will not stop worshipping (*kifina*) the calf until Moses return to us' and Q.20:97, 'look at your *ilāh* to which you have been devoted, *ākifan*.'" Albayrak, "The Qur'anic Narratives of the Golden Calf Episode," 67. The same verb is also used in 7:138, in which the people see others worshipping idols, and they ask Mūsā for something similar. Rubin, "Traditions in Transformation," 205.
52. One may also look at 20:115 as introducing the story and its themes. See Bodman, "The Poetics of Iblīs," 109. For an example of a merging of time and space elsewhere in the Qur'ān, see Cuypers, *The Banquet*, 172.
53. Naddaff, *Arabesque*, 49.
54. Naddaff, *Arabesque*, 76.
55. Naddaff, *Arabesque*, 50, 91.
56. Naddaff, *Arabesque*, 54, 60.
57. Naddaff, *Arabesque*, 54, 60.
58. Naddaff, *Arabesque*, 108.
59. Naddaff, *Arabesque*, 113.
60. The verses are "These people are a puny band––they have enraged us" (26:54–55).
61. Here is the root *w-ḥ-y*, also discussed in the second chapter of this book, in the context of Mūsā's mother being inspired by God.
62. Booth, *The Rhetoric of Fiction*, 377.

## Chapter 5

1. See, e.g., Walid Saleh: "One was always engaged in detective guess work, trying to find the source of this bit of information or that. Finding origins became the telos of modern Quranic scholarship." Saleh, '"What if you refuse, when ordered to fight?,'" 266. See also Waldman, "New Approaches to 'Biblical' Materials in the Qur'ān."
2. Reynolds, *The Qur'ān and Its Biblical Subtext*, 2.
3. In works on *i'jāz al-Qur'ān* by Arabic rhetoricians such as al-Jurjānī, al-Bāqillanī, and al-Rummānī.
4. Reynolds, *The Qur'ān and Its Biblical Subtext*, 1–2.
5. Saleh, '"What if you refuse, when ordered to fight?,"' 266.
6. Saleh, '"What if you refuse, when ordered to fight?,"' 266 for "coherent vision"; "web of design" from Alter, "Sodom as Nexus," 1.
7. Alter, "Sodom as Nexus," 33, 36, 37.
8. Alter, "Sodom as Nexus," 38.
9. This was first suggested to me by Robert Alter, personal communication.
10. Stetkevych, "Solomon and Mythic Kingship in the Arab-Islamic Tradition," 6, 25.
11. al-Maḥallī and al-Suyūṭī, *Tafsīr al-Īmamayn al-Jalālayn*, 71.
12. al-Tha'ālibī, *al-Jawāhir al-Ḥisān*, 1:251–2.
13. al-Ṭabarī, *Jāmi' al-Bayān*, 3:1773.
14. al-'Amārī, *Tafsīr Abī al-Su'ūd*, 2:33.
15. Quṭb, *Fī Ẓilāl al-Qur'ān*, 4:2303.

16. al-Ghazālī, *A Thematic Commentary on the Qur'an*, 326.
17. al-Dimashqī, *Mukhtaṣar Tafsīr Ibn Kathīr*, 2:444.
18. al-Maḥallī and al-Suyūṭī, *Tafsīr al-Īmamayn al-Jalālayn*, 397.
19. al-'Amārī, *Tafsīr Abī al-Su'ūd*, 5:258.
20. al-Ṭabarī, *Jāmi' al-Bayān*, 7:5456–8.
21. Quṭb, *Fī Ẓilāl al-Qur'ān*, 4:2303.
22. Parts of this section are modified from Ozgur Alhassen, *Qur'ānic Stories.*
23. The translator here has translated *ṣawm* as "to abstain from conversation," although a more literal translation of this word would be "to abstain," without adding "from conversation."
24. Mir, *Understanding the Islamic Scripture*, 84. Reynolds mentions that angels address Zakariyyā and Maryam, but they address God in 3:40 and 3:45–47. He explains: "Once again, it seems that God is present, somehow, in the midst of the messengers." Reynolds, *The Qur'ān and Its Biblical Subtext,* 88.
25. Maybudī writes about how unique it is to be called or addressed directly by God: Maybudī, *Kashf al-Asrār*, 111.
26. Abboud, "Mary, Mother of Jesus and the Qur'anic Text," 130. Parts of this section are modified from Ozgur Alhassen, *Qur'ānic Stories.*
27. al-Maḥallī and al-Suyūṭī, *Tafsīr al-Īmamayn al-Jalālayn*, 38; al-Tha'ālibī, *al-Jawāhir al-Ḥisān,* 1:144; al-Ṭabarī, *Jāmi' al-Bayān*, 2:925–6.
28. Osman, *Topics of the Quran*, 625.
29. Neuwirth, *Scripture, Poetry and the Making of a Community*, 319.
30. Abdel Haleem, *Understanding the Qur'an,* 208.
31. Robinson, *Discovering the Qur'an*, 233.
32. Neuwirth, *Scripture, Poetry and the Making of a Community*, 319.
33. A further avenue of research would be to see if this verse (and consequently all the verses discussed) is also connected to "Your Lord says, 'Call on Me and I will answer you; those who are too proud to serve Me will enter Hell humiliated" ' (40:60).
34. Neuwirth, "The House of Abraham and The House of Amram," 512.
35. Ernst, *How to Read the Qur'an*," 184.
36. Parts of this section are modified from Ozgur Alhassen, *Qur'ānic Stories.*
37. al-Ṭabarī, *Jāmi' al-Bayān*, 6:4370; al-'Amārī, *Tafsīr Abī al-Su'ūd*, 4:224; Quṭb, *Fī Ẓilāl al-Qur'ān*, 4:1912; and Asad, *The Message of the Qur'ān*, 3:365, note 101.
38. Saleh, ' "What if you refuse, when ordered to fight?," ' 268.
39. Saleh, ' "What if you refuse, when ordered to fight?," ' 269. The larger point that Saleh makes is that by depicting thirst, rather than hunger, this story would have been more striking to its audience, and it is thus not merely a corruption of the biblical story (Saleh, ' "What if you refuse, when ordered to fight?," ' 271).
40. al-Ṭabarī, *Jāmi' al-Bayān*, 4:3113.
41. al-Tha'ālibī, al-Jawāhir al-Ḥisān, 1:463.
42. al-Zamakhsharī, *al-Kashshāf*, 1:654.
43. al-'Amārī, *Tafsīr Abī al-Su'ūd*, 3:97. Cuypers also explains this, Cuypers, *The Banquet*, 415 and 421. For more on this, Asad, *The Message of the Qur'ān*, 2:193, note 137.
44. al-Ṭabarī, *Jāmi' al-Bayān*, 4:3114.
45. al-Ṭabarī, *Jāmi' al-Bayān*, 4:3115; al-Maḥallī and al-Suyūṭī, *Tafsīr al-Īmamayn al-Jalālayn*, 160.
46. al-Tha'ālibī, *al-Jawāhir al-Ḥisān*, 1:463; Abū'l-Su'ūd adds, if they believe, al-'Amārī, *Tafsīr Abī al-Su'ūd*, 3:97.

47. al-Ṭabarī, *Jāmiʿ al-Bayān*, 4:3114.
48. al-Ṭabarī, *Jāmiʿ al-Bayān*, 4:3120.
49. al-Ṭabarī, *Jāmiʿ al-Bayān*, 4:3117 and 3120; Quṭb, *Fī Ẓilāl al-Qurʾān*, 2:999.
50. al-ʿAmārī, *Tafsīr Abī al-Suʿūd*, 3:99; Quṭb, *Fī Ẓilāl al-Qurʾān*, 2:999.
51. Quṭb, *Fī Ẓilāl al-Qurʾān*, 2:999.
52. Quṭb, *Fī Ẓilāl al-Qurʾān*, 2:999.
53. Quṭb, *Fī Ẓilāl al-Qurʾān*, 2:1000.
54. Quṭb, *Fī Ẓilāl al-Qurʾān*, 2:1000.
55. Asad, *The Message of the Qurʾān*, 2:194, note 138.
56. Cuypers, *The Banquet*, 421.
57. Cuypers, *The Banquet*, 352.
58. Cuypers, *The Banquet*, 415.
59. The same phrase occurs in the following verses, which are not stories, 3:126, 8:10, and 13:28.
60. See Bauer, "Emotion in the Qur'an," *Journal of Qurʾanic Studies* 19, no. 2, 15 for more on the heart in the Qur'ān.
61. al-Zamakhsharī, *al-Kashshāf*, 1:391; al-Thaʿālibī, *al-Jawāhir al-Ḥisān*, 1:202; al-ʿAmārī, *Tafsīr Abī al-Suʿūd*, 1:256.
62. al-Ṭabarī, *Jāmiʿ al-Bayān*, 2:1533.
63. al-Thaʿālibī, *al-Jawāhir al-Ḥisān*, 1:201.
64. al-Zamakhsharī, *al-Kashshāf*, 1:391 and al-ʿAmārī, *Tafsīr Abī al-Suʿūd*, 1:256.
65. al-Tustarī, *Tafsīr al-Tustarī*, 37.
66. al-Tustarī, *Tafsīr al-Tustarī*, 37.
67. al-Tustarī, *Tafsīr al-Tustarī*, 38.
68. al-Thaʿālibī, *al-Jawāhir al-Ḥisān*, 1:202.
69. Verses that use the word *rabbika/rabbaka* but are not in stories and do not have people making requests are 4:65 and 26:175.
70. al-ʿAmārī, *Tafsīr Abī al-Suʿūd*, 1:106.
71. Quṭb, *Fī Ẓilāl al-Qurʾān*, 1:74.
72. Quṭb, *Fī Ẓilāl al-Qurʾān*, 1:78.
73. al-Zamakhsharī, *al-Kashshāf*, 1:605; al-Thaʿālibī, *al-Jawāhir al-Ḥisān*, 1:423.
74. al-Thaʿālibī, *al-Jawāhir al-Ḥisān*, 1:423.
75. al-ʿAmārī, *Tafsīr Abī al-Suʿūd*, 3:25.
76. al-Ghazālī, *A Thematic Commentary on the Qur'an*, 96.
77. al-Ṭabarī, *Jāmiʿ al-Bayān*, 4:2812.
78. al-Tustarī, *Tafsīr al-Tustarī*, 81; al-Thaʿālibī, *al-Jawāhir al-Ḥisān*, 2:158.
79. al-Ṭabarī, *Jāmiʿ al-Bayān*, 6:4547; al-ʿAmārī, *Tafsīr Abī al-Suʿūd*, 4:280.
80. al-Zamakhsharī, *al-Kashshāf*, 2:322; al-Thaʿālibī, *al-Jawāhir al-Ḥisān*, 2:158.
81. al-Zamakhsharī, *al-Kashshāf*, 2:322.
82. Quṭb, *Fī Ẓilāl al-Qurʾān*, 4:1992.
83. al-Ṭabarī, *Jāmiʿ al-Bayān*, 6:4560; al-Maḥallī and al-Suyūṭī, *Tafsīr al-Īmamayn al-Jalālayn*, 311; al-Thaʿālibī, *al-Jawāhir al-Ḥisān*, 2:160; al-ʿAmārī, *Tafsīr Abī al-Suʿūd*, 4:284.
84. al-Ṭabarī, *Jāmiʿ al-Bayān*, 6:4562.
85. Quṭb, *Fī Ẓilāl al-Qurʾān*, 4:1995.
86. Other instances include 2:260, 3:35–36, 3:38, 3:40–41, 3:47, 5:25, 5:117, 6:76–78, 6:80, 6:161, 7:44, 7:62, 7:68, 7:79, 7:89, 7:93, 7:125–126, 7:143, 20:73. Among these, e.g., there is the story of Mūsā asking to see God (7:143).

## Chapter 6

1. Shahid, "Another Contribution to Koranic Exegesis," 1; Shahid, 'The "Sūra" of the Poets, Qur'ān XXVI. See also Zwettler, "The Sura of the Poets."
2. The root is absent from the introduction to the *sūra*, but it is present many times in the construction *rabbi al-'ālamīn*, discussed earlier. The first time this phrase is present, God labels Himself thus. This phrase is also in the introductory refrain to many of the stories (26:16, 26:23, 26:47, 26:77, 26:98, 26:109, 26:127, 26:145, 26:164, 26:180, and 26:192).
3. This root appears seven times in the *sūra*, only one of them outside of the story of Mūsā (26:32, 26:43 twice, 26:44, 26:45, 26:46, and 26:223).
4. Ozgur Alhassen, *Qur'ānic Stories*, Chapter 5.
5. Ozgur Alhassen, "A Narratological Analysis of the Story of Ibrāhīm in the Qur'ān."
6. Ozgur Alhassen, *Qur'ānic Stories*, Chapter 5.
7. Izutsu, *The Structure of Ethical Terms in the Quran*, 113.
8. Izutsu, *The Structure of Ethical Terms in the Quran*, 113.
9. The four non-repeated roots that stand out in the story of Mūsā are *k-f-r* (26:19), *s-j-n* (26:29), *k-n-z* (26:58), and *d-r-k* (26:61). Three of them end the verses and accordingly stand out more.
10. This is my translation.
11. For more on the layers of narration in Qur'ānic stories, see Ozgur Alhassen, *Qur'ānic Stories*, Chapter 1.
12. These sections of the verses are almost the exact same, although Abdel Haleem translates them differently. This is the translation from 22:5.

## Chapter 7

1. For more on the end-rhyme and meter in the *sūra*, see Stewart, "Divine Epithets and the Dibacchius."
2. Neuwirth, *Scripture, Poetry and the Making of a Community*, 92.
3. Ozgur Alhassen, *Qur'ānic Stories*.
4. Qutb, *Fī Ẓilāl al-Qur'ān*, 6:3428.
5. Qutb, *Fī Ẓilāl al-Qur'ān*, 6:3427.
6. Qutb, *Fī Ẓilāl al-Qur'ān*, 6:3428.
7. al-Ghazālī, *A Thematic Commentary on the Qur'an*, 600.
8. Qutb, *Fī Ẓilāl al-Qur'ān*, 6:3425.
9. In Islamic history, the issue of the createdness of the Qur'ān becomes highly controversial; it would be interesting to analyze this *sūra* in that historical context.
10. See the introduction in Ozgur Alhassen, *Qur'ānic Stories*.
11. I also write about this narrative technique in Ozgur Alhassen, *Qur'ānic Stories*.

## Appendix A

1. Al-Kallās includes 7:103–171 only in his chart; al-Kallās, *Mūsā 'Alayhī al-Salām*, 17.
2. Al-Kallās includes 11:96–99 only in his chart; al-Kallās, *Mūsā 'Alayhī al-Salām*, 17.
3. Al-Kallās includes 14:5–8 only in his chart; al-Kallās, *Mūsā 'Alayhī al-Salām*, 17.

4. Al-Kallās includes, under the heading of "briefly," 17:4–8 only in his chart; al-Kallās, *Mūsā ʿAlayhī al-Salām*, 17.
5. Al-Kallās includes 20:9–99 only in his chart; al-Kallās, *Mūsā ʿAlayhī al-Salām*, 19. Also, Robinson mentions the similarity between 20:25–30 and 94:1–5, Robinson, *Discovering the Qur'an*, 158.
6. Al-Kallās does not include this in his chart; al-Kallās, *Mūsā ʿAlayhī al-Salām*, 19.
7. Ernst, *How to Read the Qur'an*, p. 151 includes verses 28:1–54. Al-Kallās additionally includes 28:76–82, which is the story of Qārūn, in his chart; al-Kallās, *Mūsā ʿAlayhī al-Salām*, 19.
8. Al-Kallās does not include this in his chart; al-Kallās, *Mūsā ʿAlayhī al-Salām*, 19.
9. Al-Kallās includes 40:22–54 in his chart.
10. Al-Kallās includes 44:17–29 only in his chart; al-Kallās, *Mūsā ʿAlayhī al-Salām*, 21.
11. Al-Kallās includes 51:30–40 in his chart; al-Kallās, *Mūsā ʿAlayhī al-Salām*, 21.
12. Al-Kallās includes 54:41–42 only in his chart; al-Kallās, *Mūsā ʿAlayhī al-Salām*, 21.
13. Ernst gives the following summary of *Sūra* 79: punishment story of Moses' call, 79:15–20; Pharaoh's rejection, 79:21–26; and God's power, 79:27–33. Ernst, *How to Read the Qur'an*, 79.
14. Alford T. Welch mentions that while other prophets are described in the Qur'ān as being sent to a people or tribe, Mūsā is described as being sent to Firʿawn. Welch, "Formulaic Features of the Punishment-Stories," 109.
15. Robinson, *Discovering the Qur'an*, 313, footnote 27.
16. Ernst, based on Farrin, summarizes 2:40–103 as "Moses delivers law to Children of Israel." (Ernst, *How to Read the Qur'an*, 167.) Instead, I included the following stories: Mūsā with his people, 2:49–74, and Mūsā's people and the golden calf, 2:92–93. 2:40–48, 2:83–86, and 2:102 can be seen as being about Banī Isrā'īl. I included 2:87 in the category of verses that are difficult to categorize. Al-Kallās includes 2:40–96, 2:101–103, 2:111–112, 2:122–123, 2:211, and 2:246–251 in his chart; al-Kallās, *Mūsā ʿAlayhī al-Salām*, 17.

    Albayrak writes: "The 'golden calf' episode is discussed in verses Q.20:83–98 and Q.7:148–151. In addition to this there are two short versions in Q.2:51, 54, 92–3 and Q.4:153." Albayrak, "The Qur'anic Narratives of the Golden Calf Episode," 47.
17. Al-Kallās includes 5:20–32, 5:43–46, and 5:70–71 in his chart; al-Kallās, *Mūsā ʿAlayhī al-Salām*, 17.
18. 7:103–74 are also in the Mūsā and Firʿawn table.
19. 14:4–8 are also in the Mūsā and Firʿawn table.
20. 20:9–100 are also in the Mūsā and Firʿawn table.

    Albayrak looks at the story's structure in *Sūra* 20 thus: Section I: 20:83–84 (Introduction, 20:83–85); Section II, God's test: 20:85; Section III, Moses and the Israelites: 20:86–89 (story begins in 20:86); Section IV, Moses and Aaron: 20:90–94; Section V: 20:95–98 (20:95–97, Moses and Sāmirī); conclusion: 20:99. Albayrak, "The Qur'anic Narratives of the Golden Calf Episode," 47–62.
21. He is often called al-Khiḍr in Islamic tradition.

# Bibliography


Abboud, Hosn. "Mary, Mother of Jesus and the Qur'anic Text: A Feminist Literary Study." Ph.D. dissertation. University of Toronto, Canada, 2006.

Abdel Haleem, Muhammad. *The Qur'ān: English Translation and Parallel Arabic Text*. Oxford University Press, 2010.

Abdel Haleem, Muhammad. "Qur'anic "*jihād*": A Linguistic and Contextual Analysis." *Journal of Qur'anic Studies* 12, no. 1–2 (2010): 147–166.

Abdel Haleem, Muhammad. *Understanding the Qur'an: Themes and Style*. I.B. Tauris, 1999.

Abou El Fadl, Khaled. *Conference of the Books: The Search for Beauty in Islam*. University Press of America, 2001.

Abou El Fadl, Khaled. *Speaking in God's Name: Islamic Law, Authority and Women*. Oneworld, 2005.

Abu-Deeb, Kamal. "Studies in the Majāz and Metaphorical Language of the Qur'ān: Abū 'Ubayda and al-Sharīf al-Raḍī." In *Literary Structures of Religious Meaning in the Qur'an*, edited by Issa J. Boullata. Curzon, 2000, 310–353.

Abu-Zayd, Nasr. "The Dilemma of the Literary Approach to the Qur'an." *Alif: Journal of Comparative Poetics* no. 23, Literature and the Sacred (2003): 8–47.

Abu-Zayd, Nasr, and Esther R. Nelson. *Voice of an Exile: Reflections on Islam*. Praeger, 2004.

Afsar, Ayaz. "A Discourse and Linguistic Approach to Biblical and Qur'ānic Narrative." *Islamic Studies* 45, no. 4 (2006): 493–517.

Afsar, Ayaz. "A Literary Critical Approach to Qur'ānic Parables." *Islamic Studies* 44, no. 4 (2005): 481–501.

Afsar, Ayaz. "Plot Motifs in Joseph/Yūsuf Story: A Comparative Study of Biblical and Qur'ānic Narrative." *Islamic Studies* 45, no. 2 (2006): 167–89.

Ahmed, Shahab. *What Is Islam? The Importance of Being Islamic*. Princeton University Press, 2016.

Albayrak, Ismail. "The Classical Exegetes' Analysis of the Qur'ānic Narrative 18:60–82." *Islamic Studies* 42, no. 2 (2003): 289–315.

Albayrak, Ismail. "The Qur'anic Narratives of the Golden Calf Episode." *Journal of Qur'anic Studies* 3, no. 1 (2001): 47–69.

Algar, Hamid. "Q. 21:78–9: A Qur'anic Basis for Ijtihād?" *Journal of Qur'anic Studies* 4, no. 2 (2002): 1–22.

Ali, Kecia. *The Lives of Muhammad*. Harvard University Press, 2014.

Alter, Robert. *The Art of Biblical Narrative*. Basic Books, 1981.

Alter, Robert. "Sodom as Nexus: The Web of Design in Biblical Narrative." *Tikkun Magazine* 1, no. 1 (1986): 30–38.

al-'Amārī, Abū Su'ūd Muḥammad ibn Muḥammad. *Tafsīr Abī al-Su'ūd*. 9 vols. Dār al-Ḥayā' al Turāth al-'Arabī, 1994.

Asad, Muhammad, trans. *The Message of the Qur'ān*. Book Foundation, 2003.

Asad, Talal. *Formations of the Secular: Christianity, Islam, Modernity*. Stanford University Press, 2003.

Auerbach, Erich. *Mimesis: The Representation of Reality in Western Literature*. New and expanded edition. Princeton University Press, 2013.

Austin, J. L. *How To Do Things with Words: The William James Lectures Delivered at Harvard University in 1955*. Oxford University Press, 1975.

Ayoub, Mahmoud. "Literary Exegesis of the Qur'ān: The Case of al-Sharīf al-Raḍī." In *Literary Structures of Religious Meaning in the Qur'an*, edited by Issa J. Boullata. Curzon, 2000, 292–309.

Ayoub, Mahmoud. *The Qur'ān and its Interpreters*. Vol. 1. State University of New York Press, 1984.

Bal, Mieke. *Death and Dissymmetry: The Politics of Coherence in the Book of Judges*. University of Chicago Press, 1988.

Bal, Mieke. *Narratology: Introduction to the Theory of Narrative*. 3rd ed. University of Toronto Press, 2009.

Barlas, Asma. "The Qur'an and Hermeneutics: Reading the Qur'an's Opposition to Patriarchy." *Journal of Qur'anic Studies* 3, no. 2 (2001): 15–38.

Barthes, Roland. "Mythologies." In *Literary Theory: An Anthology*, edited by Julie Rivkin and Michael Ryan. Blackwell, 2004, 81–89.

Barthes, Roland. *S/Z: An Essay*. Translated by Richard Miller. Noonday Press, 1974.

Bashir, Shahzad. "Everlasting Doubt: Uncertainty in Islamic Representations of the Past." *Archiv für Religionsgeschichte* 20, no. 1 (March 2018): 25–44.

Bashir, Shahzad. "On Islamic Time: Rethinking Chronology in the Historiography of Muslim Societies." *History and Theory* 53 (December 2014): 519–544.

Bauer, Karen. "Emotion in the Qur'an: An Overview." *Journal of Qur'anic Studies* 19, no. 2 (2017): 1–30.

Beaumont, Daniel. "Hardboiled: Narrative Discourse in Early Muslim Traditions." *Studia Islamica* 83 (1996): 5–31.

Bellamy, James A. "The Mysterious Letters of the Koran: Old Abbreviations of the Basmalah." *Journal of the American Oriental Society* 93, no. 3 (1973): 267–85.

Ben Abdeljelil, Jameleddine. "Ways of the Intellect: Forms of Discourse and Rationalization Processes in the Arabic-Islamic Context." In *Worldviews and Cultures: Philosophical Reflections from an Intercultural Perspective*, edited by Nicole Note, Raúl Fornet-Betancout, Diederik Aerts and Josef Estermann, translated by Ursula Bsees and Anthony Lowstedt. Springer, 2009, 11–29.

Benjamin, Walter. *Illuminations: Essays and Reflections*. Edited by Hannah Arendt, translated by Harry Zohn. Schocken Books, 1969.

Ben Nabi, Malik. *The Qur'anic Phenomenon: An Attempt at a Theory of Understanding the Holy Qur'an*. Translated by Abu Bilal Kirkary. American Trust, 1983.

Blatherwick, Helen. "Textual Silences and Literary Choices in al-Kisā'ī's Account of the Annunciation and the Birth of Jesus." *Arabica* 66, no. 1–2 (2019): 1–42.

Bodman, Whitney S. "The Poetics of Iblīs: Narrative Theology in the Qur'ān." Harvard Theological Studies, 2011.

Booth, Wayne C. *The Rhetoric of Fiction*. 2nd ed. University of Chicago Press, 1983.

Boullata, Issa J. "Sayyid Quṭb's Literary Appreciation of the Qur'ān.' *Literary Structures of Religious Meaning in the Qur'an*, edited by Issa J. Boullata. Curzon, 2000, 354–371.

Böwering, Gerhard. "The Concept of Time in Islam." *Proceedings of the American Philosophical Society* 141, no. 1 (March 1997): 57–58.

Brooks, Peter. *Reading for the Plot: Design and Intention in Narrative*. Harvard University Press, 1984.

Chatman, Seymour. *Story and Discourse: Narrative Structure in Fiction and Film*. Cornell University Press, 1978.

Cuypers, Michel. *The Banquet: A Reading of the Fifth Sura of the Qur'an*, edited by Rafael Luciani, translated by Patricia Kelly. Convivium Press, 2009.

Cuypers, Michel. "Semitic Rhetoric as a Key to the Question of the *naẓm* of the Qur'anic Text." *Journal of Qur'anic Studies* 13, no. 1 (2011): 1–24.

Dayeh, Islam. "Al-Ḥawāmīm: Intertextuality and Coherence in Meccan Surahs." In *The Qur'ān in Context: Historical and Literary Investigations into the Qur'ānic Milieu*, edited by Angelika Neuwirth, Nicolai Sinai, and Michael Marx. Brill NV, 2010, 461–498.

al-Dimashqī, Abū al-Fidā' Ismā'īl ibn Kathīr. *Mukhtaṣar Tafsīr Ibn Kathīr*. 3 vols. Dār al-Qur'ān al-Karīm, 1981.

Eagleton, Terry. *Literary Theory: An Introduction*. Basil Blackwell, 1983.

El-Awa, Salwa. "Repetition in the Qur'ān: A Relevance Based Explanation of the Phenomenon." *Islamic Studies* 42, no. 4 (Winter 2003): 577–593.

El-Awa, Salwa. *Textual Relations in the Qur'ān: Relevance, Coherence and Structure*. Routledge, 2006.

Elder, E. E. "Parallel Passages in the Koran (The Story of Moses)." *The Muslim World* 15 (1925): 254–259.

Ernst, Carl W. *How to Read the Qur'an: A New Guide, with Select Translations*. University of North Carolina Press, 2011.

Farrin, Raymond. *Structure and Qur'anic Interpretation*. White Cloud Press, 2014.

Firestone, Reuven. "Abraham." *Encyclopaedia of the Qur'ān*. Edited by Jane Dammen McAuliffe. Georgetown University, Brill Online, 2015.

Geissinger, Aisha. "Mary in the Qur'an: Rereading Subversive Births." In *Sacred Tropes: Tanakh, New Testament, and Qur'an as Literature and Culture*, edited by Roberta Sterman Sabbath. Brill, 2009, 379–392.

Genette, Gerard. *Narrative Discourse: An Essay in Method*. Translated by Jane E. Lewin. Cornell University Press, 1980.

al-Ghazālī, Muḥammad. *A Thematic Commentary on the Qur'an*. Translated by Ashur A. Shamis, revised by Zaynab Alawiye. International Institute of Islamic Thought, 2000.

Goldfeld, Yeshayahu. "The Development of Theory on Qur'ānic Exegesis in Islamic Scholarship." *Studia Islamica* 67 (1988): 5–27.

Goody, Jack. *The Domestication of the Savage Mind*. Cambridge University Press, 1977.

Greifenhagen, F. V. "The *qamīṣ* in *Sūrat Yūsuf*: A Prolegomenon to the Material Culture of Garments in the Formative Islamic Period." *Journal of Qur'anic Studies* 11, no. 2 (2009): 72–92.

Hasan, Ahmad. "The Qur'ān: The Primary Source of 'Fiqh.'" *Islamic Studies* 38, no. 4 (1999): 475–502.

Heath, Peter. "Creative Hermeneutics: A Comparative Analysis of Three Islamic Approaches." *Arabica* 36, no. 2 (1989): 173–210.

Hoffmann, Thomas. "Agnostic Poetics in the Qur'ān: Self-referentialities, Refutations, and the Development of a Qur'ānic Self." In *Self-Referentiality in the Qur'ān*, edited by Stefan Wild. Wiesbaden, Harrassowitz Verlag, 2006, 39–57.

Ibn al-'Arabi. *The Bezels of Wisdom*. Translated by R. W. J. Austin. Paulist Press, 1980.

Ibrahim, Celene. *Women and Gender in the Qur'an*. Oxford University Press, 2020.

Ibrahim, M. Zakyi. "Ibn Ḥazm's Theory of Prophecy of Eomen: Literalism, Logic, and Perfection." *Intellectual Discourse* 23, no. 1 (2015): 75–100.

Izutsu, Toshihiko. *God and Man in the Qur'an: Semantics of the Qur'anic Weltanschauung*. Islamic Book Trust, 2002.

Izutsu, Toshihiko. *The Structure of Ethical Terms in the Quran*. ABC International Group, 2000.

Johns, A. H. "A Humanistic Approach to *i'jāz* in the Qur'an: The Transfiguration of Language." *Journal of Qur'anic Studies* 13, no. 1 (2011): 79–99.

Johns, A. H. "Joseph in the Qur'ān: Dramatic Dialogue, Human Emotion and Prophetic Wisdom." *Islamochristiana* 7 (1981): 29–55.

Johns, A. H. "Narrative, Intertext and Allusion in the Qur'anic Presentation of Job." *Journal of Qur'anic Studies* 1, no. 1 (1999): 1–25.

Johns, A. H. "Reflections on the Dynamics and Spirituality of *Sūrat al-Furqān*." In *Literary Structures of Religious Meaning in the Qur'an*, edited by Issa J. Boullata. Curzon, 2000, 188–227.

Johns, A. H. '"She desired him and he desired her" (Qur'an 12:24): 'Abd al-Ra'ūf's treatment of an episode of the Joseph story in *Tarjumān al-Mustafīd*." *Archipel* 57 (1999): 109–34.

al-Jurjānī, 'Abd al-Qāhir. *Asrār al-Balāgha*. Dār al-Madanī, 1991.

al-Kallās, Ṣalāh al-Dīn Khalīl. *Mūsā 'Alayhī al-Salām wa Qawmahu Banū Isrā'īl*. Dār ul-Bashā'ir, 2007.

Kant, Immanuel. *Anthropology from a Pragmatic Point of View*. Springer Netherlands, 2012.

Kazmi, Yedullah. "The Notion of History in the Qur'ān and Human Destiny." *Islamic Studies* 37, no. 2 (Summer 1998): 183–200.

Kazmi, Yedullah. "The Qur'ān as Event and as Phenomenon." *Islamic Studies* 41, no. 2 (Summer 1998): 193–214.

Keeler, Annabel. "Towards a Prophetology of Love: The Figure of Jacob in Sufi Commentaries on *Sūrat Yūsuf*." In *The Spirit and the Letter: Approaches to the Esoteric Interpretation of the Qur'an*, edited by Annabel Keeler and Sajjad Rizvi. Oxford University Press, 2016, 125–153.

Kennedy, Philip. *Recognition in the Arabic Narrative Tradition: Discovery, Deliverance and Delusion*. Edinburgh University Press, 2016.

Kermani, Navid. "The Aesthetic Reception of the Qur'ān as Reflected in Early Muslim History." In *Literary Structures of Religious Meaning in the Qur'an*, edited by Issa J. Boullata. Curzon, 2000, 255–276.

Kermani, Navid. "From Revelation to Interpretation: Nasr Hamid Abū Zayd and the literary study of the Qur'ān." In *Modern Muslim Intellectuals and the Qur'ān*, edited by Suha Taji-Farouki. Oxford University Press, 2004, 169–192.

Kermani, Navid. *God Is Beautiful: The Aesthetic Experience of the Quran*. Polity, 2015.

Khalafallāh, Muḥammad Aḥmad. *al-Fann al-Qaṣaṣī fī al-Qur'ān al-Karīm*. Arab Diffusion, 1999.

Khan, Irfan Ahmad. "The Qur'ānic View of Moses: A Messenger of God from the Children of Israel to Pharaoh." *Islamic Studies* 45, no. 1 (Spring 2006): 5–20.

Klar, M. O. *Interpreting al-Tha'labī's Tales of the Prophets: Temptation, Responsibility and Loss*. Routledge, 2009.

Laude, Patrick. "Reading the Quran: The Lessons of the Ambassadors of Mystical Islam." *Sophia: The International Journal for Philosophy of Religion, Metaphysical Theology and Ethics* 46, no. 2 (2007): 147–162.

Lord, Albert B. *The Singer of Tales*. Harvard University Press, 1960.

Lybarger, Loren D. "Prophetic Authority in the Qur'ānic Story of Maryam: A Literary Approach." *Journal of Religion* 80, no. 2 (2000): 240–270.

al-Maḥallī, Jalāl al-Dīn Muḥammad bin Aḥmad and Jalāl al-Dīn 'Abd al-Raḥmān bin Abī Bakr al-Suyūṭī. *Tafsīr al-Imamayn al-Jalālayn*. Dar El-Marefah, 2002.

Martensson, Ulrika. '"The Persuasive Proof": A Study of Aristotle's Politics and Rhetoric in the Qur'ān and in al-Ṭabarī's Commentary." *Jerusalem Studies in Arabic and Islam* 34: 363–420.

Martin, Richard C. "Inimitability." *Encyclopaedia of the Qur'ān*. Edited by Jane Dammen McAuliffe, Brill, 2002.

Maybudī, Rashīd al-Dīn. *Kashf al-Asrār wa 'Uddat al-Abrār: Unveiling of the Mysteries and the Provision of the Pious*. Abridged version. Translated by William C. Chittick. Fons Vitae, 2015.

McAuliffe, Jane Dammen. "Chosen of All Women: Mary and Fāṭima in Qur'ānic Exegesis." *Islamochristiana* 7 (1981): 19–28.

McAuliffe, Jane Dammen. "Text and Textuality: Q. 3:7 as a Point of Intersection." In *Literary Structures of Religious Meaning in the Qur'an*, edited by Issa J. Boullata. Curzon, 2000, 56–76.

Merguerian, Gayane Karen, and Najmabadi, Afsaneh. "Zulaykha and Yusuf: Whose 'Best Story'?" *International Journal of Middle East Studies* 29, no. 4 (1997): 485–508.

Mir, Mustansir. *Coherence in the Qur'ān*. American Trust, 1986.

Mir, Mustansir. "Dialogue in the Qur'ān." *Religion & Literature* 24, no. 1 (1992): 1–22.

Mir, Mustansir. "Humor in the Qur'an." *The Muslim World* 81 (1991): 179–193.

Mir, Mustansir. "Irony in the Qur'an: A Study of the Story of Joseph." In *Literary Structures of Religious Meaning in the Qur'an*, edited by Issa J. Boullata. Curzon, 2000, 173–187.

Mir, Mustansir. "The Qur'an as Literature." *Religion & Literature* 20, no. 1 (1988): 49–64.

Mir, Mustansir. "The Qur'anic Story of Joseph: Plot, Themes, And Characters." *The Muslim World* 76, no. 1: 1–15.

Mir, Mustansir. "Some Aspects of Narration in the Qur'an." In *Sacred Tropes: Tanakh, New Testament, and Qur'an as Literature and Culture*, edited by Roberta Sterman Sabbath. Brill, 2009, 93–106.

Mir, Mustansir. *Understanding the Islamic Scripture: A Study of Selected Passages from the Qur'ān*. Pearson Longman, 2008.

Morris, James W. "Dramatizing the Sura of Joseph: An Introduction to the Islamic Humanities." *Journal of Turkish Studies* 18 (1994): 201–224.

Mourad, Suleiman A. "On the Qur'ānic Stories About Mary and Jesus." *Bulletin of the Royal Institute for Inter-faith Studies* 1, no. 2 (1999): 13–24.

Naddaff, Sandra. *Arabesque: Narrative Structure and the Aesthetics of Repetition in the 1001 Nights*. Northwestern University Press, 1991.

Najmabadi, Afsaneh. "Reading—And Enjoying—'Wiles of Women' Stories as a Feminist." *Iranian Studies*, 32, no. 2 (1999): 203–222.

Nasr, Seyyed Hossein, Caner K. Dagli, et al. *The Study Qur'an: A New Translation and Commentary*. HarperCollins, 2015.

Netton, Ian Richard. "Towards a Modern *Tafsīr* of *Sūrat al-Kahf*: Structure and Semiotics." *Journal of Qur'anic Studies* 2, no. 1 (2000): 67–87.

Neuwirth, Angelika. "The House of Abraham and the House of Amram: Genealogy, Patriarchal Authority, and Exegetical Professionalism." In *The Qur'ān in Context: Historical and Literary Investigations into the Qur'ānic Milieu*, edited by Angelika Neuwirth, Nicolai Sinai, and Michael Marx. Leiden: Brill NV, 2010, 499–532.

Neuwirth, Angelika. "Mary and Jesus—Counterbalancing the Biblical Patriarchs. A Re-reading of Sūrat Maryam in Sūrat Āl 'Imrān (3:1-62)." *Parole de l'Orient* 30 (2005): 231–260.

Neuwirth, Angelika. "'Oral Scriptures' in Contact. The Qur'ānic Story of the Golden Calf and Its Biblical Subtext Between Narrative, Cult, and Inter-communal Debate." In *Self-Referentiality in the Qur'ān*, edited by Stefan Wild. Wiesbaden, Harrassowitz Verlag, 2006, 71–92.

Neuwirth, Angelika. "Orientalism in Oriental Studies? Qur'anic Studies as a Case in Point." *Journal of Qur'anic Studies* 9, no. 2 (2007): 115–127.

Neuwirth, Angelika. "Qur'an and History—a Disputed Relationship: Some Reflections on Qur'anic History and History in the Qur'an." *Journal of Qur'anic Studies* 5, no. 1 (2003): 1–18.

Neuwirth, Angelika. "Referentiality and Textuality in *Sūrat al-Ḥijr*. Some Observations on the Qur'ānic 'Canonical Process' and the Emergence of a Community." In *Literary Structures of Religious Meaning in the Qur'an*, edited by Issa J. Boullata. Curzon, 2000, 143–172.

Neuwirth, Angelika. *Scripture, Poetry, and the Making of a Community: Reading the Qur'an as a Literary Text*. Oxford University Press, 2014.

Neuwirth, Angelika. "Two Views of History and Human Future: Qur'anic and Biblical Renderings of Divine Promises." *Journal of Qur'anic Studies* 10, no. 1 (2008): 1–20.

Newby, Gordon D. "The Drowned Son: Midrash and Midrash Making in the Qur'an and *Tafsīr*." In *Studies in Islamic and Judaic Traditions*, edited by William M. Brinner and Stephen D. Ricks. Scholars Press, 1986, 19–32.

Nguyen, Martin. "Exegesis of the *Ḥurūf al-Muqaṭṭaʿa*: Polyvalency in Sunnī Traditions of Qur'anic Interpretation." *Journal of Qur'anic Studies* 14, no. 2 (2012): 1–28.

Obiedat, Ahmad Z. "Defining the Good in the Qur'an: A Conceptual Systemisation." *Journal of Qur'anic Studies* 14, no. 2 (2012): 110–120.

Ong, Walter J. *Orality and Literacy: The Technologizing of the Word*. Routledge, 1988.

Osman, Fathi. *Topics of the Quran: A Topical Reading*. 2nd ed., revised and with additions. MVI, 1999.

Ozgur Alhassen, Leyla. "Islam and Iconoclasm: Ibrāhīm and the Destruction of Idols in the Qur'ān," *Religion and the Arts* 23, no. 3 (2019): 195–216.

Ozgur Alhassen, Leyla. "A Narratological Analysis of the Story of Ibrāhīm in the Qur'ān: Faith, Family, Parents and Ancestors." *Religion and Literature* 49, no. 3 (2019): 49–76.

Ozgur Alhassen, Leyla. *Qur'ānic Stories: God, Revelation and the Audience*. Edinburgh University Press, 2021.

Ozgur Alhassen, Leyla. "A Structural Analysis of *Sūrat Maryam* Q. 19:1–58." *Journal of Qur'anic Studies* 18, no. 1 (2016): 92–116.

Ozgur Alhassen, Leyla. "'You Were Not There,' the Creation of Humility and Knowledge in Qur'ānic Stories: A Rhetorical and Narratological Analysis." *Comparative Islamic Studies* 11, no. 1 (2015 [2017]): 65–94.

Quṭb, Sayyid. *Fī Ẓilāl al-Qur'ān*. 6 vols. Dar al-Shorouk, 2007.

Reda, Nevin. *The Al-Baqara Crescendo: Understanding the Qur'an's Style, Narrative Structure, and Running Themes*. McGill-Queen's University Press, 2017.

Rendsburg, Gary A. "Literary Structures in the Qur'anic and Biblical Stories of Joseph." *The Muslim World* 78, no. 2: 118–20.

Reynolds, Gabriel Said. *The Qur'ān and Its Biblical Subtext*. Routledge, 2010.

Riddell, Peter G. "The Transmission of Narrative-Based Exegesis in Islam: al-Baghawī's Use of Stories in his Commentary on the Qur'ān, and a Malay Descendent." In *Islam: Essays on Scripture, Thought and Society: A Festschrift in Honor of Anthony H. Johns*, edited by Peter G. Riddell and Tony Street, Brill, 1997, 57–80.

Rippin, Andrew. "'Desiring the Face of God': The Qur'ānic Symbolism of Personal Responsibility.' In *Literary Structures of Religious Meaning in the Qur'an*, edited by Issa J. Boullata. Curzon, 2000, 117–124.

Rippin, Andrew. Review of *Studien zur Komposition der mekkanischen Suren* by Angelika Neuwirth. *Bulletin of the School of Oriental and African Studies, University of London* 45, no. 1 (1982): 149–150.

Robinson, Neal. *Christ in Christianity and Islam*. State University of New York Press, 1991.

Robinson, Neal. *Discovering the Qur'an: A Contemporary Approach to a Veiled Text*. 2nd ed. Georgetown University Press, 2003.

Robson, James. "Stories of Jesus and Mary." *The Muslim World* 40, no. 4 (1950): 236–243.

Rosenberg, Joel. "Biblical Narrative." In *Back to the Sources: Reading the Classical Jewish Texts*, edited by Barry W. Holtz. Summit Books, 1984, 31–82.

Rubin, Uri. "Traditions in Transformation: The Ark of the Covenant and the Golden Calf in Biblical and Islamic Historiography." *Oriens* 36 (2001): 196–214.

Ruf, Frederick J. "The Consequences of Genre: Narrative, Lyric, and Dramatic Intelligibility." *Journal of the American Academy of Religion* 62, no. 3 (1994): 799–818.

Saheeh International. *The Quran: Arabic Text with Corresponding English Meaning*, 1997. https://www.islamawakened.com/quran/20/39/.

Sakaedani, Haruko. "The Correlation Between Definite Noun Phrases and Verb Forms in Qur'anic Narrative Texts." *Journal of Qur'anic Studies* 6, no. 2 (2004): 56–68.

Saleh, Walid. *The Formation of the Classical Tafsīr Tradition: The Qur'ān Commentary of al-Thaʿlabī (d. 427/1035)*. Brill, 2004.

Saleh, Walid. '"What if you refuse, when ordered to fight?' King Saul (Ṭālūt) in the Qur'ān and Post-Quranic Literature." In *Saul in Story and Tradition*, edited by Carl S. Ehrlich, Tübingen: Mohr Siebeck, 2006, 261–283.

Saussure, Ferdinand de. "Course in General Linguistics." In *Literary Theory: An Anthology*, edited by Julie Rivkin and Michael Ryan. Blackwell, 2004, 59–71.

Sells, Michael. *Approaching the Qur'ān: The Early Revelations*. White Cloud Press, 1999.

Sells, Michael. "A Literary Approach to the Hymnic Sūras of the Qur'ān: Spirit, Gender, and Aural Intertextuality." In *Literary Structures of Religious Meaning in the Qur'an*, edited by Issa J. Boullata. Curzon, 2000, 3–25.

Sells, Michael. "Sound and Meaning in *Sūrat al-Qāriʿa*." *Arabica* 40, no. 3 (1993): 403–430.

Shahid, Irfan. "Another Contribution to Koranic Exegesis: The Sura of the Poets (XXVI)." *Journal of Arabic Literature* 14 (1983): 1–21.

Shahid, Irfan. "Fawātiḥ al-Suwar: The Mysterious Letters of the Qur'ān." *Literary Structures of Religious Meaning in the Qur'an*, edited by Issa J. Boullata. Curzon, 2000, 125–142.

Shahid, Irfan. "The 'Sūra' of the Poets, Qur'ān XXVI: Final Conclusions." *Journal of Arabic Literature* 35, no. 2 (2004).

al-Shidyaq, Ahmad Faris. *Leg over Leg: Volumes One and Two*. Reprint edition. Translated by Humphrey Davies. New York University Press, 2015.

Silvers, Laury. '"In the Book We Have Left out Nothing': The Ethical Problem of the Existence of Verse 4:34 in the Qur'an." *Comparative Islamic Studies* 2, no. 2 (2008): 171–180.

Smith, Andrew C. "Deliberate Alternation of Time: Verbal Enallage or *Iltifāt* as Rhetorical Poetics in Surah 54 (al-Qamar)." Presentation, IQSA, 2016.

Smith, Jane I., and Yvonne Y. Haddad. "The Virgin Mary in Islamic Tradition and Commentary." *The Muslim World* 79, no. 3–4: 161–187.

Stern, David. *Midrash and Theory: Ancient Jewish Exegesis and Contemporary Literary Studies*. Northwestern University Press, 1996.

Stern, M. S. "Muhammad and Joseph: A Study of Koranic Narrative." *Journal of Near Eastern Studies* 44, no. 3 (1985): 193–204.

Sternberg, Meir. *The Poetics of Biblical Narrative: Ideological Literature and the Drama of Reading*. Indiana University Press, 1985.

Stetkevych, Suzanne Pinckney. "Solomon and Mythic Kingship in the Arab-Islamic Tradition: Qaṣīdah, Qur'ān and Qiṣaṣ al-anbiyā'." *Journal of Arabic Literature* 48 (2017): 1–37.

Stewart, Devin J. "Divine Epithets and the Dibacchius: Clausulae and Qur'anic Rhythm." *Journal of Qur'anic Studies* 15, no. 2 (2013): 22–64.

Stowasser, Barbara Freyer. *Women in the Qur'an, Traditions, and Interpretation*. Oxford University Press, 1994.

Syamsuddin, Sahiron. "*Muḥkam* and *Mutashābih*: An Analytical Study of al-Ṭabarī's and al-Zamakhsharī's Interpretations of Q.3:7." *Journal of Qur'anic Studies* 1, no. 1 (1999): 63–79.

al-Ṭabarī, Abū Jaʿfar Muḥammad ibn Jarīr. 10 vols. *Jāmiʿ al-Bayān ʿan Ta'wīl al-Qur'an*. Dār al-Salām, 2007.

al-Ṭabrisī, Abū ʿAlī al-Faḍl ibn al-Ḥasan. *Majmaʿ al-Bayān fī Tafsīr al-Qur'an*. Accessed at www.altafsir.com/Tafasir.asp?tMadhNo=4&tTafsirNo=3&tSoraNo=28&tAyahNo=14&tDisplay=yes&Page=2&Size=1&LanguageId=1.

Taji-Farouki, Suha, ed. *Modern Muslim Intellectuals and the Qur'ān*. Oxford University Press, 2004.

Tlili, Sarra. *Animals in the Qur'an*. New York: Cambridge University Press, 2012.

al-Thaʿālibī, Abū Zayd ʿAbd al-Rahmān b. Muḥammad b. Makhlūf. *al-Jawāhir al-Ḥisān*. 3 vols. Dār al-Kutub al-ʿIlmiyya, 1996.

Toorawa, Shawkat M. "*Sūrat Maryam* (Q. 19): Lexicon, Lexical Echoes, English Translation." *Journal of Qur'ānic Studies* 13, no. 1 (2011): 25–78.

Tottoli, Roberto. "About Qur'anic Narratives: A Review Article Koraniceskie skazanija (Qur'anic narratives) by Gianni Capra; M.B. Piotrovskij." *Oriente Moderno* 72, no. 7–12 (1992): 87–91.

Tottoli, Roberto. *Biblical Prophets in the Qur'ān and Muslim Literature*. Translated by Michael Robertson. Curzon Press, 2002.

al-Tustarī, Abī Muḥammad Sahl bin 'Abd Allah. *Tafsīr al-Tustarī*. Dār al-Kutub al-'Ilmiyyah, 2002.

Wahyudi, Jarot. "Literary Interpretation of the Qur'ān: 'Fawāṣil al-Āyāt,' 'Qasam' and 'Istifhām,' Three Examples from Bint al-Shāṭi''s Tafsīr." *Islamic Studies* 37, no. 1 (1998): 19–28.

Waldman, Marilyn R. "New Approaches to 'Biblical' Materials in the Qur'ān." *The Muslim World* 75, no. 1: 1–13.

Ward Gwynne, Rosalind. *Logic, Rhetoric, and Legal Reasoning in the Qur'ān: God's Arguments*. RoutledgeCurzon, 2004.

Welch, Alford T. "Formulaic Features of the Punishment-Stories." In *Literary Structures of Religious Meaning in the Qur'an*, edited by Issa J. Boullata. Curzon, 2000, 77–116.

Welch, Alford T. "Review of *Studien zur Komposition der mekkanischen Suren* by Angelika Neuwirth." *Journal of the American Oriental Society* 103, no. 4 (1983): 764–767.

Wheeler, Brannon. "Arab Prophets of the Qur'an and Bible." *Journal of Qur'anic Studies* 8, no. 2 (2006): 24–57.

Wheeler, Brannon. *Moses in the Quran and Islamic Exegesis*. RoutledgeCurzon, 2002.

Wheeler, Brannon. "Moses or Alexander? Early Islamic Exegesis of Qur'ān 18:60–65." *Journal of Near Eastern Studies* 57, no. 3 (1998): 191–215.

Wheeler, Brannon. *Prophets in the Quran: An Introduction to the Quran and Muslim Exegesis*. Continuum, 2002.

White, Hayden. *The Content of the Form: Narrative Discourse and Historical Representation*. Johns Hopkins University Press, 1987.

Wolf, C. Umhau. "Moses in Christian and Islamic Tradition." *Journal of Bible and Religion* 27, no. 2 (1959): 102–108.

Yazicioglu, Isra. *Understanding the Qur'anic Miracle Stories in the Modern Age*. Pennsylvania State University Press, 2013.

Zadeh, Travis. *The Vernacular Qur'an: Translation and the Rise of Persian Exegesis*. Oxford University Press, 2012.

Zahniser, A. H. Mathias. "Major Transitions and Thematic Borders in Two Long Sūras: *al-Baqara* and *al-Nisā'*." In *Literary Structures of Religious Meaning in the Qur'an*, edited by Issa J. Boullata. Curzon, 2000, 26–55.

Zahniser, A. H. Mathias. "The Word of God and the Apostleship of 'Isa: A Narrative Analysis of Al-'Imrān (3):33–62." *Journal of Semitic Studies* 36 (1991): 77–112.

al-Zamakhsharī, Abū al-Qāsim Maḥmūd ibn 'Umar. 4 vols. *Al-Kashshāf*. Dār El-Fikr, 2006.

Zebiri, Kate. "Towards a Rhetorical Criticism of the Qur'ān." *Journal of Qur'anic Studies* 5, no. 2 (2003): 95–120.

Zubir, Badri Najib. "Departure from Communicative Norms in the Qur'an: Insights from al-Jurjānī and al-Zamakhsharī." *Journal of Qur'anic Studies* 2, no. 2 (2000): 69–81.

Zwettler, Michael J. "The Sura of the Poets: 'Final Conclusions'?" *Journal of Arabic Literature* 38, no. 2 (2007): 111–166.

# Index

*For the benefit of digital users, indexed terms that span two pages (e.g., 52–53) may, on occasion, appear on only one of those pages.*
Tables and figures are indicated by *t* and *f* following the page number


acceptance, 79, 145
ʿĀd, 123, 127, 130, 141–42
adopt, adoption, 26, 42, 43, 73–74, 102, 109, 145–46
afterlife, 63, 96–97, 101–2, 105, 106, 108, 109–10, 112, 114–15, 117, 120–21, 124, 130, 133–35, 139, 143, 146–47
agency, 10, 18–19, 145
Alter, Robert, 2, 5, 36, 38–45, 49–50, 54, 77–78
analysis, narratological, 2 , –3, 95, 97, 146
analysis, rhetorical, 2–3, 33, 41, 62, 97
ancestors, ancestry (ʾ-*b*-*w*), 96–97, 98–101, 105–6, 108, 112, 114, 139
angels, 11, 79, 80–81, 85–86
annunciation, 78–79, 83*f*
authority, 27, 53, 58, 145–46

baby, 10, 11, 15, 16, 20–21, 20*f*, 22*t*, 28–29, 43, 53, 85–86
Banī Isrāʾīl (Children of Israel), 24, 31–32, 32*f*, 53, 58, 59, 69, 70, 73–74, 98, 99*t*, 107–8, 109, 112, 141, 150, 155*t*
Bashir, Shahzad, 64, 67
ʿ-*b*-*d*, *ʿabd*, *ʿibād*, 82–84, 111, 127, 141, 160*t*, 163*t*, 164*t*
belief, beliefs (theological), 1, 3, 5–6, 8, 9–10, 14, 62, 64–65, 75, 77–78, 95, 146
betray, betrayal, 26, 33–34, 81
blame, 17–18, 26, 48–49, 53, 58, 70–71, 75, 92–93, 117, 156*t*
blending of various registers, 127
*b*-*n*-*y*, 106, 139
brevity, 44
*b*-*sh*-*r*, 11–12, 116, 143
*b*-*ṣ*-*r*, 126*t*, 131
*b*-*y*-*n*, 101–2, 159*t*, 164*t*

calf, cow, 4–5, 11, 17, 24, 69–70, 85–86, 92, 149, 150, 151*t*, 156*t*
camel, 114, 127–28, 130, 140, 141
celestial bodies, 27, 28
character, characterization, 4, 5, 10, 14, 16, 26, 28, 33–34, 38, 39–40, 43, 44–45, 48–49, 50, 53, 54–55, 56, 58, 59–61, 64, 66, 70, 71, 74–75, 84, 102, 106, 112–13, 116–17, 120, 131, 135–36, 137–38, 145–47, 158*t*
Chatman, Seymour, 62–63
chest, 15, 110–11, 116
children, 10–14, 15–21, 22*t*, 33–34, 53, 55, 73–74, 77–95, 98, 99*t*, 102, 105–6, 109, 145
Children of Israel. *See* Banī Isrāʾīl
choice to believe or not, 96–97, 108–13, 136
chronological, 5, 32–33, 41, 60–61, 62–63, 139
comfort, 42, 43, 48, 49*t*, 67, 68, 80, 90, 91, 115, 132, 151*t*
commentators, 18–19, 67, 68, 70, 79, 80, 82, 86, 91, 92–93, 94
communication, breakdown of, 6–7, 29
comparison, 7, 10, 16, 25, 36, 55, 58, 102, 118, 122–44, 153, 161
concentric circles, concentric construction, 9, 41, 42*t*, 147
context , 13, 27, 29, 37, 39–40, 48–50, 52, 54, 59–60, 72–73, 80–81, 82, 84, 89, 91, 92, 97, 98, 117, 130, 150
contradiction, 35, 36, 143–44
criteria, 127–28
Cuypers, Michel, 9, 41, 89–90

Day of Judgment, Judgment Day, 32–33, 63, 105, 106, 124–26, 127, 128–29, 139, 142–43

despair, 53
ʿ-*dh-b*, 130, 160*t*, 161*t*, 164*t*
dialogue, 5–6, 27–28, 50–51, 52, 55, 59, 60–61, 65, 66–67, 68, 69–70, 71, 80–81, 105, 106, 109–10, 116, 118, 130, 136, 137–38, 139–41
didactic, 5–6, 64, 75, 146
disciples, ʿĪsā's, 16, 87–95
disconnected letters, 31, 33, 147
discourse, 2, 36, 37, 62–63, 70, 72, 73, 74, 75, 139
disobey, 56–57, 69, 70–71, 91–92, 156*t*
displaced, displacement, 1–2, 29, 105
divine, 44–45, 63–64, 67, 72–73
*ḍ-l-l*, *ḍāllīn*, 109, 127–28, 143, 160*t*, 162*t*, 164*t*
dream, 15, 16–17, 18, 31, 93
dynamic, 123, 124–26, 133–34, 135, 136

echo, echoes, echoing (words and phrases), 1–2, 3, 4, 6, 7, 11–12, 14, 17, 25, 28–29, 37, 77–95, 104–5, 115, 117, 122, 133–34, 137, 146, 148
ellipsis, 62–63, 66–67, 68, 72, 73, 75, 146
empower, 28, 41, 99*t*, 123, 129, 132–33
empty, 43
end-rhyme, 49–50, 122, 123
eternal, 68, 72–73, 125–26
exclusion, 9–10, 44
extraordinary, 38, 123, 124–29, 142, 143–44
eye, eyes, 15, 45, 72–73, 102, 124, 125–27, 130, 131, 132, 134, 138

*fa-dhūqū* (taste), 130, 134–35
fallible, 132–33
families, 14, 16, 145, 147
family members, doing counterintuitive things, 9–10, 15–21
fasting (*ṣiyām*, *ṣawm*), 6, 77–95, 146, 148
fear, 11, 15, 21, 24, 27–28, 39–40, 41, 42, 43, 45, 50, 51*t*, 52, 53, 54, 55, 56, 65, 66–67, 71–72, 73–74, 86, 87, 93–94, 96–97, 98, 99*t*, 107, 109, 110–11, 116, 123, 130, 131, 132–33, 140, 142–43, 151*t*, 155*t*
feasting, 77–95
feelings, 53, 61, 64, 116, 125–26, 131
fickleness, 124–25
Firʿawn's wife, 43, 56, 59, 151*t*
fire, 39, 43–44, 50, 51*t*, 66–67, 69, 116, 151*t*
flashback, 62–63, 69, 70–72, 75
flashforward/prolepse, 62–63, 66, 68, 72, 75, 146
flood, 126–27, 132
focalization, focalizer, 5, 7, 38, 51–54, 60–61, 137–38, 144, 145–46, 147
food, 11–12, 77–95, 106, 156*t*, 158*t*
*f-s-d*, 98
*f-t-ḥ*, 101–2, 118

Genette, Gerard, 62–63
gesture, 40, 79
*gh-l-b*, 104–5, 163*t*
gift, 11, 78, 102–3
God, answering people's prayers, 82
God, at the center, 2
God, central to human lives, 14
God, involvement in people's lives, 72
God's promise, 42, 64
guide, guided, 10, 24, 27, 36, 53, 56, 61, 74–75, 81, 94, 99*t*, 105–6

*ḥadīth*, 18–19, 36, 64, 92–93
Hāmān, 42, 57–58, 59–60, 151*t*
heart, 36, 42, 43, 80, 87, 88, 90–91, 104–5, 124–25, 129, 132–33, 156*t*
history, historical, 1, 2–3, 5, 31–32, 35, 36, 44–45, 50–51, 54, 60–61, 63–64, 82, 89, 145–46, 149
holistic, 1, 148
Hūd, 96–121, 123, 123*t*, 126*t*, 128, 130, 136–37, 138*t*, 140, 141–43, 159*t*, 160*t*, 161*t*, 162*t*, 163*t*
human weakness, 123, 129–32, 142
hypocrisy, 53

Ibrāhīm's father, 6–7, 11, 105, 139, 145
Ibrāhīm's son, 16
*imām*, 13, 14, 33–34
information, selective giving and withholding of, 38
inherit, inheritance, 10, 11, 14, 109, 112, 139
injustice, 71–72
innocence, 18–19, 70
inspiration, 6–7, 17–18, 19–20, 96–121, 136, 146–47
interact, interactive, interacting with the Qurʾān, 1, 3, 4–5, 10, 15, 18, 20–21, 33–34, 72–74, 77, 83–84, 92–93, 136, 137, 139, 145
intimate, 5, 27–28, 61, 80–81, 82–83, 105, 131
intratextual, 2, 37
irony, 55, 84–85

Ismāʿīl, 19–20

*j-n-n*, 125–26, 126*t*
joy, 42, 43
judge, 24, 27, 48–49, 75, 82, 117, 125–26, 128–29, 142
judgment, 118, 139–40
Judgment Day. *See* Day of Judgment
justice, 18–19, 71–72, 75

Kaʿba, 13–14, 20*f*, 20–21, 22*t*, 33–34, 101
*k-dh-b*, 118–19, 127–28, 142–43, 159*t*, 161*t*, 164*t*
Kermani, Navid, 4
*k-f-r*, *kuffārukum*, 108–9, 134–35, 137–38, 162*t*, 164*t*
al-Khiḍr, al-Khaḍir, 26, 158*t*
*kh-l-d*, 107–8
*kh-w-f*, 116, 164*t*
kill, 15, 21, 24, 25–26, 28–29, 42, 43, 51–53, 55–56, 73–74, 87, 91–92, 93–94, 108, 116, 130, 140, 143, 151*t*, 156*t*, 158*t*

legal, verses, 33, 84, 95, 146, 148
*Leitwort*. *See* root letters
lengths, 2, 37–38, 56
liar, calling others, 6–7, 54, 56, 65, 73, 96–97, 111–12, 116–17, 119, 120, 128, 130–31, 142–43
limitlessness of God, 50–51
limits of human language, 50–51
linear, 36, 63–64
*ʿ-l-m*, 102, 106, 117, 159*t*, 163*t*, 164*t*
local, 27–28
logic, 9–10, 33, 63–64, 127–28
L/lord, *rabb*, *rabbanā*, *rabbuka*, *rabbi*, 11–12, 39, 50, 77–95, 101, 103–4, 106, 109–10, 112–13, 116, 117, 118, 119
loss, 43, 99*t*
loyalty, 14, 105–6, 109
*l-q-y*, 4–5, 17
Lūṭ, 85–86, 95, 96–121, 122–44, 159*t*, 160*t*, 161*t*, 162*t*, 163*t*
lying, liar, 6–7, 54, 56, 65, 73, 96–97, 111–12, 116–17, 118–19, 120, 128, 130–31, 142–43

*al-madīna*, 25
Madyan, 24, 25–26, 151*t*
majestic, 28
*al-Mālik*, 32–33, 32*f*
manipulate, manipulative, manipulating, 53, 55, 61, 73–74, 75, 98, 109, 120–21, 145–46
Maryam's mother, 11, 20*f*, 20–21, 22*t*, 33–34, 85, 95, 145
meaning, layers of, meaning making, 1–2, 3, 4, 29–30, 31, 63, 72–73, 93, 114, 115, 126–27, 135–36, 144
Meccan, *sūras*, 32–33
mercy, 11, 16, 32–33, 32*f*, 54, 58, 67, 69, 80, 81
metanarrative, 5–6, 62, 77–79, 95, 146
miracle, 24, 41, 88, 89–90, 97, 101–2, 108, 124, 139
misguide, misguided, 53, 73, 98, 101–2, 120, 127–28, 138, 140
mistake, 24, 48–49, 52, 53, 71–72, 109, 125, 134–35, 143
*ʿ-m-l*, 117
moon, 16, 27, 31, 124–25, 128–29, 132–33
motif, 38, 40–42, 42*t*, 77–79, 84
Muḥammad, Prophet, 18–19, 29, 44–45, 50, 56–57, 58, 71–72, 92, 97, 103–5, 110, 112–13, 115, 116, 118, 124–26, 128, 130, 133, 134–35, 137–38, 141, 143–44
multiple readings, 2
Mūsā's mother, 10, 15, 16, 17, 19–21, 22*t*, 33–34, 43, 55, 145, 151*t*
Mūsā's sister, 43, 151*t*
*al-muṣawwir*, 68
*mustaqirr*, 132

Naddaff, Sandra, 2, 5, 36, 38, 39, 40, 44–45, 54, 66, 72–73
*nadhīr*, 26, 101–2
nature, 27–28, 36, 86, 107, 124–25, 126*t*, 127, 128–29, 131, 142–43, 145–46, 148
*n-dh-r*, 127–28, 161*t*, 164*t*
near, 29, 39–40, 44, 56, 81, 82, 94, 104–5, 124
Neuwirth, Angelika, 63, 82, 83, 84–85, 122
*n-ṣ-r*, 126*t*, 131, 160*t*, 162*t*, 164*t*
*n-z-l*, 119

Ong, Walter, 4
oral, orality, 4, 36, 39, 148
ordinary, 116, 119–20, 123, 124–29, 142, 143
organizational logic, pattern, 31–32, 33
original, 9–10, 27–28, 35, 77, 103–4
outlier, 4–5, 9–10, 28–30, 33, 94, 119, 144

pair, paired concepts, 6–7, 30, 33, 36, 102, 113–14, 133–34

parallel, 2, 9–34, 36, 50, 103–4, 110–12, 120–21, 128–29, 146–47
parent, 10–14, 15–21, 22*t*, 71–72, 105–6, 139, 145, 158*t*
patient, 26, 137–38, 158*t*
performative, 4, 5–6, 64, 67
personal, 28
poets, poetry, 96–97, 110, 143–44
prayer, supplication, *du'ā'*, 11, 14, 16, 43, 56, 67, 73–74, 79–80, 82, 83*f*, 83–84, 85–86, 87, 89, 92, 94–95, 104–5, 106, 112, 114–15, 118, 139
presence, 29, 39–40, 41, 57–58, 64, 65, 66–67, 68, 75, 132
prison, 17, 18–19, 92–93, 99*t*, 101, 102, 109–10, 145
privilege, 6–7, 18–19, 41, 56, 71–72, 96–98, 99*t*, 102–3, 105, 108, 112, 120–21
prophecy, 2, 44–45, 96–97, 136
prostrate, 48, 49*t*, 104–5, 151*t*

Qārūn, 57–58, 59–60
*qaṣīdah*, 78
*q-dh-f*, 4–5, 17
*q-d-m*, 98–101, 106, 139
*q-d-r*, 132, 161*t*, 164*t*
*q-l-b*, 104–5
*q-r-b*, 104–5
*q-ṣ-y*, 1–2, 28–29
Qur'ān explains the Qur'ān (*al-Qur'ān yufassir ba'ḍuhu ba'ḍan*), 2
Qur'ānic audience, 26, 56, 84, 115
*q-w-m*, 114–15, 159*t*, 162*t*, 164*t*

*al-Raḥīm*, 32–33, 112–13
*al-Raḥmān*, 32–33
*r-b-b*, 112–13, 159*t*, 164*t*
*r-dh-l*, 116–17, 118
Reda, Nevin, 9, 31–32
refocus, 53
regret, 139, 151*t*
rehearse, 68
relationship, between the audience and the Qur'ān/text, 1, 123, 142, 144, 147
  relationship, between people and messengers, 142, 144, 147
  relationship, with God, 3, 105
repetition, aborted, 38, 45, 48–49
  repetition, deployed, 38, 45–47
  repetition, suppressed, 38, 45, 49–51, 137
repetitive, repetitiveness, 12, 35, 140, 144
request, 64–65, 66–67, 75, 87, 88, 89–90, 91, 95, 102–3, 146, 151*t*
resonance, 4, 9, 36
retell, 53, 54
return, 15, 17–18, 27–28, 39–40, 41, 42, 43, 46, 47, 51–52, 68, 69, 71–72, 85–86, 99*t*, 104–5, 108, 117, 128, 151*t*
revelation, 96–121, 122–44
reward (*'-j-r*), 2, 43, 45, 47, 48–49, 49*t*, 94–95, 96–97, 99*t*, 102–3, 104–5, 107, 108, 111, 112, 113–14, 115, 118, 119, 120–21, 128–29, 130, 131, 132, 136, 142–43, 146–47, 151*t*, 156*t*
*r-ḥ-m*, 112–13, 164*t*
ritual exchange, 78
root letters, 4, 6–7, 38, 39–40, 42, 57, 83–84, 96, 104–5, 120, 127–28, 144, 146–47, 159*t*, 160*t*, 161*t*, 162*t*, 163*t*, 164*t*
*r-s-l*, *al-mursalīn*, *rasūl*, 57, 93, 96–97, 98, 113, 119, 141, 159*t*, 161*t*, 164*t*

sacrifice, 14, 15, 16, 17, 20–21, 20*f*, 22*t*, 33–34, 78–79, 80, 86, 87, 88*t*, 90, 95, 156*t*
sadness, 10, 43
Ṣāliḥ, 97*t*, 102, 107–8, 113, 114, 116, 118–20, 123, 123*t*, 126*t*, 127–28, 130–31, 135, 136–38, 138*t*, 140, 141–44, 159*t*, 160*t*, 161*t*, 162*t*, 163*t*
salvation, 123, 132–33
al-Sāmirī, 4–5, 17, 24, 156*t*
*sāriqūn*, 17–18
scale, 1–2, 4–5, 6–7, 9, 10, 28, 32–33, 36, 38, 39, 40, 42, 43, 45, 62, 96, 114–15, 120, 122, 141–42, 144, 145, 146–47
scripture, 43, 13, 31, 36, 58, 128, 130, 138, 150, 155*t*
*ṣ-d-q*, 119–20, 160*t*, 163*t*, 164*t*
second-person singular, 133, 137–38, 141
seduce, 17–18, 26
Sells, Michael, 4
semantic, 2, 4–5, 12, 17, 21, 25, 33–34, 37, 39, 95, 97, 146, 148
senses, 106, 125, 126*t*, 131
sequence, 3, 7, 38, 43–44, 96, 105, 122, 136–37
series of stories, 4, 6–7, 10, 96, 120, 123, 125–26, 146–47
shape, shaping, 5–6, 30, 31, 52, 53, 54, 62, 67, 68, 72, 104–5, 136–37
Shayṭān, *shayāṭīn*, devil, devils (*sh-ṭ-n*), 17, 96–97, 103, 106–7, 108, 119, 142–43

*sh-k-r*, 131, 163*t*
*s-ḥ-r*, 96–97, 102, 124–25, 159*t*, 164*t*
Shu'ayb, 97*t*, 102, 111–12, 113, 114–15, 116, 117, 118–20, 136–37, 138*t*, 141, 159*t*, 160*t*
sign, signs, *'-y-y*, *āya*, 11–12, 18–19, 27–28, 30, 31, 31*f*, 39–40, 46, 47, 50, 56, 57, 58–59, 65, 66–67, 73, 78, 79–81, 83–84, 83*f*, 88, 107–8, 111–13, 114, 117, 124–25, 127–29, 132, 134–35, 138, 142–43, 151*t*, 159*t*, 164*t*
slave, slavery, enslave, 6–7, 24, 27–28, 53, 73, 98, 99*t*, 109, 111, 139, 145, 147
snake, 27–28, 39–40, 41, 51*t*, 101–2, 151*t*
sorcerers, sorcery, 45–47, 48–49, 58, 99*t*, 102–3, 104–5, 124–25
stability, 123, 124–25, 127, 129, 132–33, 144, 147
star, stars, 16, 27, 31
storytelling, 5–6, 35, 60–61, 64, 75, 145–46
strangers, 9–10, 21–26, 33–34
style, 2, 5, 8, 15, 29–30, 33, 48–49, 54, 56, 71–72, 77, 82, 88–89, 105, 122, 123, 124–26, 133–34, 135, 136, 144, 149
successor, 10
Sulaymān, 78
sun, 16, 27, 31, 99*t*
*Sūrat 'Abasa*, 71–72
*Sūrat al-Fātiḥa*, 32–33, 32*f*
*Sūrat al-Kahf*, 26, 54
*Sūrat Maryam*, 3, 9–14, 20–21, 30, 30*f*, 35
*Sūrat al-Najm*, 122
*Sūrat al-Qamar*, 7, 105, 107–9, 112–13, 120, 122–44, 147, 161
*Sūrat al-Raḥmān*, 122
*Sūrat al-Shu'arā'*, 6–7, 8, 48–49, 66, 72–75, 96–121, 122–44, 147, 159, 161
*Sūrat Ṭaha*, 15, 17, 37, 66–72, 73, 74–75
*Sūrat Yūsuf*, 10, 15–21, 30, 31*f*, 33, 48–49, 63, 77, 147
swerve, 9–14, 18, 20–21, 20*f*, 22*t*, 26, 27–28, 29–30, 33, 105, 145

*tafsīr*, 2–3, 36, 80
*taghlīb*, 67
Ṭālūt, 86–87, 95
Thamūd, 119, 123, 141–42
theft, 10, 17–19, 145
thematic, 4–5, 6, 9, 11–12, 21, 25, 28–29, 33–34, 36, 54, 78–79, 84, 95, 142
theocentric, 64
timeline, 62–63
tongue, 54, 73, 101–2, 110–11, 116
tongue-twister, 117
translate, translation, translator, 15, 17, 39–40, 50, 65, 70–71, 108–9, 132
triangle, triangles, 3, 4–5, 9–10, 30–33, 136–37, 145, 147
trust, 21–26, 29–30, 33–34, 52, 87, 142–43, 145–46
truth, 5, 17, 18–19, 36, 45, 46, 53, 56, 61, 88, 89–90, 91, 107–8, 110–11, 118, 119–20, 124, 125–26, 127, 132, 142–43, 145–46
type-scene, 38, 44–45, 149

usurp, 74, 75, 107–8, 128–29, 141, 145–46

variation, 10, 19–20, 48–50, 54, 55, 56, 60, 78–79, 85, 86, 88–89, 95, 112–13, 118, 128, 130, 134–36, 137–38, 140, 144
victorious, victory, 1–2, 29, 47, 48–49, 68, 87, 88*t*, 95, 97, 99*t*, 102–3, 104–5, 108, 110, 113, 127, 130–31, 134, 138, 143–44, 155*t*

water, 16, 24–25, 33–34, 43, 53, 55, 86–87, 88*t*, 95, 126–29, 131, 132–33, 151*t*
weaknesses, 50–51, 55, 94, 120–21, 123, 129–32, 142
wealth, 97, 106, 108, 112
Western (academics, Qur'ānic studies scholarship), 4, 35, 148
whims, 124–25, 129, 132–33, 143–44
*w-ḥ-y*, 15, 16, 19–20, 88, 98, 110. *See also* inspiration
*w-l-d*, 98–101, 106
word play, 82, 93, 126–27
*w-q-y*, 113–14, 159*t*, 164*t*
*w-r-th*, 98–101, 106, 112, 139

Ya'qūb, 10, 17, 20*f*, 22*t*, 92–93
*yu'aqqib*, 39–40
Yūsuf's brothers, 4–5, 10, 16–21, 20*f*, 22*t*, 26
*'-y-y*, *āya*. *See* sign, signs

*ẓ-l-l*, 111–12
*'-z-z*, 103–4, 112–13, 159*t*, 164*t*